Buddha Behind Bars

What Readers Are Saying

"This book was a two-tissue-box affair: so vivid, emotional, and very intelligent, too. I was right there with her through the whole amazing journey. It will make a great movie or TV series!"

— Mila A

"Buddha Behind Bars is spellbinding and transformative–a literary gem that entertains and enriches the reader's perspective. From the raw vulnerability of despair to the soaring heights of hope, Collin provides a beacon of inspiration with her profound narrative of triumph over adversity. Drawing readers into a world fraught with challenges yet imbued with an unyielding spirit, this book offers a tapestry of insight that lingers long after the final page."

— Akshay P

"Collin's skillful and eloquent writing feels like a story taken out of a captivating movie. Looking at her environment as a Buddhist Monastery offers tremendous insight into living and surviving through difficulties with equanimity. She demonstrates how personal practice elevates us to embody exceptional qualities beyond race, gender, status, and economics."

— Ralph S

"Collin's journey touched my heart so much. So many times, I felt tears welling at all she was going through. I felt inspired by this courageous woman's daily decisions to make her experience one of growth. I will be ordering lots of copies for gifts this Christmas. A must-read."

— Kare N

COLLIN RUIZ

Buddha Behind Bars

—A Memoir—

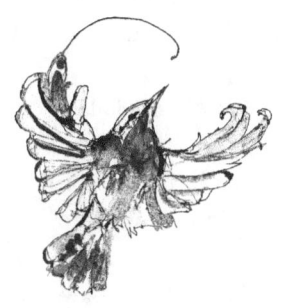

Ft. Collins PRESS

Buddha Behind Bars: A Memoir

Copyright © 2023 by Collin Ruiz

Developmental Editor: Max J. Miller
Copy editing by Diedre Hammond
Book interior layout and cover design by Mario Lampic
Cover illustrations by Julia Duclos (Juh D.)
Back cover photo by Cara Faith (Soulgraphy)

First print edition
Printed in the United States of America

ISBN: 979-8-9880505-0-6

www.BuddhaBehindBars.com

Fort Collins Press
www.FtCollinsPress.com

DEDICATION

For my brother, Kenge:
You gave me confidence, courage, and strength.
You gave my life dimension.

I miss your laughter and your reassuring presence.
I miss your care and concern for those around you.
I can't imagine a world without you in it.

Whether you're still somewhere on this earth,
Or if you are off on a new adventure,
I always keep a light shining in my heart for you.

I miss you, brother.

TABLE OF CONTENTS

One:
PRISON OR MONASTERY—YOU CHOOSE

I'M TEETERING ON A PRECIPICE. Behind me, the life I've known is coming apart. Ahead of me, life stretches out into the unknown—the abyss of prison.

It's one week until I surrender myself. I've been crying around the clock. I keep telling myself to be strong, all the time thinking, *I'm forty-nine years old! How in the world am I going to make it?*

A friend once said, "It doesn't matter if you think you can't handle the future—you can handle this moment." There's truth in that: I know I'm less fearful when I focus on the present. But *this* moment goes way beyond other times of stress in my life. Going to prison for two years is bad enough. But I am leaving behind Jera, my fourteen-year-old special-needs son. I must put my whole life on pause. *Is this really happening to me?*

I heard somewhere that we are always living in whatever future we see coming at us. If I had a ticket to Hawaii, for example, I'd already be picking out my bathing suit, anticipating the feel of the sand under my feet, and relaxing as if I were already there.

My mother understood this. Once while I was at college, I was home for a visit, and she said, "Collin, don't let your future steal your present."

"What do you mean?" I asked.

"You still have two more days here, yet you've already left." She was spot on. No matter what I had to do when I got back to school, enjoying the present moment with my mother meant that I had to be *present*. I get it.

Unfortunately, it's no different with a future that you dread. Instead of a ticket to Hawaii, I've got a reservation to check into prison, and it feels

1

impossible not to think about prison every moment of every day. I want to enjoy each moment I have with my son, but in a very real sense, I'm already in prison.

Today I'm visiting my psychologist, Ralph, in Santa Fe. My sister Greta introduced us. Jera and I have met Ralph a couple of times together. Ralph generously offered some free private sessions leading up to my incarceration. I took him up on his offer to try to find ways to cope with this stress.

I've barely settled in my seat in his office and I'm already sobbing. He patiently hands me a box of tissues and says, "Take your time."

"Oh, my God." I said blowing my nose, "I could easily just cry through the whole hour. I've been crying for weeks. Months, really."

After a couple minutes, he said, "Take a few deep breaths. The body can't cry and breathe at the same time. Inhale for a count of four: one, two, three, four. Pause. Now exhale for six: one, two, three, four, five, six. Repeat that a few more times."

I remember when Greta worked with Ralph, she told me Ralph used breathing exercises and incorporated both mind and body for healing. As a former Buddhist monk, Ralph has a comforting presence with a smile in the corner of his eyes, calm and welcoming.

When I start to calm down and catch my breath, Ralph says, "This emotion is about going to prison; is that correct?"

"Yes," I reply, still breathing unevenly, "but I'm not as upset about prison as I am about how Jera will cope without me."

"That makes perfect sense," he says, smiling compassionately, "you are his mother."

"As a single mother since he was ten months old, I've never been away from him for more than a few days. We have been through so much together. I know him, his wants, and his needs. I keep asking myself, is he going to be alright?" I burst into tears again.

"Breathe through it. One, two, three, four, pause, and one, two, three, four, five, six. And again."

"He's the love of my life," I said, holding back another wave of tears. "Jera is my life."

"From what I've seen of Jera so far, I'd say he's an extraordinary young man. He's aware and sensitive."

"Yes! He's amazing!" I said, almost jumping out of my seat. "I just want to have all the bases covered for him. My lawyer asked me to compile a professional history of my son's diagnoses and a road map of his emotional struggles. Over the years, he's had so many diagnoses: sensory integration disorder, depressive anxiety, and ADHD. Some of his early years were unbelievably difficult. Finally, they determined that he fit on the Asperger's spectrum."

Jera will be living in more than one place while I'm gone, with my siblings. I'm the oldest of five. After me, there's my sister Greta, then my sister Dante, followed by my brother Kenge, and then my brother Mesa. We're all spread out geographically, so Jera will live in Colorado with Dante while he goes to school and in New Mexico with Greta and Mesa on school breaks. I'm happy he has the support of all my siblings, but a new school will be a big change for Jera."

"These are the concerns of a responsible, loving parent," he said reassuringly. "You are doing all the right things. And I'm sure getting this all set up is keeping you very busy."

"It's a nonstop frenzy," I said. "I've been going through the motions of daily life with my mind racing 24/7. I'm always on-task asking myself, 'What do I need to get done? What needs to happen? What should I do to make sure nothing goes awry when I'm gone?' I also feel like no matter how much I get done it won't be enough. When I'm in prison and unable to do anything, it will feel worse."

"What are the big pieces you need to handle?" Ralph asked.

"Well, Greta helped me pack up my house. I'm so grateful for that because I felt overwhelmed. I have a shed behind my house to store all my belongings. How am I supposed to know what I will still want two years from now? I'm keeping what I love and selling off everything I can."

"It's all been so exhausting." I continued, "One day, I went to visit a friend. He made us some lunch and we talked. Afterward, we sat down to watch TV, and it dawned on me: I am exhausted. This feeling wells up inside of me and I'm suddenly on the verge of tears. I need to rest. Really, I need to lay this burden down. I ask my friend if I can take a nap on the couch. I want to take a time-out while someone I trust watches over me. 'Will everything be okay?' I wonder, 'Just for a few minutes?'"

"Do you think you're tired mainly from the activity or from the stress of all of this?"

"Both, but mainly the stress!" I reply. "Since my brother went on the run from the law over a year ago, my life has turned inside out. Being indicted and threatened with ten to forty years in prison felt like an unbearable burden of stress and anxiety. And then not knowing what is going to happen to my son and to me"

"People keep telling me to trust that everything will work out. Trust doesn't even sound like a real word right now. I've used up my trust, faith, and confidence. They are overshadowed by so much chaos in my head. I am going to prison! How am I going to make it through this? I have no answers."

"A year is such a long time to maintain that level of stress," Ralph said. "Try to be patient with yourself and with others. Sometimes people don't know what to say in situations like this."

"Oh, no kidding," I said. "I share what's going on in my life with just a few people. I have no time for acquaintances. This is when I find out who my true friends are. Everybody that I tell is shocked. To them, this is not who I am.

"People keep asking if I am cooperating with law enforcement. It's so maddening. What do they think? And the law enforcement officers insist that I know more than I do. I don't know anything at all about the other fifteen people indicted in this case and I have no idea what happened to my brother. And I don't know what's going to happen to me."

Tilting his head to one side, Ralph said, "You're facing the unknown. That's stressful and uncomfortable."

"Oh! So stressful! Six months ago, when I was indicted, I was freaking out. It felt like something was lurking around every corner. I was persistently worrying that someone was out to get me. Some new information could ruin me. Someone could squash me like a bug. Maybe somebody is listening to me, waiting to get some dirt on me, or going to snatch my son away from me forever.

"Night after night, I have awakened from a nightmare. Either someone is stalking me, watching me, scheming to trap me, or hunting me like prey.

"One day, I told my sister Greta about how paranoid I felt. She said, 'It's not paranoia if what you fear is real.' And the things I'm afraid of are real."

"And all this fear and anxiety leaves you exhausted," Ralph said.

"Yes," I said, holding back tears. "I am so tired! I just want to go deep into myself, sleep right through it, and wake up when I get out."

"Yes, that's one option," he says with kindness. "You can sleep through this, or you can use this experience to awaken.

"Spoken like a true Buddhist," I said playfully. "My mother attended Tassajara Zen Mountain Center in her younger life. She taught me a few things about Buddhism. I know Buddha means 'awakened.' She often said Buddhism is about compassion. She meditated a lot."

"Meditation is a central practice of Buddhism," Ralph said with a slight nod.

"It always looks like doing nothing. I need to do something. I feel like I have to take action and move forward to get through this."

"Meditation is surprisingly active," he said, raising one eyebrow.

"Maybe I should study Buddhism while I'm in prison." The thought left me almost hopeful.

"Here's a choice for you. Would you rather go to prison or go to a monastery?"

"Hah!" I blurt out, "That's easy, a monastery!"

5

Ralph explains, "Anyone can *learn about* Buddhism. There are lots of books and classes. However, in a monastery, one *practices* being a Buddhist. It's not just about studying."

"It still sounds better." I said, "When I envision prison, I'm afraid of whom I'll become in there. Prison has a reputation for hardening its inhabitants. I keep asking myself if I will be frozen and bitter when I get through this. Will that part of me that is caring, loving, and kind disappear in there, never to be seen again?

"By contrast," I continued, "I imagine a monastery softens its inhabitants with its tranquil and contemplative environment."

"That would be the intention of dwelling in a monastery. *Practicing* Buddhism is about being on the path out of suffering. And as your mother said, practice cultivates compassion.

"But you also might find similarities between prison and a monastery," Ralph continued. "The inhabitants of both live minimally. Life becomes rhythmic as you follow a structured routine. You are separated from the outside world. There are rules and rituals. And you're not alone; you must learn to live within a community."

"I get it. Prison and a monastery have similarities, but a monastery *has* to be better."

Ralph asks, "So you want to go to a monastery?"

"Yes!"

"Come back tomorrow ready to take your Buddhist vows," he says calmly and confidently.

Whoa! What just happened? When I walked out of Ralph's office, the swirl in my mind continued, but it took on a completely new tone from what I'd been feeling for the last year. I'm feeling a bit more confident about moving forward and maybe even somewhat hopeful about my future.

Become a Buddhist? Go to a monastery? Should I shave my head? Do I have a choice? I don't feel like I have a lot of options. Somehow, this choice feels right—in line with who I am.

The most positive thing I've ever heard about prison is that in rare cases it can be transformational. I've heard stories about Nelson Mandela. I've heard how mindset shifts and education while serving time in prison can bring about an experience of awakening. I've read about St. John of the Cross, a priest imprisoned in a monastery. He wrote about his transformative, spiritual experience in a poem that has become known as *The Dark Night of the Soul.*

Writers and speakers frequently use "dark night of the soul" as a metaphor for passing through the darkness on the way to a renewed phase of life and light. It evokes another metaphor: the phoenix rising from the ashes. Both refer to the process of becoming an entirely different being. St. John of the Cross offers a simple but profound lesson: when faced with uncertainty, we move through it by faith—just putting one foot in front of the other.

When our world becomes dark, when we lose hope, we may wallow in the dark or dig deep to discover faith. Faith seems to arise from a need, circumstances that overwhelm us. I imagine faith as trust arising naturally like the dawning of light. I've heard that faith is the first step on the path to awakening.

Faith might require a shift in our approach to life. At times in my life, when I have woken up feeling like my world is dark, I've learned to sidestep depression by taking simple actions like sitting in the sun or taking a walk in nature. These actions empower me to take a leap of faith, to feel the light in my world.

Ralph offered me a choice. I can see prison as a scary time of separation and suffering or I can choose to see it as a spiritual path. Either way, it's still a 'dark night' kind of experience because I don't know what I'm going to confront. I've never been to prison. Nor a monastery.

It's not the first time I've faced a scary, unknown future. Becoming a mother, I did not know what to expect day to day. I did not know how things would turn out. I simply said yes to motherhood as it happened.

I had Jera one month before my thirty-fifth birthday. Ten months later, I was a single mother—never knowing what tomorrow would look like. Pregnancy had been arduous. I had never worked so hard in my life! All-day morning sickness, gestational diabetes, and then an emergency C-section. Managing gestational diabetes with only diet and exercise required checking my blood glucose every two hours and swimming almost daily at the senior center.

Some days, motherhood felt like being in a race. From the moment the gunshot sounds, you're in it and running. There's no stopping. I had to lean in, step up, and commit to parenthood. For me, motherhood and being a single mother was never about being ready. I wanted to be a mother since I was a little girl, but until it happened, I had no idea what I would be like as a mother, and what it would mean to be a parent. It has always been about stepping up.

I pledged to myself to hold motherhood above all else. To hold the mindset of motherhood forefront in my being. *How many ways are there to be a mother?* I promised to do whatever I have to do to be the best mother I can be! And motherhood made me a whole different being.

Now, prison looms as an unknown future in front of me. And a monastery sounds better, but it's still an unknown. They are both foreign worlds to me just as motherhood was. *Could becoming a Buddhist be a similar choice? Could my commitment to be a Buddhist as I enter prison change my experience of prison? Could it change who I am? If so, like motherhood*, I thought, *maybe I can do this prison thing, too. I'll be a Buddhist prisoner.*

And I'm not really going into prison alone. I can already hear Ralph's words of reassurance, "Don't worry. If anybody has anything to say to you, you tell them that you have a man on the outside who's looking out for you." That makes me smile. *Somebody's got my back.*

Making that definitive choice to be a mother didn't spare me from some dark moments of anxiety and doubt. I'm betting that this choice will lead to a better life for me.

I'm stepping into a new world again. I didn't know how to be a mother, but I stepped into a foreign world and did it.

And Ralph's got my back. I know my family's got my back, too.

The night before taking my Buddhist vows, it doesn't even cross my mind to look up what the Buddhist vows are. Yet, becoming a Buddhist feels like a good thing. I don't know what it means to be a Buddhist. I don't know how to go forward; however, I'm committed to moving forward. Buddhism is calling me, like motherhood called to me. Ready or not, here I come.

THE BUDDHIST PRECEPTS:

1. I will abstain from killing living beings. A disciple of Buddha does not kill but rather cultivates and encourages life.

2. I will abstain from taking that which is not given. A disciple of Buddha does not take what is not given but rather cultivates and encourages generosity.

3. I will abstain from sexual misconduct. A disciple of Buddha does not misuse sexuality but rather cultivates and encourages open and honest relationships.

4. I will abstain from telling lies. A disciple of Buddha does not lie but rather cultivates and encourages truthful communication.

5. I will abstain from all intoxicants. A disciple of Buddha does not intoxicate self or others but rather cultivates and encourages clarity.

Two:
THE WORST TWO WEEKS OF MY LIFE

THE EXCITEMENT ALL STARTED on a Monday morning six months ago in early July. Like any other Monday, I take out the trash first thing in the morning and head to the gym to get my week rolling out right.

I start my workout with stretches and abdominal work. This time after stretching, I got up off the mats, and two tall men in street clothes came up to me.

One of them asked, "Are you Collin Ruiz?"

"Yes," I said hesitantly.

"We are U.S. marshals," they say, as my heart skips a beat. *Is this it?*

One of them asks me to go with them to answer some questions.

"Wait a minute, am I under arrest?"

"No, we just want you to come and answer some questions."

Now my brain is on fire. Obviously, this is about my brother Kenge who went on the run. It's been a whole year since he ran, and now, they are here for me.

After my brother ran, my friends and family told me to talk to a lawyer. We wondered if the authorities failed to locate my brother, who would they investigate next? Kenge and I were always close. I suspected that I could be next.

Kenge had deposited money in my account on many occasions—all for innocent purposes. Kenge and I had spent many vacations together. He would help me cover Jera's therapeutic and treatment expenses. Sometimes, he helped me get from one paycheck to the next for whatever my need was at the time, the utility bills, a medical bill.

Someone had suggested I look for a lawyer who can handle a federal case. Turns out, they're not very common. A year ago, I found Grace, an attorney up in Boulder, and set up a time to meet with her. She was very impressive, tall, wearing perfectly tailored clothes, and very articulate. I told her my situation.

"In all likelihood," she said frankly, "it's not a matter of *if* they come for you, but rather *when* will they come for you." That was a punch to the gut.

After more than an hour with Grace, I'm devastated. I leave her office, sobbing. This is so much worse than I ever could have imagined. Grace listed many likely charges and emphasized the high probability of me getting prison time.

Now, a year since I consulted with Grace, the U.S. marshals want to take me in. I tell them my son is at home, and I must go home and arrange for someone to care for him.

They clear out the locker room before I can get my purse and the keys to my car (which, of course, I am not allowed to drive.) One of the U.S. marshals drives my car and I get in the big black SUV to ride back to my house to see my son. I would never just leave my son wondering what happened to me.

When we arrived, there were three cop cars parked around my house. Because there is no female officer with them, they won't allow me to go into my house to change clothes. I'm feeling very bare in my gym clothes. They want me to leave my son at a neighbor's house and I say, "No, I have people who will come and take care of him."

They let me make a call. One officer makes the call and then I can have my phone to talk to my friend Cara. Then we wait for her to come over.

At this point, two U.S. marshals and four cops are surrounding me on my front lawn. It seems like overkill, one always standing within arm's reach. *What am I going to do? Make a run for it? Leave my son behind and take off running down the street?*

Jera must be sleeping, and because I can't go in the house, he doesn't know that I'm here. Jera is fourteen and it's summer break. I ask the U.S.

marshals if we can move to the backyard. One officer wants my driver's license. Another officer starts playing with my dog. How am I supposed to act? I've never been arrested in my life. It's hard to remember what the lawyer told me a year ago. "Don't talk!" That much I remember.

Cara arrives and goes inside to talk to Jera. Then, Jera comes running outside and I give him a big hug. He tells me not to cry, to be strong. I don't want to leave my son. I don't know if I'm going to be gone for a day or a week.

I don't know what's coming, so I better just calm down right now. Be calm and attentive. Cara takes Jera back into the house. He seems remarkably calm.

The marshals seem impatient. They take me to the car, and I leave Jera and Cara behind. Cara runs out and gives me a bag of trail mix. *Who knows when or what I will eat next?* She knows health and nutrition are important to me. I get into the SUV and look at the house, but I don't see Jera. *Probably easier for both of us, that way.*

They take me to the Fort Collins Police headquarters, not to a cell but a conference room with a table. We sit around the table. *Okay, what are we waiting for?*

One of the U.S. marshals asks me, "Have you ever been to Texas?" I know there were people involved in this case arrested in Texas.

"Well, yes, I have. I used to live in Amarillo and worked at a gym there." Suddenly, I feel the fight arising within me. *Bring it on, bring it on!*

An officer comes in. He says, "We're moving you to Denver." I'm still not arrested but we're way past "just want to talk and ask a few questions." *Was that just a line to get me quietly out of the gym? Are they going to arrest me now?*

"We have an hour-long drive to Denver," the officer says. "Do we need to put you in handcuffs?"

"Nope. I'm reasonable," I said. *What am I going to do-jump out of a moving vehicle?*

It's a waiting game now. Wait to learn what's happening. Wait to talk to my lawyer.

In Denver, I'm processed. Here, there are even more officers. They're coming and going like a French farce. One takes a picture of my tattoo. Another catalogs everything I have; they have my wallet.

I am wearing beaded bracelets that my sisters and I made. I've worn them ever since—except when I delivered Jera. Some of the beads came from a bracelet I made when my mother passed away over thirty years ago. An officer tells me he will have to cut them off. He asks me for an address and puts them in an envelope. This officer seems nice. Still, I doubt I will ever see them again.

They tell me to go with a new officer—all the others stay behind. *What happens next?* I'm taken to an office where the officer hands me a pants-and-top uniform with big maroon stripes. "Change into these." When I come out, he takes my clothes and points to a room for me to wait in. There are lots of men and women and pay phones. I don't know who to call at this point, and I have no idea what I would tell anyone, so I just sit down and wait. I'm a little disoriented.

I've always been calm under pressure. After my mother passed away, a therapist told me that I act like a soldier: calm amid chaos, showing no emotion, ready to do whatever is necessary. Sometimes emotions arise later. Some part of me seems to be living in the illusion that someone is going to swoop in and take me by the hand, show me what to do. Another part of me feels like an outsider in a very harsh foreign world. I'm thinking, *don't have any expectations, don't ask questions, don't talk, and wait until all is revealed.*

I am feeling steady but very tense in my body. It reminds me of my high school cross-country races, waiting for the shot to ring out and the race to start. I wonder how I'm going to react—if I'm going to lash out at any moment or maybe curl up in a ball instead. I am already alone and feel disconnected, even with myself.

An officer calls my name and leads me to a huge, two-story room with individual cells. I'm put in a cell and the door locks behind me. *I'm in jail, whoa!*

13

This cell has a metal toilet and a bunk with a slanted mattress and one blanket. That's it. I don't know what to do. It's late and I can't imagine sleeping, but I lay on my mattress with the blanket over my head.

When I wake up, the lights are still on. Time has passed—I'm still here. I still have no clue what's happening and no one to talk to.

I look out my window and see a few women coming and going. Some women are bringing in carts with food trays. It's early in the morning. It is hard to tell exactly what time it is; I can't see a clock and there are no windows to the outside. The cell door opens automatically. "Breakfast." I exit the cell.

Now what? No one talks to me, and I don't talk to anyone. I see a glass door off to the side propped open to an "outdoor" area. It's an enclosed space with a couple openings high on one outside wall. There's fresh air and I can hear the traffic down below. I think I'm on the third floor. No one else is out here so I pick up a basketball and walk and dribble. I'm not much of a basketball player, but I might as well move around while I can.

A few hours go by, and I hear my name being called on the intercom. When I go to the front area, an officer says, "You're transferring to Castle Rock. Change back into your street clothes."

After waiting in another holding cell for a couple hours, I'm put in shackles and led to a van that takes me to Castle Rock. I learn that this is the only Federal holding facility for women.

The holding cells at Castle Rock are ridiculously cold! This holding cell has a urinal, a metal bench, and several other women. There isn't enough room for all of us to sit on the bench, so we randomly take turns sitting on the bench, standing around, or even sitting on the floor.

I want to escape the cold, cold floor, cold bench, and there's nowhere to move. How can I describe the cold? The feeling that my body wants to shut down, all the way to oblivion. However, it does not work that way. I am trying to tune out, but the cold is relentless. My whole body is shivering! I've rarely experienced cold like this. *Holy crap, my body thinks I'm dying!*

A Native American woman with a swastika tattooed on the back of her hand is the most talkative. She tells us that she has been to jail many times but is wondering if she is going to prison now. She talks about times she got drunk and did crazy things, like driving in reverse on the highway. Finally, someone asks, "Why do you have a swastika tattooed on your hand?"

"It happened at a party. I passed out drunk, and my friends pranked me."

As the hours go by, we just sit and wait. We are all in summer clothes. My tank top is not doing much for me. One gal wearing a big t-shirt hugs her knees under her shirt. A blonde gal, also in a tank top, starts yelling, "Turn on the fucking heat! We're fucking freezing in here!" She continued this rant, and suddenly a male voice comes over the intercom, "Keep it up and you will stay in there all night."

Finally, they start processing us one by one. It's about 11 p.m. when my name is called. I have been here for six hours. The woman officer comes in wearing a winter coat (in July) and takes me to another very cold room. It's empty, like a storage closet. Then she tells me to strip.

Now I'm freezing *and* naked. I stand in front of her.

"Turn around, bend over, and spread your cheeks."

"Seriously?!" For that split second, it is impossible to believe that this is me being treated in this way. I had just been held overnight in Denver, so I have no idea what I'd be carrying inside me.

Even if I'm an inmate, I'm still a human being. Yet, everybody treats me like I've been here before. Nobody tells me how to do this.

The officer hands me a new uniform. It has big yellow and white horizontal stripes. Because it is a V-neck shirt, we must wear a white t-shirt under it and I'm grateful for an extra layer. We are not allowed to wear bras with underwire. By the time the officer takes me to a cell, everybody in the unit is asleep. A woman sleeps on the lower bunk. I get up on the top bunk and somehow, I go to sleep.

The next day, I notice each group of inmates has different colored uniforms. Turns out, it's a code. Those wearing the red ones are on lockdown twenty-three hours a day! I'm so glad I'm not wearing red. I'm grateful to be a bumblebee instead.

How long I will be in jail? Is my son alright? Did my brother talk to my lawyer? Will someone come get me out? I'm moved to another cell with the blond girl, Amy.

"Are you from Santa Fe?" Amy asks me.

"Well," I replied, "I have family there." Suddenly, it clicks in my head: *she must be connected to my brother Kenge.*

In my innocence I asked her, "Do you know my brother, Kenge?"

"Yes," she replies, "Do you know where he is?"

For a minute, I consider that someone may have put us together on purpose. Then I get uncomfortable and try to shut the conversation down.

We share a cell for the next two weeks. I entertain thoughts from time to time that if she knew Kenge, she must be cool. At times, it feels like we are in this together, which makes us more relaxed. *Is that what someone else wants us to feel?* Suddenly, I'm feeling paranoid again, like I'm being set up.

The next two weeks are some of the worst in my life. I'm transferred for court multiple times up to Denver and back, always in shackles. It's hard to walk in shackles. They slipped down as I step and slice into my ankle. Being indicted in sweatpants would have been a lot better!

The arraignment comes first. Amy and I are transferred to Denver. Then, with a couple guys, we are taken to a courtroom. The bailiff reads, "Count one: Ruiz, along with fourteen other people, are charged with conspiracy to distribute and to possess with intent to distribute marijuana."

The bailiff continues, "Count two: Ruiz, along with fourteen other people, are charged with aiding and abetting possession with intent to distribute marijuana."

Finally, I'm formally charged. I wondered, *How did they come up with this when I've never been arrested?*

Back to Castle Rock holding facility where I get my first shower. Right off the main living area, the shower stall has a door like a toilet stall. The top half is cut off, and a shower curtain is hanging down. I must put my towel and clean clothes on the table an arm's reach from the stall—the same tables where inmates eat, play cards, and sit when we are not in our cells. Just a shower curtain between me and everybody else.

The days go by. I get cold easily. I spend most of my time reading in my bunk, under my blanket. There is a cart of books, and I read a whole book each day. There is little else to do. There is always a game of cards going on at one of the tables. I've learned how to play the card game "Kings." Something I can teach Jera when I get out. But otherwise, very monotonous.

The food is horrible! It's just like I would imagine: gray slop—no one knows what it is. I lost over ten pounds in two weeks without even trying. When we get a hard-boiled egg for breakfast, I am happy.

Fortunately, there's something of a black market, like when a diabetic young woman will trade her orange for my cake. Here, oranges are not just prized as real food. One day when I was constipated, my bunkie pulled out some orange peels from beneath her pillow and gave them to me.

"What am I supposed to do with this?"

"Everybody gets constipated on jail food. Eating orange peels can make you go."

I soon discovered they can also cause some cramping, and your body adapts to eating them, so they're not 100 percent effective.

It's now Thursday, and I've been in jail since Monday. Finally, my name is called. "Your lawyer is here to see you."

As I follow the guard down the hall, I imagine my lawyer takes my hand and walks me out of here. It's a fantasy, but a woman can hope.

17

I come into the room, and Grace stands up. With a smile, she says, "Don't worry."

We sit down, and she tells me, "When your brother Mesa called me, I couldn't remember who you were. It's been a year since I've seen you. The authorities have been digging around for a year, looking for people to bring in on this case. It's ridiculous," as she shakes her head.

I have questions, but at the same time, my head feels empty. I feel like a deer in the headlights, just staring straight ahead, waiting to see what will happen next. "They picked me up 'just for questioning' and then moved me from place to place, one holding cell to another. Finally, I heard charges, and I still haven't heard anybody tell me I'm under arrest. Can we just hurry up, post bail or something, so I can get out of here?"

Grace says, "I don't have all the paperwork yet." As if she could read my anxiety, she says, "Collin, it doesn't matter what your charges are. Your charges don't define who you are."

Yes, logically, I know that, but, but, but. I keep questioning everything.

Grace says, "You will have a hearing, charges will be read again, and bail will be set. I want you to have a few friends and family at that hearing to demonstrate that you have support. It's just the process. Yes, it's tedious but hang in there."

"That shouldn't be a problem." I'm thinking of friends, as my family is far away and probably won't be able to make it up here on such short notice. Unfortunately, because Monday is a federal holiday, I probably won't get out until the end of next week.

Grace reassures me, "Don't worry, I'm working on this now. Call your brother Mesa and just hold tight."

When I call Mesa, he immediately says, "I've been waiting for your call."

I replied, "I would have called before but I didn't know what to say."

"Sis! We're here to support you," he says warmly. "I've had many conversations with Grace. We want you to know that she is working on your bond hearing, and I'm getting several friends there to support you."

"I really appreciate that, Mesa. I'm sure Cara will help out if you ask her."

"As soon as Grace knows when you're getting out on bail," he continues, "she'll let me know, and I'll have somebody there to pick you up."

"Oh, thank you, Mesa. I'm so relieved to hear that you have all this under control."

Later as I lay in my bunk, I felt more relaxed. I realized I had been tense, and I had resigned myself to undergo this on my own. I had been telling myself, *be strong, take whatever comes your way.*

Jail is a lot waiting around for something to happen, interrupted with tragic stories. I spend my days reading, hungry, and waiting. Inmates come and go.

Our cell doors are propped open during the day, and we are allowed to come and go. Most of the day, we hang out in a room of bolted-down tables and chairs. When our unit is counted, we have to go back to our cells.

One day, I'm sitting at a table reading a book when a young girl comes up to me crying. She sits herself down across from me and says, "My parents won't give up their Fourth of July camping trip to get me out."

I ask her, "What are you in here for?"

"I got busted using heroin," she tells me matter-of-factly.

I'm kind of shocked; I thought heroin was such a dangerous drug of choice.

"I was addicted to painkillers and heroin is cheaper," she tells me.

I end up hearing this sad story again and again. Drugs play a part in most incarcerations.

I've been spending most of my days reading at a table. Another inmate approaches me. She has a book in her hands. "Glad to see another reader," she says, adding, "It's kind of rare in here. I'm Kate."

"I'm Collin. What kind of books do you like to read?"

"I'm trying to learn German. I'm waiting for a German book. You know that you can request specific books or authors when they bring the book cart through? What do you like to read?"

"Science fiction and fantasy mostly," I replied. "I've seen you doing your pushups in the morning. Do you ever get outside for exercise?"

"We are supposed to get outside for an hour in the morning and an hour in the afternoon," she said with a shrug.

"What?! That hasn't happened since I've been here," I said, "I can't wait to get some fresh air!"

Finally, one afternoon a voice comes over the loudspeaker, "If you want outside time, line up by the door." I jump up and get in line. The outside consists of a concrete floor, concrete walls about two stories high, with chain-link fencing across the top.

The chance to line up and go outside becomes more regular—twice a day with random exceptions. For example, one afternoon, an inmate was cleaning a hall closet near the door. Since we are not allowed to walk within ten feet of them while they are working, we have no way to get outside.

When I do get an hour in our outside cage, I feel like an animal in the zoo. Either I walk around the edge or just lie down and look up at the sky.

One beautiful day, a few inmates are lying outside on the concrete looking at the sky and somebody starts singing. The quality of her voice took me by surprise. It was strong and smooth.

Do we have a pro singer locked up with us here? I turned to see who it was, and I chuckled to myself when I realized who was singing. I'd already formed a strong sense of this Native American gal. Every time I'd heard her speak, she cussed just about every other word. She has all the classic "butch" features: super short hair, great muscles, aggressive speech. Obviously, there's more to her than that.

She finishes her song and stops. We all applaud. "Sing another one!" says one inmate.

Others chime in, "Please, sing more."

"I don't know all the words to any other songs," she says.

"Sing it again!" several people urge.

As she repeats the song, I recognize it's the old classic song by Jan and Dean about a young guy crashing his car. Something about a yellow car and a Deadman's curve? For that short period of time, everybody is silent. Warm concrete on our backs, looking up at the patch of blue sky, silent, listening. The song takes me out, takes me to my son, wanting to tell him all about this.

We just listened. I didn't want it to end, wanting something to hold onto so badly. *Bumblebees in a cage, flying free on a song.*

I've been here for over a week, and it feels much longer. I hear my name over the intercom. They tell me to change clothes because I'm going back to Denver. *Whew, this must be my bond hearing.*

I'm the only inmate in the van. I'm taken in handcuffs into the courtroom, where I see my friends Cara and Ruthie, and Jeff, my psychologist. I'm relieved. These last few days, I've felt so alone.

Grace is here, and across from her are two men in suits, nothing casual about them at all. They're representing the state of Texas, and they oppose letting me out on bond because Kenge is my brother.

The judge turns to Grace for her response. She tells the judge, "Collin has character references and considerable family support, your honor, and her own psychologist is here to testify on her behalf." Grace has Jeff get up and talk about me. He tells the court that I'm a good mother and a well-known professional.

Grace is so sharp, so spot-on. She really knows her stuff. I feel so grateful to have her on my side.

It's a weird arrangement in this courtroom. There are three tiers of seats. They put me all the way up in the back row. I'm looking down over the scene. My attention gets pulled in many directions and I don't really know what's going on. At times I feel like I'm outside my own body.

21

The judge bangs his gavel down and people start moving around. Grace waves at me to move down toward her. She says, "You'll get out on a $50,000 bail."

"What?!" I exclaimed. "I don't have that kind of money lying around."

She reassures me, "It's just going to take some paperwork. We'll put a lien on your house. You should be out in twenty-four hours."

They take me back to Castle Rock where I fill out some paperwork. Now I'm anxiously waiting for my name to be called. I'm crossing my fingers it's only one more night here.

Meanwhile, I have become familiar with these thirty women. One sweet woman was busted for driving without a driver's license, a repeat offense because she works an hour from where she lives and must go to work. Another woman with an ugly, raw open wound on her hand burned herself on a dare for money so she could buy alcohol.

Kate comes up to me and asks, "How did your hearing go?"

"Hopefully, I'm getting out on bail tomorrow," I said.

"Good for you," she says, "I'm happy for you!"

The next morning before anyone awakens, I hear a voice calling, "Collin Ruiz, bring your stuff to the door." I'm scrambling to roll up my bedding and all my stuff. As I walk to the door, I see Kate waving cheerfully from her window. My arms are full and in the rush I didn't even respond. I wish I had acknowledged her.

I'm quickly back in my gym clothes, shackled, and driven in the van back to Denver. *Thank God, finally, I'm getting out!*

When we get to Denver, I'm put in a tiny, freezing booth to wait. I've been shivering for hours when somebody finally opens the door and says, "You're free to go. Take that elevator and turn left out the door."

I walk out onto the sidewalk looking for a friendly face. I don't know whom Mesa sent to pick me up. Finally, I recognize a friend's truck and now I know I'm going home.

We drive an hour and a half in July heat with no air conditioning. But after sitting for hours in the freezing cold, I'm not complaining.

Once back home, the first thing I do is take a shower. It's the little things that feel so good, like my face lotion, my clothes. And somehow, food tastes better than ever. Still, my brain is running in circles. *What do I have to do? What do I need to do first? What is coming up around the next corner?*

After two weeks in jail, my life has already changed dramatically. My daily life is not the same. My life is caught up with rescheduling appointments I didn't make while I was in jail and reaching out to lawyers. I didn't tell anyone I would be gone for two weeks—I didn't know to tell them! Now I must explain what happened, and most people don't even know that my brother was on the lam. *Shit just got real.*

I just want to stay close to my son, and sleep in my bed. It feels a little like when my mother died. There is this feeling of living a new life and no one else knows; no one can see that two weeks ago I lived differently. I'm wearing the same clothes I was wearing two weeks ago when those marshals brought me in. No one can see just how naked and exposed I feel right now.

My introverted nature has kicked into high gear. I don't want to be around anyone, except Jera and my family. My family is too far away, leaving only the phone as our primary means of communication. However, talking on the phone to my family is awkward; nobody knows what to say or what is safe to talk about. *Somebody might be listening?*

Greta says, "We are here to support you, but we don't know what that means yet." My niece, Isa, tells me. "You should take notes in prison because somebody will want you to write a book."

Since the case is in Texas, I will go to West Texas in a week for my first official court appearance. Grace had told me that having her at my hearings in Texas is going to be expensive. She recommends that I get a Texas lawyer.

A week later, I have another lawyer and I'm on my way to my first hearing. It's a two-day drive from Colorado through New Mexico to Texas. I'd fly there, except not only did they take my driver's license, but they also took my purse, and my passport from me. Stopping at my sister's would be a natural halfway point; however, I'm not allowed to stop. I've been told not to even talk to my family. I drive alone over the vast, flat plains to Texas.

An endless thought-loop replays in my mind: *what is going to happen to me? To my son?* A million different dreadful scenarios continue to play out. I look for anything to focus on: antelope, crows, cows. I watch the lightning in the sky, the clouds, and how the light changes day to night. Anything to distract my mind from worrying.

This arraignment hearing was an unbelievable non-event. It was just a formality and in all of ten minutes it was over. It would be the beginning of many court proceedings over many months leading up to my sentencing hearing.

On the two-day drive back to Colorado, I rehash the charges in my mind repeatedly. I was charged with breaking many laws, but not committing a crime. I kept hearing from lawyers and others over and over, "This is our justice system." It makes me feel trapped. Things can change in the blink of an eye without apparent logic. I feel outrage and disbelief at a system of so-called "*justice*" running with an unimaginably twisted mind of its own. I'm being swept along by a raging current of insanity.

The next six months are a blur. People ask me questions all the time. Even friends ask, "Where is your brother?" "Will he come forward so you don't have to go to prison?" "Are you mad at your brother for not being here?"

Every hearing is hard to bear. Anger, frustration, and sadness threaten to spill down my face. I'm not angry at my brother. I am angry at a system that makes me feel like a blank wooden piece of a puzzle that some unknown person is putting together. And who benefits from this?

The vast majority of legal cases never go to trial. Typically, the defendant pleads guilty and then goes through the process of plea bargaining to determine a sentence. In one of my hearings, the judge read my charges and asked me, "Guilty or not guilty?"

I said, "guilty," the judge banged his gavel, and the hearing was over. I walked out feeling like I had declared myself a criminal. It felt very wrong.

Not all those who work in the system are ignorant of the absurdities of it. One officer said, "I'm sorry I have to do this to you" as he took my fingerprints and pictures. Others acknowledged that the system was hard and dehumanizing. And there was the Denver officer who spoke kindly as he took my possessions when I was first processed, the one who offered to send me the beads from the bracelets they cut off my wrists.

About three months later, I had a dream about the Denver officer. I had been busy, overwhelmed, living day by day with my son, and I had given up on receiving my beads. In my dream, this officer was sitting in the bleachers at our neighborhood baseball field. I walked up, sat behind him, and spoke to him as if he was a good friend. The next day, when I went to my mailbox, my beaded bracelets had arrived!

Today is my last trip to Texas, for the sentencing hearing. This town has only one hotel. This time I'm not alone, my sister Greta, my family therapist, Jeff, who has known me for over ten years, comes with me. My lawyer told me to wear nicer, conservative clothes for this event. Both my sister and I get awesome pant suits and we look really good. When we walked out of the hotel, I felt like we were in an episode of *Charlie's Angels*. The sun is blinding and hot as we put on our sunglasses and walk in slow motion to our rental car. *Maybe we are fighting crime in this dusty little town in the middle of nowhere.*

Walking into court feels like walking into a fighting cage. I have not seen this judge before. My lawyer warns me that he has sentenced the rest of the fifteen people in this case. Most received five-year sentences. I've talked to Jera about this. Five years seems like such a long time! I'd miss all Jera's high school years; he'd be a different person by the time I got out. My lawyer thinks that there is a possibility I will get only two years. Two years sounds somehow doable. I keep assuring Jera that we will make it through this, no matter what.

After things get rolling, the prosecutor indicates to the judge that he has something to say to my lawyer. He comes over to our table and asks my lawyer if he will work with him on the larger case (beyond my personal case). These guys are friends and colleagues, and they excuse themselves from me for a brief conversation with the judge.

When my lawyer comes back to the table, he tells me that he and the prosecutor agreed to drop the severity of my changes a little bit. Then my lawyer calls Jeff to the stand. I'm watching Jeff testify and my lawyer whispers to me, "Look at the judge. He is recalculating your sentence right now."

He stops Jeff in the middle of what he was saying and asks him to sit down.

The judge was writing and calculating. He looks up and starts to rant at me, "Miss Ruiz, you're a single mother. How could you allow yourself to get caught up in all this?" He went on for quite a while and I began losing all hope of a shorter sentence.

Finally, with a long sigh of exasperation, he announced my sentence, "Two years in federal prison and three years' supervised probation." Gavel slams. We're done!

I can't wait to tell Jera that I will get to spend Christmas with him. He will complete the semester and then I must take myself to prison in the beginning of January.

Three:
LOVE AND PAIN

PRISON LOOMS. I've survived the loss of my mother, my brother, and other loved ones. I just don't know what I will look like on the other side of prison.

I feel like I've taken care of as much as I possibly can. Still the pain hovers around me, or maybe it's the anticipation of pain.

One evening I went to a local pub with a couple of friends. I sat at the bar with one of my girlfriends, next to a very handsome young man named Matt. I intended to help my girlfriend get to know this guy. However, after a few minutes, it was obvious that he wanted to talk to me. So, my girlfriend left us to go hang out with our other friends.

Matt was healing from a broken leg. This was his first day out of the cast and we made a toast to health. He was a Marine and broke his leg during a training exercise almost two months before. Matt and I end up having a very real, down-to-earth conversation. I didn't tell him that I was headed to prison. I just wanted a moment of normalness.

He told me this story of when he first became a marine. "After basic training," Matt told me, "I was standing out on the tarmac, getting ready to be shipped out for my first assignment. As I stood with a group of new soldiers in front of this big aircraft, I felt so alone. I asked myself, 'Why am I here?' I was trained and felt qualified; however, I continued to question, 'What am I doing? Maybe I don't want to be a soldier. Can I back out now? Can I not get on that plane?'"

I ask him, "What made you get on the plane?"

"I just said 'Yes,'" he replied.

Ah, that's what courage looks like: you just say, "Yes."

He really got me thinking. *Now, I'm on the tarmac, so to speak.* Me without any luggage. I'm leaving my home, my family, I'm leaving my whole life behind. I will be strip-searched again. Loss, and the anticipation of more loss leave me feeling tremendous tension. I keep asking myself, like a foxhole prayer, "How can I remain present and peaceful for these last moments of freedom?"

All I must do now is leave my son and go to prison. I wonder, *How can I do this? What force can make me move away from my son?* Courage. Inspired by the Marine I met in the pub, I say, "yes."

Matt reminds me a little of my brother. Kenge and I were always close, and it was easy to talk to him.

He was outgoing and a positive example of a hardworking family man. He built his own landscaping company. He would take dirt and scrub and turn it into an oasis of trees, ponds, and incredible rock waterfalls.

Kenge was always helping someone with something. I would call him and ask what he did that day, he'd say something like, "I had to haul some rocks, then helped Steve fix his backhoe." He was always building something, fixing something, or just being there for someone.

To Kenge, his friends were family. For him, buddies always look out for each other, help each other out whenever the need arises. That is what he did, as a brother, a father, and a friend. He operated as "I'm here for you."

Kenge parented and adopted his first wife's son before having kids of his own. Her son was only two years old when they got together. When he had his own children, he was ecstatic. Kenge loved being a father to his girls! They were his pride and joy. Kenge was protective and tough. He wanted them to have everything they could ever want. Birthdays were wonderfully fun. He would take them all to an amusement park or host big parties at his house. He loved being a family man.

I enjoyed hanging out with my brother whenever I had the chance. There were times that I would drive seven hours each way to hang out with him for the weekend. We'd take vacations together. I always felt safe with my brother.

My brother was generous, and when I was struggling, he would help me out financially. Kenge was also the person I called if I was having a crappy day as well as when I was having a particularly great day.

Kenge was also a marijuana dealer. Before states started to legalize marijuana, there had been a war on drugs, including marijuana in the U.S. Whenever the feds are going after a drug organization, they want the major players. I believe that my brother became a target to gain access to these major players. He panicked, went on the lam, and my nightmare began.

Now that I think of it, this was the beginning of my dark night of the soul. Kenge was gone a year when I was indicted. I am charged with many things; the list was as long as my arm. However, these days one does not go to trial—one pleads out. In the end, I was convicted of "aiding and abetting the possession and distribution of marijuana."

I have reason to believe an investigation is still ongoing. Therefore, I offer no explanation, other than I hold myself accountable and maintain that I was not in any way part of my brother's business.

As I've engaged the legal system up close and personal, I have thought a lot about the difference between committing a crime and breaking a law. It's generally understood that committing a crime requires an act of aggression or harm against an individual or property. While we live in a country with more laws on the books than anyone could possibly know or understand, at the time of my indictment, the five most frequently broken laws are underage drinking, littering, smoking marijuana, jaywalking, and pirating music. What will land someone in prison is rather obscure.

I've learned more than I ever cared to know about the judicial system. I'm still no expert on the subject, but the massive inconsistencies and injustices that occur within our justice system boggle the mind.

Kenge going on the lam was like my brother dying. The loss has been so great, and I miss him every day. I've been missing my mother for over thirty years, so I know this feeling won't just go away.

My life changed irreversibly when we found out my mother had a malignant brain tumor. I remember that day like it was yesterday: my stepfather called to say that my mom had three grand mal seizures today and was scheduled for surgery the next morning for a brain tumor. It was a Stage III cancerous brain tumor.

I have a picture of my mother sitting in a rocking chair and wearing a simple, embroidered dress from Mexico. I love her hands, her brown skin—such graceful hands. I love the picture for her grounded presence and simple natural beauty.

My mother was raised with traditional Mexican, Christian values. Church every Sunday. Tortillas made fresh every day. She left home as soon as she turned eighteen, eager to be free of all the strict rules. She took a big leap, leaving aspects of her culture behind. She left the church and quit speaking Spanish.

She went to a women's college and became a high school English teacher. She was the teacher who helped young men dodge the draft. She mentored several young women, taking them horseback riding on the weekends. She was the cool teacher.

I loved to hear her voice as she read us bedtime stories, always looking forward to the next chapter.

One day she announced she was changing her first name to Chama and asked us to call her by her new name. I was only about twelve and I remember how hard it was not to call her mom. I was a little bit mad.

"Why can't we keep calling you mom? Don't you want to be our mom?"

She said, "When you call me 'mom,' I can't help but think of my own mother. And I don't want to be my mom. I want to feel like I'm my own person. I want to be more myself."

Chama always seemed to be doing exactly what she wanted. Chama was a headstrong woman with a fierce, independent nature. As a kid, I remember waking up in the middle of the night while my parents were fighting. More than once that led to her loading us into the car to wake up in a new place. Then, we would live somewhere new, have a new adventure. Time would pass and then, suddenly, my father would show up. Or we would be moving again.

It's really no wonder she was always her own person. She had a thirst for knowledge, questing after personal insight, reading Joseph Campbell and Jung. When we were in high school, she went back to school to become a psychologist.

While she was studying psychology, she was processing her past. She was always open with us about what she was discovering. We would go on walks together. She would talk about something she was learning and share a colorful story from her past to illustrate the idea.

I was a student at Colorado State University when my mother got cancer. She was living in Santa Fe and working as a psychologist. It was early in the semester, and I was very unmotivated. I would go stay with my mom every chance I got. I still had a life in Fort Collins, but she was never far from my thoughts. She influenced me not only by the life she led but also by her dying process.

Chama went through rounds of surgeries, radiation, chemo, and each time they thought they got it. Then, eventually, it would come back. It was a long, hard deal.

I realized was that I had my own baggage to process to be present for my mother. It was important to be there for her, so I found a therapist. Throughout therapy, my thoughts about my mother's cancer shifted from *I can't deal with this, and I don't know how to deal with this*, to *I will show up*. Hmm, seems to be a lesson I keep needing to learn.

I was making a music tape and wondering if it was worth it to even go to school right now with my mom being sick. Then my stepfather called me. "Your mom's tumor's back, and she is done with everything." He told me, she insisted, "No more surgery, radiation, or chemo."

I wanted to be there for her and spend those last days with her, so I decided to put school on hold. Those days were spent living and crying. I knew these were the last moments of our shared experience. Everything I was about to lose was in my face.

One day I was taking her to church, and she said "I'm trying not to take death so personally. We all die." She was doing her work right up to the end. In church she would make peace with her past. With us she kept it real. I believe that my mother's wisdom consisted of, "Find yourself, be yourself, be true to yourself."

It was fall in Northern New Mexico. I went to the Santa Fe ski basin to see the aspen leaves changing from green to gold. I walked through the most beautiful yellows, my eyes puffy, my head so full of snot, it was pounding. I thought, *How can I take this beauty in? Whether my mom is dying or not dying, this beauty is here. What will my life look like without my mother in it?*

After my mother's passing, I took my youngest sibling, Mesa, to live with me. He was fourteen and I had to learn how to give him the parenting he needed and still just be his sister. A whole different kind of normal.

I had left home when Mesa was only about four years old, so now, I was nurturing a new relationship with him. Helping Mesa deal with the loss of our mother intensified my own grieving process. In some ways, Mesa had a different mother than I had. My mother had grown from parenting four children before Mesa. I frequently wondered, *How would Chama deal with this?* I wanted Mesa to have some of the ideals, principles, and values that my mother taught me. I cared for him until he finished high school and went out on his own.

My sisters and I found a therapist together to make sure Mesa had support. Jeff met with us individually and collectively. He and I talked a lot about living in a high state of stress. Jeff told me that when people

32

live in a state of high stress for a long period of time, they get used to it, and not in a good way. While my mother suffered with cancer and after she passed away, my brain was expecting something bad to happen every day. As I was processing my mother's death, I also had to learn to relax again. I had to quit imagining that something terrible was going to happen tomorrow.

At times, I comprehend that pain and loss are essential to having people you love in your life. I've lived without my mother and now I live without my brother. Still, I can't imagine living without my son. I can't imagine not being in his presence every day.

In addition to what I've lost already, the anticipation of the pain yet to come lies in wait like a scary, black tar pit. I'm tiptoeing around it and often catch myself holding my breath. When I read this passage by Jeff Foster it hit home and gave me some insight into what I was experiencing.

"'Pain' is a label that thought gives to what it perceives as a threat to the well-being of the body, and therefore a threat to 'me' (since we are so identified with the body). Take away the description 'pain,' and what is there, in the moment? Intense sensation, tingly, burning, sharp, hot, vibrating, dancing, moving. The word 'pain' made it sound like a solid lump, fixed in time and space, separated from you, unchanging and unmoving and dead, but upon closer investigation, with loving and close attention, it is felt to be an alive dance, changing from moment to moment, moving, never the same twice. But you have to pay attention and not rush into assumptions. The moment is alive. The word 'pain' doesn't even begin to capture this mystery. Plus, the word 'pain' has an opposite, and these intensely alive sensations have no opposite in the moment, for life itself has no opposite. These sensations are not against life, they are life, however strange that may be to hear."
— Jeff Foster, *The Deepest Acceptance* (2012)

This passage reminds me that there are not enough words for pain. Like the Eskimos, who have hundreds of words to describe different types of snow, there should be at least a hundred words to describe different types of pain. Motherless pain, worry pain, heavy-burdens pain, acute-longing pain, intense-fear pain, helplessness pain, tiptoeing pain that lands for a second and then disappears, and breaking-heart pain.

Pain does not sit still. It dances within my body from the loss of my mother to the impending loss of being able to hold my son. Integrating my past pains and losses has chiseled my character. Pain has the power to shape us just as love does. And to keep these people in my life, shaping me with pain and love, I willingly love and love some more.

Opening my eyes first thing in the morning has become arduous. December days are short and cold. During these last weeks before going to prison, the days are strenuous as I search for more strength. At day's end, my body is weary but I'm unable to relax into sleep. *Is this a test?* If it is, I'm failing. Each step, every step of the process is my greatest challenge. When one requirement is dealt with, it only leads to another task. And I must do all this in front of my son. I'm leaving him, and every moment I'm looking at him, my leaving is unfathomable.

Jera was only ten months old when I became a single parent. He could have been a limitation in my life. Instead, Jera has been my lifeline so many times over. He made every day remarkable.

My relationship with his father had soured considerably through my pregnancy, and once Jera was born, our relationship was over. I knew single mothers who never had a moment to do anything besides parenting. My sister and friends said they would *never* be single parents. I was happier focusing all my energy on my son.

Jera was a high-need child with Asperger's tendencies, but no matter how hard the days were, I always wanted to have Jera with me. I liked mom-responsibilities and mom-purpose in my life, and I've always wanted to be his mother.

I can't imagine what prison will be like but imagining not having my son with me is beyond comprehension. Life is hard for most of us, but it's impossible to describe *this* kind of hard. I am going to prison! The tears shake my body. I have felt pain before in my heart, but nothing like this.

I feel the pain alive inside me, ripping me apart, bleeding, and raw. So much of what makes me, me, is breaking and even though the earth feels less than solid, somehow, I move forward. It's a cold winter day. I'm packed, and I will drive Jera to school and leave him. *I don't think I can do it. I must do it.*

I've done everything to prepare for today—the day I leave Jera behind. We have a plan and we've talked about it. I told Jera I would drop him off at school and he didn't have to stay there; I assured him if he wants to leave, my sister will come and get him.

I am awake. The dreaded day is here. It is happening. If only I could stop time.

I give Jera his Batman underwear to wear and say, "You are my superhero today! I love you!"

"Yes, Momma," he says. Holding each other, we cry and cry. It's hard to talk, it's hard to breathe. Yet, somehow, we both are alive and moving forward.

We get in the car together. Parked in front of the school, I wonder, *How can I let him go?* I say over and over, "I love you." As he walks in, I get back in my car and drive away, *I have to.* I can't stop crying.

Everything I see makes me cry harder. I pass a barn with a big mural painted on it. It is an eagle over the American flag. I start thinking of that eagle, with its wings spread and how I am going to have to make my love fly to my son on big strong wings.

I don't know what tomorrow looks like. I just know I am willing to say yes.

DARK NIGHT OF THE SOUL

Once in the dark of night
When love ignited me, I yearned and rose
(O the fires burned)
In the remote darkness I arose
Leaving behind all that is familiar

In the shadows my broken heart weeps
Shedding tears even in my dreams
(O the fires burned)
Wailing from my depths
My very soul disappears

And under the lucid water
I find the divergent one
We embrace with tenderness
And I loved him for my own
Breathing gentle and easy

On the mountain, above the tallest mountains
The deep green wind blows
Nobody lived there, the graves are tended,
I went without my sight
I find a way, a prayer in the night

At the edge, so far to fall
I've chosen to lay my body down on the earth
My fingers reach for her reassuring warmth
My cares fall away
Forgotten among her roots

Mourning, on the first rays of sunshine
Searing my throat with sadness
A glimmer of promise to guide me
Prayers of hope love and desire
Letting go of my happiness

And from the roads in Dreamtime
You walked in, I cried out
I've been shredded
Fiber after fiber pulled away
A shattered heart feels everything

Look at me, look at me
There is nothing left
Impossible to fill the void with words
Find yourself
I love you

—Collin Ruiz, ©2010

Four:
THE DAY I WENT DOWN

I WOKE UP IN A 4-STAR HOTEL in a luxurious bed. It isn't flat, but poofed up with softness. The sheets felt soft and smelled fresh. I yearned to go back to sleep (for about two years).

However, today is the day that I am "self-surrendering." That means I will walk into the Federal Prison Camp of my own volition. It is a Sunday morning in January.

My brother Mesa and my sister Greta have driven me here to Phoenix. I'm walking into prison a day earlier than was required of me so that they can drop me off and drive back on Sunday instead of Monday (and not miss a day of work). I am aware that this process is hard not only for me but for my family as well.

Today is that day. Freedom doesn't feel so free anymore. I've left my home packed into a shed, taken my Buddhist vows, and said goodbye to my son. There's nothing left to do except walk into prison.

I am anticipating what it will be like inside prison. My brain seems to be operating in a frantic, slow-mo mode, like I'm moving underwater. Everything is dampened down. I want to resist the temptation to go unconscious. I am determined to live wide awake during my time in prison. In my monastery.

Anticipating life in prison, it's the basics, the physical things like food and human touch that preoccupy my mind. For this reason, I consciously chose to spend this weekend in a luxurious resort and pamper myself. I want to wake up my senses and hold onto memories of what I won't have in prison. I want to go in with Spirit wrapped around my shoulders, like a bearskin holding me, keeping me solid.

38

The resort lays out this awesome gourmet breakfast bar. Fresh raspberries, looking so red, smelling so wonderful, as many as anyone could want, a bottomless bowl of raspberries. *What do I want with my raspberries?* I have so many options: oatmeal and granola with numerous toppings, eggs prepared to order. I ate until I thought I would burst. The resort seeks to satisfy its guests with all of this food and I'm painfully aware I won't get pampered like this for a long time. I will somehow have to find my own satisfaction! *But will I be satisfied?*

Just last week, Ralph talked to me about desire and the human tendency to be dissatisfied. Discernment, he told me, was the challenge—distinguishing between what is supportive to our practice and what hinders it. We desire food when we're hungry. We desire sleep when we're tired. But what is enough? Finding enough is what Buddhists call 'the middle way.'

Ralph instructed me to let go of anything and everything that could be used against me by guards and other inmates. The third Buddhist precept says, "I will abstain from sexual misconduct. A disciple of Buddha does not misuse sexuality but rather cultivates and encourages open and honest relationships."

Ralph said, "No sex! No thinking about sex! No contemplation, daydreaming, or ruminating about sex, past, present, or future." *No* sex!

Though everything he said made sense, I wondered how reasonable it is to completely disconnect from one's sexual nature. Nevertheless, I'm committed to remove all distractions and hindrances from my monastic path.

Everything in these last couple weeks is a goodbye: goodbye to raspberries, goodbye to being with my son, goodbye to sex. I am preparing myself to let go. I am hoping I'll feel ready to let go. I keep repeating a mantra: "*I am ready to let go of the physical nature of my world.*" I will walk a spiritual path. Detach from the human inclination for physical touch. *Can that really be done? Is it just a decision? Can I choose to let it go?*

This past week, when I took my Buddhist vows, I contemplated shaving my head. What if I walked into prison as a nun? If I did, would the spiritual nature of Buddhism be more palpable to me? I think about how a child's demeanor changes when he puts on a cape. I could really use some superpowers right now.

After breakfast, I'm getting a massage. I feel like I am sleepwalking. Everything is vivid, and at the same time, just out of reach as if in a dream. The massage room is a calm blue, very quiet, and heavily curtained. Before I know it, it is over. I step outside into the bright light.

As I walk back to my room, I think, *Every step I take I know is getting closer to prison.*

Mesa and Greta are waiting for me. Knowing they must leave me behind and go back to their lives, I am so grateful they are here at this moment with me.

Since Kenge went on the run, much of this trek has felt very lonely. I don't have a significant other and my family members are very far away. There is no one that I can talk to about how I'm doing through this process. Phone conversations don't feel safe to me; I always wonder if someone is listening, especially when it comes to Kenge and my case.

My family members experience a range of feelings about this whole situation. We all feel grief over Kenge's disappearance. However, we are each responding differently to the fallout. Some feel anger, others feel some mixture of bewilderment, betrayal, anguish or worry. I appreciate how Greta walks a middle ground with her supportive attitude towards me. She says we don't have to see eye to eye to help each other.

As Greta and I grew into adulthood, we got along better and better. As a mother herself, Greta is deeply empathetic. Traveling with Greta always feels easy and enjoyable. Maybe that's because both of us are mutable astrology signs; astrology rules say that we adapt to change easily. I'm counting on this now.

Ever since Kenge left, Mesa has reached out to me, offering me his support. He included me in his spiritual community and organized a sweat lodge for me. He encouraged me with prayer and ceremony.

Mesa had told me that he had a dream about walking with me up to the doorway of prison and leaving me to go through the door. When I think of entering prison, I have this image of me walking up wooden stairs to stand on a platform, like the structures used for a hanging. *That's not good!*

Then I remember this passage about the god Thor from Ralph Blum's *The Book of Runes*:

> "Visualize yourself standing before a gateway on a hilltop. Your entire life lies out behind you and below. Before you step through, pause and review the past: the learning and the joys, the victories and the sorrows—everything it took to bring you here. Observe it all, bless it all, release it all. For in letting go of the past you reclaim your power. The quality of your passage depends upon your attitude and upon the clarity of your intention. Be certain that you are not suffering over your suffering." (pp. 133-134, ©1982 Ralph Blum)

Great rune!

Mesa has been out walking around, praying all morning. He will hold the space and give a moment to Spirit. This feeling of vulnerability leaves me feeling physically weak. My legs are strong, and at the same time, I need them both to help me walk to the doorway. Knowing I must step over the threshold myself and so unsure I can make it to the doorway.

I remember what Ralph taught me and I focus on my breathing. Anytime I got into a mind loop such as *What is it going to be like in prison,* breathe! I think, *Air is coming in, air is leaving.* Thoughts of Jera, *Breathe.*

Mesa takes us to a spot on the hotel grounds that has a small tree and semi-circle brick wall. He does a ceremony and what stands out, is their voices, the actual sound, and their way of speaking stays in my head. I don't remember the words, but I move forward with their presence.

Ceremony is a form of communication to Spirit. We give all of our desires and our sorrows over to Spirit and we pray for strength. I feel Mesa and Greta supporting me. I feel the energy in their words, and their bodies' energy is strong.

As we leave the resort, I notice there are flowers here, in January! *What kind of world am I walking into?* Driving to the prison, I feel Greta and Mesa, but we remain silent on this ride. I don't know whether there's a hundred things to say or nothing at all to be said. We pull up to the front of the prison and park. Still no words between us.

All that's left is to walk in. Compared to when I left Jera, I'm calm, cool, and collected. Greta and Mesa expose their grief with tears in their eyes.

I can't let myself remain in the goodbyes as I walk through that door. I can't walk into prison crying. To get through this I must get past the goodbyes. I tell Mesa and Greta not to get out of the car when we get there. It feels like one moment I'm with them and the next I'm not. Here's the moment I've been imagining. I walk through the door. Suddenly, I'm in prison. I don't look back.

In the entryway, a woman stands crying and holding onto a man. He leaves and we walk into the office together. Two women self-surrendering at the same time. Something about the transition gave us a common bond that continued throughout our stay. She talks first and an officer takes her away. Then I step up and tell the officer my name.

The officer wrinkles his brow saying, "You're a day early!"

"Yep," I blurt out, "time to get this party started!"

I'm processed one more time. When I change into uniform this time, I know I'm leaving more than clothes behind. The officer asks, "Do you want your clothes held during your sentence?"

I imagine my sweaty clothes in a zipped plastic bag for two years. *Eww.* I tell him, "No."

At this point, they've taken everything from me. There are no remnants of my life left. I ask to keep my hair tie and a piece of paper with my important phone numbers on it. If I forget my sister's phone number, even for a moment, I feel like the stress will overwhelm me.

I'm about to put on my uniform which makes me look like every other inmate. Army-green pants and light green t-shirts. My identity is washed away. I know who I am but what do I look like to these people? Does the brown color of my skin—my Mexican heritage—make me a Mexican to them? I don't even speak Spanish. And how can I tell who these women are? Will their skin color shape my view of them? How can I see past the surface and truly know them?

Once I've changed into my new clothes, an inmate is waiting outside the door. The guard hands me a stack of bedding and uniforms and tells me to follow the inmate to my unit. The elastic waistband of my pants is too tight. My arms are full, holding a pillow, sheets, a blanket, a few pairs of pants, and t-shirts.

This inmate I'm following is the first inmate I see up close. She's got her hair pulled back tight, slick, and black like her boots, her high-top boots laced to the top with her pants tucked in. She is silent. I follow her up a concrete path to a two-story building. I see dirt, cacti, and fellow inmates watching from afar. Nobody walks past us. In fact, nobody is on this walkway except us. On one hand, I feel like I'm on display, and on the other hand, I'm thinking, *Where is everyone?* I thought it would be crowded. I had visions in my head, like in the movies where the newbie is walking down the hall, inmates hanging out of their cells yelling. *Nobody is yelling at me. That's a good start.*

As we enter the building, the hallways seem very dark, maybe because the Arizona sun is so bright? Later, I would watch others come and I wonder about their first impressions, because once settled in, the halls never seem so dark as on that first day.

I see inmates staring at me. I'm glancing around at everybody and everything. I see the bathroom at the far end of the hall. Walking down the hall, I notice that the cells have no doors. They're rooms with only a partial wall, so I see an inmate lying on her bunk, another sitting at her desk bolted to the wall. I see everyone! Suddenly, I'm aware of how completely exposed I am 24/7.

I'm a stranger in someone else's home. That helps me cope with all the watchful stares. Here, with no pretense of privacy, people lose their filters: they stare, they're blunt, and they make no attempt at politeness. It's unsettling, and it will take some time to get used to the things inmates say and do in here.

In the hall just in front of the bathroom, two bunks sit side by side with a locker in between. This is my new house, the bottom bunk in the hall.

"Here you go," my inmate guide says. She turns and leaves and now there is no one to tell me what to do. *Is there a handbook that I'm supposed to read, telling me what to do next?*

The gal on the top bunk is looking down at me. She smiles and asks, "So who are you?"

I reply, "Collin."

"I don't have extra flip-flops, but I'll find some for you. You can't walk the halls barefoot, *ever*, because there are scorpions all over."

I look down at the floor thinking, *I'll bet they're well camouflaged on this off-white floor.*

"I'm your new bunkie," she says, "I'll introduce you to some of the other girls."

"And your name?" I ask.

"Just call me Bunkie."

Later that evening, Bunkie asks me, "Do you need a coat?"

"Yes, please! I get cold easily and I can't see how I'm going to make it with only t-shirts."

I'm so grateful to have a warm coat. January in Phoenix is warmer than Colorado when the sun is out, but winters are still chilly here.

I make my bed, put my clothes in my locker, and sit on my bunk. A neighboring inmate comes over to ask if I need anything else. *Do I?* I'm not sure yet. She looks like the lady that cleaned my hotel room. I imagine her in a hotel uniform, asking me if I need an extra towel.

Other women are coming by, saying hi. Too many faces for me to remember who's who. One young woman comes by and says, "I hear you need flip-flops." She hands me the shower flip-flops. She tells me, "You can buy the cool kind with a band over the toes so that you can wear them with your socks at night. If you have money on your books," she added, "then you will be allowed to go to the first available commissary."

Wow. I wasn't expecting everybody to be so nice to me. It kind of throws me off. I'm here in their world—my new world.

The commissary opens twice a week. Half the population goes on Wednesday, while the other half goes on Thursday. I'm told that in the next few days, I will have to attend an orientation. I'll finally receive the handbook with all the rules in it. For now, I watch and listen.

I go outside and sit at an empty concrete table. Everything looks so well-kept. The dirt is raked like in a Japanese garden. There are pretty designs made with the rocks on the dirt. Some trees and cacti. Women walking around, talking, and laughing.

If I squint just a little bit, I can see that this is a monastery. These nuns have lots of tattoos and scars, though. The women don't look mean or as serious as I imagined. *And so far, nobody is yelling at me. Whew.*

A young girl comes and sits down with me. She is beautiful, a Native American, and so young, must be in her twenties. Of course, I'm trying to imagine what she did to land here. *Should I be afraid of her?* "First day?" Her voice is friendly and direct.

"Yep."

"What unit did they put you in?"

"That one," I say, pointing at my building.

"Do you have children?"

"Yep."

"Did you come from a different prison?"

"No." I feel her assessing me. Fortunately, she seems to lose interest quickly and walks away.

I get the feeling that she came over to see me up close, see how old I am, and if am I going to be her companion. *Do I look like someone that needs a companion?* I want to laugh! Maybe I should have shaved my head before I entered my new prison-monastery. I imagine how this conversation would go if I had. But would she have guessed in a million years that I shaved my head for spiritual reasons?

In Buddhism, shaving one's head when entering a monastic lifestyle visibly indicates one's commitment to leave the ego and worldly ways behind in pursuit of a higher spiritual life.

Already, the life I left on the outside feels so far away. I'm in this new world for the next two years. *What will it do to me? Who will I become?*

In here my identity is being given to me; I'm wearing my uniform, and my name's replaced by a number. I'm a prisoner.

That's the role they've assigned me to play. But in my monastery, if I can shape my inner world, maybe I'll find freedom to become my best self. I want that.

Of course, Ralph told me, "You cannot 'want' anything!" *Really, how is that possible?* Is wanting to be home and wanting to be with my son hindering my inner growth?

I can't help but wonder, *Is Jera still able to be himself without me there?* Immediately, I feel like crying, so I stand up and breathe. *"Don't want anything"* *is an absurd demand! Or maybe it's powerful instruction. And wise. I can't decide right now.*

I think he was trying to teach me about non-attachment, one of Buddhism's central concepts. It's not just about self-denial. It's about not allowing things to own you. It includes relationships, emotions, and the clothes on your back. Buddhism teaches that when you let go of every-thing, you can enjoy the world just as it is.

Despite the awkwardness of being in this strange new place, I do have this odd sense of opportunity here. It's something akin to the feeling I had when I would go on vacation or work conferences. I would challenge myself to reinvent myself as more confident or outgoing.

Nighttime comes and my first day is done. Once we are on lockdown, I'm thinking I'll go to sleep as quickly as possible to leave this place be-hind for a while. Then I remember, I *must wait until we are counted, then I can sleep.* Finally, I lay down, the lights are still on, they are always on. I can hear people breathing or snoring all around me.

The lights allow the guards to see women sleeping on their bunks. Face out to protect your back or face the wall with the illusion of privacy. *Will sleep take me away? What will my dreams bring to me?*

After about two weeks, they assign Bunkie and me to a room upstairs. I still have the bottom bunk, which makes me happy. I hear that the scor-pions drop down from the ceiling. The bunks are up against the far wall with a window on the left side. I sleep with my head away from the win-dow while Bunkie sleeps with her head at the window side. Just a small measure of privacy.

Prison world has its own culture, rules, and expectations. The days are still so new and weird. At my orientation, the guard says, "You'll all be required to take classes. Most of you will take classes to prepare for the GED exam."

He's shuffling papers and suddenly calls out, "Ruiz?" I raise my hand. He asks, "Ruiz, did you graduate from high school?"

Oh, boy, what do I say here? I tell the truth, "No. I didn't graduate high school and don't have a GED, but I have bachelor's and master's degrees." Everybody laughs and stares at me. He shakes his head and says, "we'll figure out what classes you need later." I feel like the odd-ball here.

I do get a handbook of sorts, which I read cover to cover, and I still am so stressed about where I need to be every minute of the day. Check-in, lockdown, meals, and everything is different on the weekends. Also, I must listen for my name over the intercom. Every time that thing goes off, I jump. *Is it me? Am I in trouble?* Inmates assume someone is in trouble if their name is heard over the intercom.

I want to talk to my family, my son, but I'm waiting for phone privileges. We submit a list of phone numbers. Phone numbers must be checked out and approved before calls can be made.

Waiting for phone privileges seems to be the source of enormous tension I feel in my body. I'm trying to practice patience. I'm telling myself, *connectedness comes from inside. I'm still a mom, and I still have a family on the outside.* However, no matter what pep talk I give myself, I'm afraid I'll disappear into this prison system.

Patience might be seen in Buddhist philosophy as letting go of expectations, practicing non-attachment, and being in the present moment. Yet, letting go is never a simple formula that guarantees a specific outcome. The practice takes time and effort. Patience arises gradually.

When I am finally able to call my family members, it is such a relief. I talk to Jera—it's a ray of sunshine. When I talk to my siblings, I feel calmer. Greta ordered a magazine subscription for me. Mesa put money on my books. Knowing that people remember me matters. Knowing that I'm still Mom to my son matters.

Self-care takes a whole different meaning here. I do the basic life things: sleep, eat, shower. However, everything feels a little unnatural; things are always subject to outside regulation and control and I'm always aware of the lack of privacy. There are very few doors here. The bathroom has an open floor plan with two sinks and two toilet stalls on one side and three shower stalls on the other side. Prison rules dictate no showering before 7 a.m., or after last count and, of course, no showering together. Just imagine thirty women sharing three showers.

At least these were stalls where you could step in a couple of feet, remove your clothes, and then step into the shower.

The inmates have shower rules, too: when someone is in the shower and you want to be next, you put your towel on their stall door and yell out your name. Then when that person gets out, they yell your name, and you better jump in because, most likely, someone else is waiting to take your place.

The showers get crowded after work and just before lockdown. And if you want to take a shower after hours or with someone, you get a lookout. The lookout hangs out above the stairwell, next to a window, announcing loudly if a guard is coming toward our unit.

Compared to the hardness and the pace of prison, showering is as close to normalcy as we get. When the water hits my skin, I feel. When the water pours over me and I breathe, just me, just water. I remember myself for maybe a second. Yet, it is only a momentary thing that can be overwhelmed by everything on the other side of the stall door: women using the toilets, talking non-stop on the other side of the stall.

In here, naked is no longer normal, even for a few minutes. I don't ever really let my guard down. Showers are rushed. Quick, quick, get clean, move on. The intimacy with our own bodies is washed down the drain.

One day, I'm in the bathroom, and a gal asks me to look at the underside of her boob. She has just taken a shower and felt something there. She tried to look at it in the mirror, but the mirror above the two sinks is a shiny metal mirror like the ones at a rest-stop restroom. She tells me that she wears a bra 24/7, and she is concerned that she might have a splinter. I can't find anything, just a lesion.

Many women here wear their bras 24/7. I can't imagine not having "bra off" time. At home, "bra off" means downtime. It means, "No, I'm not going out." It means, "No, I'm not going to exercise." It means, "I'm done." At home, I'd think of my bathroom as a private place; I'd think of my body as private. I'd even believe that nighttime is my private time. In prison, bra off at night feels like I'm taking back a narrow measure of privacy.

Even though I am five rooms away from the bathroom, I hear the toilets flushing. I wonder how anyone can stand living right next door to the bathroom. Besides the sound, the smell carries. I learned right away about "the courtesy flush." My Bunkie says, "If something, anything, is leaving your body, you are flushing so that the smell is flushed away!" It really does prevent the smell from leaving the area; however, sometimes, a visit to the toilet takes quite a few flushes.

One day, I'm walking down the hall on my way to the bathroom. The gal living in the room next to the bathroom looks up from her bunk and says, "This is Alma's fiftieth fucking flush!" This gal is livid, cursing up a storm, "Fifty fucking flushes!"

So, I started counting flushes. Eventually, I could tell who was using the toilet just by the number of flushes. Nobody could compete with Alma! I'd usually lose track after she reached fifty flushes. The average woman flushes about twenty-five times every time she sits down on the pot.

A notice posted on our bulletin board downstairs talks about conserving water here in the desert. It makes me laugh. Many of these inmates don't read English. I think that water conservation is the least concern of any inmate. And, even if they know about the issue, flushing may be a sort of silent rebellion. Conservation is their world. Keeping the smells down is our world. My Bunkie says, "Even just a fart should be flushed."

Peeing at night is problematic. First, I have my shower shoes right beneath my bunk so that I do not step on any scorpions barefoot. Then, as I get out of bed, sliding my feet into my slippers, I pause. The rule is that if you happen to be in the bathroom and you hear the guards on the floor, you must stay in the bathroom at the door until you are counted. You never know if the guards were going to be on time or not, so if you decide to wait until the guards are done with count, it could be a while.

Most of the time, I make a run for it, pee as quickly as possible, and race back to bed.

Some guards were terrible about the whole thing, making a huge deal, yelling at women when they were in the bathroom and not in their bunks. Like it was such a *huge* inconvenience to them that we had to pee. A friend of mine woke up one night while she was menstruating; she had leaked on her sheets. She ran to the bathroom, and suddenly, she heard the guards. She came out of the stall, blood on her nightgown, and stood there to be counted. The guard reprimanded her for being out of bed. She cried and cried.

Here we are, hundreds of women being treated worse than animals. When normal bodily functions are seen as a major annoyance, where is dignity? Where is modesty? Where is respect? *Where is the sacred?* We are simply being dehumanized.

Word passes among the inmates when there is a new arrival or departure. We have two new arrivals today. I rarely notice the arrivals, it's not like I'm expecting a friend to show up.

Inside this world, leaving is more significant than arriving. Watching an inmate leave makes us all cry. Usually, inmates will watch their friends leave, yelling at them and crying.

When I watch someone leave, I envision our walls as a tall, jagged mountain with a raging waterfall. Behind the waterfall is a tunnel leading outside to another world. The leaving inmate walks through the veil of water, enters the tunnel, and finally emerges on the other side where a new world awaits.

I made a point to watch one woman leave. Weeks in advance, many inmates were talking about her leaving. I didn't really know her at all. I hadn't had any conversations with her, but I couldn't help thinking about her. She had been down for twenty years! She was going to ride a bus to Florida and surprise her family. I imagine her awe at how the world has changed so much in the last twenty years. *What will leave her breathless? What feeling will fill her up when she is reunited with her family?*

While she changes her clothes, I watch the door. Lots of women show up for this departure, crowded on the sidewalk opposite her pathway. The women yell, "Take care!" or "I'll miss you!" I cry watching her walk out. I'm so happy for her! I can't pray any harder for her to make it on the outside and to live happily ever after!

Then I feel it: one leaves, and it changes the whole vibe of our prison life. That voice is no longer with us. For me, leaving here seems such a long way away.

I must find my own routine, my rhythm. When I read books and magazines, I pull words and phrases and write them on the piece of paper I brought in with me. I never go without what I call my "pocket notes."

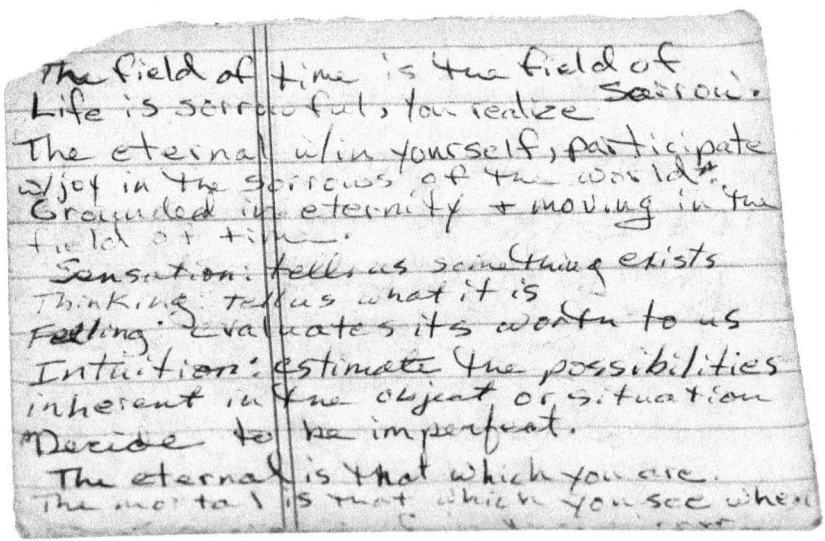

When a pocket note gets full and hard to read because of the fading ink, I start a new piece of paper. Over time, I write smaller and smaller, filling the paper with various inspiring mantras, quotes, and thoughts.

I've extracted highlights from my collection of pocket notes and refor-
matted them like this:

POCKET NOTE:

> Sensation: tells us something exists
> Thinking: tells us what it is
> Feeling: evaluates its worth to us
> Intuition: estimate the possibilities inherent in the
> object or situation

Greta starts writing to me right away. She writes, "I hardly write anymore, so it has been great fun to find cards for you! And images seem so
much better than words sometimes."

I look forward to getting her cards. It always means so much that
she is reaching out. Usually, they are simple notes, telling me what they
are up to.

Often, she includes a poem. I know reading it I will likely cry. Even
though I have never sought out poetry to read, never owned a book of
poetry, the poems she finds for me always resonate. Her notes and poems
reconnect me to feelings of real human contact and love.

In one note she wrote, "Poems, the great ones, touch places inside of
us. I hope some of these poems touch you deeply and stay with you like a
friend." It invites us to change a viewpoint.

Inside, poetry was a gift, the best shaft of light, the potential for something to touch me. Greta says poetry is expansive. Poetry offers solace.
Greta is never trite.

Buddha Behind Bars

SPACE

What is space? Where am I? I feel the distortion in my blood
Unoccupied regions with the capacity to hold substance
Lightening dancing in the sky, filling up the space for only a moment
Shackles rattling in my head, razors around my ankles
Sensory deprivation, holes where there should be wholes

Is this where space comes from?
Identity stripped like the clothes from my back
Naked, shaking from hunger, can't sleep
Too much noise, too much light, too many bad dreams, too many lines
being drawn
Go in, go deep, go home, hold on,

Absolute space, existing whether there is matter present or not
Our system of Justice rolls over me like an angry ocean wave
I can't fight it, can't define it, can't control it
I'm walking through the days like a ghost...formless, imposed structure
I may not look like what you believed in

Nerves and blood, that's all that's left of me
The bearskin is draped over my shoulders, to remind me who I am
The outside owns the inside
I am owned by the land
My heart is this body's world

Space is a relationship between entities
Continuously space connects you and me /between

THE DAY I WENT DOWN

A hand reaching through the pool of blood I'm in
Finding beauty in negative space, expanding from the center
Show me your language of love

Designing our free space to fit our new lives not with goodbyes
But pounding the drums, shaking the rattles
The effort to change, the forgiving, the prayers
My heart tears, fighting raw maternal instinct
We create with our will to love, commitment to "love in action"

After 69 days the Chilean miner holds his wife
Arms holding the space for comfort, holding on and on
Allowing space to dream, to become daring, gentle and fearless
Lay me down, let me rest, freed from my own darkness
We can make it whatever we want it to be

Creating free space where love can travel without obstructions
Looking to the heart to wake me up, what is my core made of?
Learning to float, sleeping whales, surrendering
The popping sounds you hear are grains of sand exploding
Never forgetting the beauty of the world, breathing out the blackness

Time in space being measured by the speed of light
An interlude in space, time for discrimination
Space is boundless, spirit is unbound
My breathing space, the rabbit hole
Keep me whole, please keep me whole

Wholes in space

— Collin Ruiz ©2011, revised ©2014

Buddha Behind Bars

The first poem Greta sent me:

For Mimi in Jail

Brave as you were, you will only get braver
Just as colors ring and deepen in the dusk
Keep out an ear for the wild voice inside you
As you sit up steeping in the city's musk

Narrow the walls, the locked walls that surround you
While they're taking your time for breaking their rules
But wide is the sky, and it's all hidden inside you
Like a file in a pie, starry dome of your mind

And don't mind the doubt and keep to your counsel
Don't you worry about all that wasted time
'Cause day in day out with your hands tied behind you
You touch more than you see, you are working our way free

And narrow the path, it is wished we would follow
Looking neither up nor down
Enlightened horizon or dim bloody hollow
Just swallow, Just swallow
But wide is the sky, and it's all hidden inside you
Unexplored, unconfined, starry dome
Of your mind

—Myshkin

Five:
STAY STRONG, STAY HUMAN

*I*S THAT MY NAME BEING CALLED? That intercom stresses me out! I can't tune it out because if they page me and I don't show up immediately, they'll assume I've broken out of prison. Yeah, right. Word has it one inmate escaped a while back. She made it to the Mexican border in less than six hours. So, now they count us every five hours.

When I do hear my name, my heart skips a beat, even though they only call me when my boss leaves me a message or when I have an appointment with my counselor.

The intercom reminds me of a machine that a physical therapist used on me. It contracted muscles by delivering an electronic impulse. No matter how hard I tried to relax, the anticipation made me more tense than the machine! In here, it's the same: I'm hooked up, but I don't know when the next shock will come.

Ms. Juanita, our permanent camp director, gets so angry when an inmate doesn't immediately show up after being called on the intercom. We all jump each time we hear it. When someone fails to respond, then all hell breaks loose.

One day, at the three o'clock lockdown, an elderly black woman in a nearby room is absent. A couple of guards show up and ask us when we last saw her. They shakedown her room, tearing her bed apart, going through her locker and all her letters. Once the guards leave, inmates start talking and the inmate who drives people says she took the woman to the dentist that morning.

Cora, the missing woman, has only a couple months left on her sentence. I don't know her at all, but all the inmates were saying that there was no way she would run. They called the driver down to the office and she came back crying. Ms. Juanita had yelled at her even though she forgot to send her to pick up Cora. It's always the inmate's fault.

Bunkie rants, "This is so fucked up! They don't care about us. Cora sat in the dentist's office all day starving." According to the rules, Cora couldn't accept anything from civilians, and, of course, she had no money to use a vending machine.

Bunkie continues, "We're not humans to them, just things." She's stating the obvious. We stay on lockdown until Cora returns. I notice the tightness in my body and take a deep breath. In the monastery of my mind, prison drama is just more tension to be breathed out of my body.

Our lives in prison are exposed and public. Guards will rarely use our given names. To them, I am an eight-digit number. Numbers don't carry rhythm quite like names. A number doesn't remind me of *Bertha* or *Hope*. A person's name becomes intimate information. Names are personal. Names evoke faces.

JOURNAL:

Inside, names are strangely protected. Most inmates do not call each other by their names. Some women call everybody "friend" or "mama." Many women go by nicknames. The common way of getting to know someone starts with an introduction: "Hi, my name is Collin." In prison: "Hi, I *go* by Collin." It's the name I choose today.

The story behind a name can be very significant to the one named. Names are important. Traditionally, parents name children thoughtfully, and baby names are full of meaning and significance. Siddhartha means "accomplished goal." Jacob was named "heel catcher;" as the second of two twins, he came out holding his brother's ankle.

According to numerology, your birth name contains your abilities, talents, and other characteristics. Because names carry such significance and meaning, I consider the use of someone's name a sign of respect. I want to be respectful and respect the privacy of a person by calling them by the name they want, birth name, nickname, etc. I lean toward calling someone by their last name. In that way, I'm recognizing the person *and* giving them privacy.

Names do get used and that has its challenges as well, in this melting pot of prison. Mimi, who is really Naomi, says nobody can pronounce her name. I thought I knew how to pronounce Naomi, but she pronounces it "No-Emmy," not "Nay-oh-mee."

Another name that confused me was Yoli. One day I was talking to Bunkie. "You know Yoli with the dark hair, on the first floor? Where does she work?"

She says, "That's not Yoli; that's Oli. It's short for Olivia. Oli is pronounced Oh-lee. Yoli is 'Yo-lee,' like "Hey, yo lee, short for Yolanda."

"No wonder, I thought there were too many Yoli's," I said. "This is so confusing,"

Now instead of going around thinking that there is an awful lot of Yoli's, I ask, "Is your first name Olivia or Yolanda?"

JOURNAL:

Do we have an unconscious need to have someone see who we are (even if we are afraid to see and know our authentic self)? A "relationship" starts with a perceived intimacy. Any two women in the same space tend to tell each other things about their past.

Once I have a name for a particular woman, then I want to ask, "What's your story?" But the question just rolls around in my head gathering lint because "What's your story?" is *not* appropriate inmate conversation. Without street clothes to reveal their identity, and no trust to share stories, I feel like I'm constantly playing that game where you make up a story for the strangers nearby. For example, when you are waiting for your food at a restaurant, looking at the strangers at the next table in the restaurant, you wonder, *Is this their first date? Do they have children? Are those two in love?*

JOURNAL: Inmates tell me that I don't *look* like I belong in prison. Well, I am an inmate and the property of the state, just like every woman here. But what are they noticing when they say I don't look like I fit in? My walk, my talk, my "*energy?*" What makes me different? Could it be that I am living in a monastery and therefore I'm having a different experience than most inmates? Have I acquired a different way of being because of my new point of view? Is that what others see?

The mood rarely changes day to day. The stress, tension, and apprehension of prison feel like something physical running through my body keeping me rigid. However, this morning, inmates are talking about a shakedown. Someone has seen the guards suiting up in bulletproof vests. Feeling a little panicky, inmates pass contraband to other inmates to hide. *Do I have any contraband or food that I shouldn't have? What about the extra t-shirts I have?*

Bunkie suggested I take my plastic knife to work to get it out of sight. When I go outside, I see a herd of guards fully suited-up and walking into our yard. At the end of the day, I find out I have been written up for keeping crocheted slippers in my locker. *Oops! I forgot that those were contraband.*

A lot of women crochet while in prison. Needlepoint and card-making are also popular. One rule forbids us from keeping arts and crafts projects in prison for more than thirty days. Every shakedown follows a theme based on whatever the newest member of our guard detail thinks is over the top for us criminals. In this shakedown, they were prosecuting the heinous crime of "too much crocheted stuff!"

Slippers are common on our floor. They make them from shower flip-flops. After removing the Y-shaped strap, they crochet a slipper onto a flip-flop sole. My slippers were gray with a white design, and they were warm! That's all I cared about. One evening on my way to the bathroom, an inmate said, "Ah, the skull and crossbones slippers—those were mine for a minute." *Oh, I hadn't noticed the skull and crossbones design.*

I got my first "shot" for having contraband slippers. A shot gets placed in an inmate's file as a strike against her record. Shots mean you can lose privileges like buying food at the commissary, using the phone, or having visitors. I lost commissary privileges for thirty days.

Bunkie told me write-ups could add up and cause trouble for me down the road. It's not that I break a rule and then spend all my time looking over my shoulder. It's the fact that I'm looking over my shoulder wondering if I did something against the rules I don't yet know about. The rules are not always common sense to me. Like, why does an art project become contraband when it remains in your room for over thirty days? The apprehension around being written up contributes to the ongoing stress of prison.

I try to counteract the stress by imagining a more relaxed atmosphere where colorful blankets adorn every inmate's bunk. Now that would transform this cold prison. When I get into bed every night, I think about replacing the thin, cotton prison blanket with a warm, beautiful, cozy blanket. Imagine walking down the hall seeing colorful blankets on every bunk. That would be so cool. However, as I was told over and over, the rules are in place for a reason. *Whatever.*

POCKET NOTE:

> The most transformative thing is being okay with everything.

Whenever I feel particularly tense, like the walls are closing in, I look at my pocket notes. I want to remind myself to expand. Checking my pocket notes becomes a daily practice. First, I breathe out. Then, with the inbreath, I imagine the words of pocket note flowing through me.

Breathing techniques are an integral component of yoga and meditation to support the mind-body connection. Intentional breathing leaves me feeling more flexible and resilient. Sometimes, I contemplate what I have written down and create an affirmation such as, "I choose to be okay with the numerous intrusions into my personal space today."

The day after the shakedown, six women were sent to county jail. For excess contraband? I'm not sure why. Going to county jail meant you likely wouldn't return to this minimum-security camp. The higher security institutions are generally much worse for the prisoners. The few who returned after being in other prisons told stories that made us feel like we had it pretty good: the food was horrible, you stay in your cell all day, and your bunkie will probably make you crazy.

One day while I'm sitting outside reading and writing, an inmate I know comes by to let me know that recycling is looking for a worker. The recycling job pays better than Water Ops and offers more free time. I go to the main office to let them know I'm interested in the recycling job.

Back in my room, I'm fretting, Will my new "shot" prevent me from landing this new job?

JOURNAL:

The rules continually reinforce our identity as prisoners. The "system" has become "they" and now I'm part of the "we." Despite learning about Buddhism and non-duality, I'm feeling like I've been sucked into the undertow. In here, the us/them duality serves to assert authority and to dehumanize. How do I avoid becoming bitter? Bitterness, a chronic state of pervasive, smoldering resentment takes root when we feel trapped or bound and when we feel cut off from joy. I imagine bitterness like being a starving wolf that won't let go of a bone. I'm not there yet.

A couple days later, I'm called to the office to speak to the recycling boss, Mr. Thomas. He asks me if I have any write-ups. I tell him that I was written up for having crocheted slippers and he laughs.

"You having slippers," he chuckled, "is the last thing I'm worried about."

I laughed along with him. We talked a little more and he said, "You got the job."

So much hassle and anxiety over a silly pair of slippers! But now I need to find myself a new pair of slippers. I'll be watching the trash can. Inmates share unwanted items by leaving them next to the trash can. New inmates have only what gets assigned to them. Over time, we acquire more of the stuff in circulation. Inmates generate very little trash. Our system of circulating used items was a way to care, to reassert our humanity to each other.

There's a Buddhist teaching here, too: human beings should display compassion to each other as part of a global community. Wealth is also seen as a great opportunity for generosity: give freely and take only what is being offered. The Buddhist vow of poverty amounts to a practice of living a simple life, simply.

> JOURNAL:
> What is mine? Every physical thing is not mine. What is mine doesn't define me. What happens when more than the physical things are taken away? The system has defined me as a number. Even my name has been taken away.

Some inmates, like me, subscribe to magazines. Magazines are in high demand. A few women read the articles, but the pictures were the real prize. The women who make cards would swoop up *National Geographic* and leave them again with half the pages cut into.

Mama J has a subscription to *USA Today*. When she was finished with them, she passed them on to me. I have never been much of a newspaper reader. However, now I'm really into it. It gives me a sense of what was happening outside in the big world. I always have a stack waiting for me.

At first, I am surprised how few inmates read. As I get to know their stories, I realize many women have limited education. Often responsible for their younger siblings, parents, or their own children, they scarcely had time for reading or for being children.

I am reminded how lucky I was to have had parents that encouraged reading time. Growing up, we rarely had TV, but we always had books. While I finish a book in a few days, Bunkie takes three or four months to read the same book.

JOURNAL:

There is us and there is them. Inmates and guards.

Guards are a special breed of people. Many have military backgrounds. Most are big guys. Every guard wears a badge with their last name on it. Inmates typically refer to specific guards by their last name. Guards work on three-month rotations. This way inmates never get too friendly with guards, nor guards with inmates. One guard works kitchen detail for three months, and then he could be working only on weekends in the visitor room.

The leniency of a guard depended on the unit he was patrolling and his own perspective of "the rules." I learn many of the rules from other inmates. Among the first rules I learned: don't get caught in someone else's room, don't take a shower after evening count, and don't take food from the dining hall.

Most of the time, guards are just walking around and watching. Inmates rarely have any reason to directly interact with a guard, with a few exceptions like mail call. If you are expecting mail, you go to mail call outside a small office after dinner. Anybody who is expecting mail is crowded around waiting for their name to be called. The guard calls someone's name and that inmate steps up to get their mail. Some guards knew our names. "Ruiz, where's Ruiz?" he'd ask. I'd step forward and he would give me my mail.

One guard, Mr. Johnson, would call out an inmate's number and that inmate couldn't just say, "Yes, that's me." Mr. Johnson would not give out mail unless we repeated our number to him. It felt so wrong saying, "I'm 05-327565."

Behavior like that seemed to reveal a lot about a guard's character. That proved true in the case of Mr. Johnson who made it abundantly clear how he felt about inmates. He would remind us that he was our "correction officer," and clearly, being here meant we needed correction. He knew right from wrong, and in his eyes, we were wrong, and *always* needed correction. I avoided him whenever possible, and around him, I made sure to keep it simple: "Yes, sir. No, sir."

When I worked in recycling, my work partner and I drove all over the compound in an electric golf cart. We also drove between our compound and the outlying warehouses.

One day as we are finishing up work, we pass Mr. Johnson in our compound. He says, "Wish I had a cart to drive around all day." I ignored the comment, however my workmate responded, "We need the cart to do our job!" Mr. Johnson barked some comment back to my workmate. He just wouldn't let her have the last word. At the end of our shift that day, we parked the cart as usual and hooked it up to charge the battery.

The next day, we couldn't find our golf cart. We searched everywhere, near and far. We finally walked out to the farthest field, the Boneyard, and there it was. I had a hunch this was Mr. Johnson's handiwork.

There was one guard, Mr. Henry, that everybody liked. He got sick and passed away. An inmate got a card and passed it around to other inmates who knew Mr. Henry. They wanted the card to go to his family and I said that I would take the card to Ms. Juanita. However, I was told that was not allowed. I still have the card.

Count happens every evening and midday on the weekends. In addition to daily counts, there are also check-ins depending on your work assignment, how much of the day you are at work, and how much time you spend in the compound.

I stand with Bunkie at our doorway, holding up our IDs. Most of the time, the officers would just walk by clicking their counter. Other times, they'd take our IDs and look at us. Being counted reminds us daily that they see us as numbers and not humans.

Our day starts at 5:30 a.m., so by 9 p.m. I'm ready for sleep, but we are not allowed to sleep until after the 9 p.m. stand-up count. Unfortunately, officers frequently show up late—anywhere between 9:30 and 10:30 p.m.

Sometimes I can't help but fall asleep. I heard an inmate got a shot when her bunkie didn't wake her up for count, so I feel lucky that mine would wake me when she hears the guards. An inmate who doesn't get along with her bunkie is out of luck.

It's difficult to develop a natural rhythm when the guards mess with our sleep schedules this way. We're held accountable while *they're* not. Sleep (or lack thereof) can be a source of frustration because it affects all other aspects of well-being.

It is part of my Buddhist practice to be mindful of frustration (and all emotions). Thoughts and feelings will inevitably arise like, *I am not a person to them. I'm just their job, just a head to be counted.* Yet, stewing in my annoyance will prevent me from easily falling asleep once count is finally done.

From a Buddhist standpoint, emotions cannot be controlled and it's not bad to feel emotions.

Mindfulness allows one to attend to emotions arising without suppressing or indulging them. Initially, I find it challenging to acknowledge them with no judgment. Buddhism teaches that with practice, we can free ourselves from reactivity and allow emotions to pass. I can't wait!

Before I had a job, I had to check in down at a booth throughout the day. The first week down, I missed a check-in. The guard on duty was Mr. Miguel, a Hispanic man. When I realized that I had missed the check-in an hour late, I ran over to the office and Mr. Miguel gave me a warning.

I didn't think too much about it until a couple weeks later when a white girl on my floor missed a check in and got a shot. She came walking into our unit pissed off and crying. "He only gives white girls shots!" I didn't tell her that I had missed check-in and didn't get a shot. I knew she was right—I lucked out because of the color of my skin.

I'm confounded by the large amount of voluntary segregation between the inmates, which I've heard is even worse in the men's prison. Not only between the white, black, and brown populations, but also between numerous divisions within each group.

When I think of the word "segregation," I think of the separation or isolation of a race, class, or ethnic group. In prison, the system attempts to erase personal identity: the inmates are all charged or convicted of something, all inmates wear the same (green) uniform, while the guards all wear the same (blue) uniform, asserting their authority.

Nevertheless, racism is out in the open here. I was shocked when I heard a new inmate, a white woman, say, "They better make sure I don't have to bunk with a nigger."

Outside, people attempt to downplay or deny their racism. Since college, I've had friends make comments about Mexicans and then turn to me and say, "But you're different." However, in here the color of my skin defines me as Mexican. Here, the color of our skin is meaningful for both inmates and guards. There are a lot of references to "your kind." And the uniform doesn't diminish the racism—it may, in fact, accentuate it.

JOURNAL:

It's interesting to me how people perceive a character or personality from the color of our skin. It's true for both guards and inmates. The color of a person's skin shapes others' perceptions of who that person is. I have the Mexican blood of my mother and the white blood of my father coursing through my body. I look Mexican; however, I was raised white, I don't speak Spanish, and I was raised with very little Mexican culture. Still, I feel closer to my mother's heritage, it resonates with me. Maybe being raised "off the grid" not being in school insulated me from the Mexican labels. On the other hand, maybe being raised white left me with unconscious bias that I'm just beginning to discover here in prison.

Buddhism teaches that separateness is an illusion. As I cultivate empathy, kindness, and compassion, for myself and those around me, the separateness dissolves.

Some inmates only speak Spanish. I think it's odd that not all guards speak Spanish. Mr. Thomas would say things like, "Do you understand what I'm saying because if you get this wrong, I'm going to be so pissed." Was he ever thinking that he should consider the challenges of our Spanish-speaking population? His dismissiveness is another example of judging by skin color. Today, we call this behavior a "microaggression."

One day each year, the guards come to work in their street clothes. Seems weird; I never understood the reasoning behind that. The guards' uniform asserts authority while the inmates' uniform establishes sameness. I did notice that a petite, quiet, white female guard liked motorcycles and Buddhism! She wore Harley clothes and a Buddha necklace. Bunkie confirmed the rumor that she was a Buddhist. It made her more human, and perhaps more humane in my view. In her line of sight I feel I could relax a bit, but I never tested the theory.

There are rules about "contact" with guards, even walking by them. These rules constrain inmates so that we do not come off as threatening. Therefore, if you are about to cross paths with a guard, the inmate always walks against the wall while the guard walks on the outside. No eye contact allowed.

One day, I'm walking toward the phones and a guard, Mr. Aaron, walks the other way toward the dining room. As we pass each other, Mr. Aaron, said "Hi, Ruiz." I almost tripped. *Whoa, what just happened? Was that genuine human contact?*

A guard being normal is so rare, that moment stuck with me. I remember everything about it. I remember I was wearing "weekend" clothes: shorts, a t-shirt, and tennis shoes. It was early morning and there was a cool breeze.

Funny how one moment of humanity awakens me to its general absence from this place. As a Buddhist, I'm called to bring compassion to everyone and every situation. Lord knows, these people—inmates and guards—need compassion.

Mr. Aaron suffered from elephantiasis on the right side of his body. His right arm was huge, and you could tell his right leg was also larger than normal. He usually wore a brace/cast on his right arm. I wondered if Mr. Aaron's own suffering made him more compassionate (and human).

JOURNAL:

Sometimes the things I miss are immediate, urgent, and palpable, like missing my son. Other times feelings like loneliness kind of sneak up on me. I miss talking to someone, anyone, just talking about real things without worrying about who can overhear my conversation or whether the person I'm talking to is trustworthy.

Whether I'm moving around in my unit or outside, there is always a feeling of the perimeter—the line you can't cross. In my unit, you can't go into anybody else's room. Stepping over the threshold to someone else's room is not allowed. That makes it hard to talk to someone. I can sit on my chair while someone else stands *outside*. These little things add up so that I am always on the alert, anxiously wondering, *What is going to happen next?* Never a time or a place to relax.

How can I expand my perimeter? When I am outside, walking around the track or at work, I look around and wonder what it would be like to keep walking. What if the perimeter was the top of the hill behind us? What would I see from there? From my work areas outside our compound, I can see a small section of the highway with the cars and trucks driving by. Even though they are far away, I imagine that *they* never look in, wondering about my life, as I wonder about theirs.

JOURNAL:

> The first few months are like a drive-by. I'm driving in a new neighborhood at night looking into the houses as I go by. I see people sitting around a table. I wonder, what are they having for dinner? I see someone passing in the light and maybe going to relax and watch a movie with a loved one. After being down for months and months, it feels like I'm only looking out from my house—never going out

A young woman flies by me all giggles. She has a handful of hearts, cut out of colored construction paper that she is going to put on her sweetie's bunk. Walking by another room, I see someone has strung up a whole lot of hearts above the top bunk.

It is Valentine's Day, my first *holiday* in prison. After breakfast, I came back to my unit and there are hearts everywhere. I am a little surprised. I believe the desire to be connected is innate in all of us, but I wasn't yet aware of the relationships around me.

Early into my sentence, I heard an interesting statistic from a TV show about prison life: Twenty-five percent of women going into prison are gay while seventy-five percent of women leaving prison are gay. While that statistic is dubious, it made me reflect on how sexuality functioned here in prison. I saw many different options for being *gay*. The saying, "Gay for the stay" had a myriad of meanings: gay for sex, gay for "best friend," gay for "man substitute," or gay as in sexually attracted to other women.

Some women were considered couples because they were always hanging together: to study the bible together, go to church together, and all sorts of companionship. Some women seem to choose sex as a means of connection, period.

JOURNAL:

I'm gaining new perspectives on the relationships I see forming in here. These women are living in an isolated environment that allows for development beyond any previously perceived boundaries. Exploring connections in new ways. In here, women put the opinions of friends and family on hold. What kind of expansion does that allow?

Given the variety of relationships women experience in prison, what does the statistic, "seventy-five percent of women leaving prison are gay" really imply? I hear women say they never had women friends before prison. I see women learning new things about themselves all the time. I wonder how the exploration of self and connections to other women might allow some women to discover new types of relationships that feel right for the first time.

Exploration of self. Sounds like a meditation to me. We are all here on retreat, exploring who we are. Interesting. Buddhism asks us to awaken to the world and to ourselves. Buddha = Awake. Meditation provides a means to awaken. Techniques or approaches to meditation include mindfulness, visualizations, and practicing an attitude of loving-kindness.

I heard stories and saw women who said this is the first time in their lives that they've had a chance to become who they were. Most carried such heavy burdens of responsibility before prison. Caring for their children, their siblings, their mothers, that they didn't know what it felt like to "just be."

This statistic (seventy-five percent of prisoners leave prison gay) gives me a lot to think about. Some inmates found something comfortable and safe in these intimate relationships, maybe for the first time. Some of those will continue in gay relationships while others will look for a new kind of relationship with men. So many of these women came from abusive relationships, even in childhood. By coming to prison and discovering something of themselves that felt better than ever before, they might just want to hold onto that. For others, the prison environment allowed for an inherent truth to be discovered and they will continue to identify as gay.

JOURNAL:
A Buddhist moment. I know I'm a Buddhist nun. This place demands it of me; it's the only option. When I look at other inmates, relationships form and break. I know I won't entertain thoughts of intimacy in here. This secrecy without privacy is not for me, not who I am. I've chosen to give up parts of myself (my sexuality) for the sake of the environment. Nuns and monks are no less human for being celibate. I choose passionate celibacy.

I read somewhere that Buddha's teachings don't forbid laypeople from having sex or make celibacy a prerequisite to awakening. However, for monks and nuns, craving for sensuality and sex has been seen as an obstruction to awakening. Celibacy also provides a level of security and trustworthiness for monks and nuns living together.

Many, many years ago, I was at a wedding. After the ceremony, the groom took off his fancy shirt, and underneath, he was wearing a t-shirt that said, "I'm married, not dead." When I became a single mom, I modified this to be, "I'm celibate, not dead." Before I came to prison, Ralph admonished me to let go of sexual actions, desires, and ruminations. It took about three months of wrestling with my thoughts, but then I found that I was free from these thoughts. *I'm celibate and still fully human and fully alive.*

Valentine's is always about love, yearning for love, or feeling filled up with love. I feel alone and I'm trying to ignore that fact. I think of myself walking around this place as if everyone is in inner spiritual contemplation, as nuns might be. I feel grateful to love: I love my son, love my family, love the birds, and I love the sun. The sunsets are amazing here! When I walk around the track, watching sunsets, the sky, trees, and birds, it is almost peaceful.

Occasionally we get a brief reprieve from the rules. When that happens, I soak it up. Rules about the unit include keep it clean, don't go into someone else's room, and keep the windows shut at all times. Some try to sneak their windows open; however, other inmates jump at the chance to bitch, so it rarely happens.

My first springtime in Arizona. One day the electricity goes off completely. Of course, that means that we are on lockdown. No going to work or anything else. The biggest boon: we can open our windows! The weather is slightly cool, with a light breeze on the morning air. Everybody seems unusually chill, so it is relatively quiet.

I lay on my bunk, reading newspapers, looking out at the trees and sky, with the window open! It was so peaceful. Suddenly, as I relax, I feel that my body has been holding its breath. *Since the day I met Ralph, I've been trying to be more conscious of my breath and now I sense how often my breath has been constricted. Interesting.*

Without people to trust, to talk to, to process this world, time passes laboriously. I've been down for four months now, and time is weighing me down like a coat that is too heavy. *How am I going to make it another fifteen months?* I read something about the courage to keep Spirit inside/in your center and how it can transcend the illusion of time. I'm left wondering if I have the courage I need because I need a way to transcend time!

JOURNAL:

On some level, I continually feel vulnerable. Inmates getting in trouble daily, getting shots, getting sent out. Am I next? There are plenty of days that I want to climb into a rabbit hole and tell everyone to leave me alone. I want to sleep it off, this prison, like a bad hangover. Maybe I'll feel better tomorrow.

There are days I long to step across that cattle guard, up the hill, over the fence, and wander anywhere but here. I know I can't walk away from this place. I am not planning an escape. I am thinking that I had a life out there! I had my own life!

JOURNAL:

The rules here are made to strip us of our humanity, so I'm constantly exploring what makes me feel human and what makes me feel a human connection. Mostly a game of we against them. *They* make sure we don't get comfortable, *they* make sure we are limited, telling us what we cannot have, what we cannot do. We do what we can to create normal.

Every spring and fall, the inmates organize a softball tournament. The tournament is certainly an experience. This is the only time anyone can be on the grassy infield of the track.

Of course, we don't have regular access to bats and softballs, so there's been no opportunity to practice. All the fit (or at least, not obese) inmates were asked to play. Despite the prison drama, softball tournaments are celebrations. It's a block party: loud music, women laughing, and cheering each other on.

I have been asked to play several times, but competition doesn't interest me, and I have very little experience playing softball. And I'd rather watch, instead of play. By nature, I'm an introvert. I find a place to sit in the bright sun to watch and listen. I find it interesting to observe other inmates.

Supposedly, Buddhist insight comes from self-observation and reflection. Who knows what I'll learn about myself today?

Guards rarely come out to watch. It is kind of our own thing. Women playing softball, yelling, and laughing like kids on the playground. There are only a few good players, but everybody has a good time!

There's a woman in her fifties from my floor who plays in the tournament. We have talked a few times, little more than, "Hi, where are you from?" It turns out she is from New Mexico. A place near where my family once lived. After one of the games, she and I were walking back to our unit, and she looked radiant. She told me that she had never had so much fun in all her life.

There are times when I hear laughter on the warm breeze, and I close my eyes imagining that I'm at a resort. A resort by the sea, the sound of waves and laughter is so relaxing. Reminds me of the visualizations when you imagine your happy place. Just by visualizing your happy place, your brain believes you are there. Now my perimeter is boundless!

One time, a Christian band came and played for us on the volleyball court. We sit in the bleachers, and they play Christian pop music. I watch each person very carefully. After being down for a while, I couldn't help but wonder what "normal" people were like. Watching the men, the women, what are they thinking of us? *How do we appear to them? Is there any individuality left to us? Are we just faces in a uniform? All criminals? Are we all nefarious women? Are they afraid of us?* As these questions circled my brain, I would stare at one person at a time and wonder what I could decipher about who that person was based on their manner, their clothes, their body language, and their facial expressions.

As these people play their instruments, creating music, I think about this dynamic relationship between person and instrument. I watch their hands, their bodies, creating music, and I close my eyes to listen. I enjoy the sound, feeling like I could ride the music to a different environment, where there is calm and beauty. Music can transport us mysteriously, to another place. *Yummy.*

When it is all over, we are required to go back to our units for count. I wonder if any other inmates enjoyed the music as much as I had. On the outside, I probably wouldn't have gone to hear a Christian band. They came to us—that is meaningful. There's something about music and art that personalizes life. Except for these rare moments, art is not supported in prison.

There is always noise around me. Sound becomes music. I enjoyed that.

JOURNAL: When I read a story or listen to music, or even watch a movie, I forget for a moment that I'm in prison. For that brief time, I'm in another world and another life. That is the idea behind transforming prison into a monastery. I'm always looking for ways to visualize this place in another context.

One day we are working, driving the cart from the warehouse to the compound, and we see an elderly man walking on our road. I don't think he realizes he's inside a prison. I had heard that there was an old folk's home somewhere down the road from us. Somehow, he crossed the cattle guard and just walked up the road. I look at my workmate, as if asking, "Should we stop, talk to this man, or just ignore him and drive by?" The rules are always in the back of my mind.

I stopped, my work partner decided to get out, and I followed. We went up to him and asked him what he is doing walking around here. He says that he'd like a cup of coffee and asks if we could point the way to the cafeteria. We tell him, "No, this is a prison and there is no coffee served here." We directed him toward the main office. Amazingly, he did not seem afraid of us inmates, just puzzled.

I feel this curious contradiction between my inmate self and my old self. I want to help him out. Yet, the rules and the punishments are always looming overhead making me cautious. Even talking to him could be misconstrued as something else. As a prisoner, I'm conditioned to be alert to the rules. They constantly buzz in the background of my mind.

JOURNAL: I find myself on many occasions, asking myself and the world around me, What is "here?" My point of view has a lot to say about that. I can be in prison, or I can be in a monastery. It's the same with the question, Who am I? I get to answer that for myself. Who do I strive to be? How do I strive to be seen in here? How do I want to be seen outside? I see and feel the spirit of the individuals around me. Beautiful and scarred, wounds profoundly deeper than the skin. Human spirit feels so strong with so much wounded beauty.

I feel like prison has become my initiation to deepen my relationship with myself and the world. All change is an initiation. I am an inmate, but I'm so much more than an inmate. I'm living the question: how much of what I choose to be is what I become? Buddhism encourages me not just to react to things but also to observe, reflect, and choose. I choose new behaviors. I choose new responses. I'm redefining myself on so many levels, accepting prison as a doorway to my own core.

Greta sent me a Valentine's poem.

OF LOVE

I have been in love more times than one,
Thank the Lord. Sometimes it was lasting
Whether active or not. Sometimes it was all but ephemeral, maybe only
An afternoon, but not less real for that.
They stay in my mind, these beautiful people,
Or anyway people beautiful to me, of which
There are so many. You, and you, and you,
Whom I had the fortune to meet, or maybe
missed. Love, love, love it was the
Core of my life, from which, of course, comes
The word for heart. And, oh have I mentioned
That some of them were men and some were women
And some now carry my revelation with you
Were trees. Or places. Or Music flying above
The names of their makers. Or clouds, or the Sun
Which was the first, and the best, the most
Loyal for certain, who looked so faithfully into my eyes, every morning.
So I imagine
Such love of the world—its fervency, its shining, its
Innocence and hunger to give of itself—I imagine
This is how it began.

—Mary Oliver

Six:
LIKE WHAT YOU GET

"EVERYTHING IS HARD OR HAS THORNS." When a fellow inmate said this one day, I thought, *The Buddha could have said that*. It reminds me of the first of the Buddha's Four Noble Truths: "Life is suffering." This teaching may be more obvious inside prison.

Everywhere I'm allowed to go, I'm surrounded by concrete, steel, and hard surfaces: cement walls and plastic chairs inside, concrete tables and benches outside. What's not hard is sharp: thorny mesquite and acacia trees, saguaro, and prickly pear—and I was told the short cacti with the pretty flowers are jumping cacti. *I'm not ready to believe that a cactus can jump!*

We instinctually avoid suffering and seek comfort. In prison, however, comfort is elusive. I haven't been sleeping very well with all the noise, the lights, the continuous traffic, and my extremely uncomfortable bed. I wake up because my body hurts. I shift my body and try the other side. Fifteen minutes later, I wake up again, unable to get comfortable.

My rock-hard bed reminds me of camping and sleeping on the ground without adequate padding. Makes me wonder, *What are the beds like in a monastery?* Monks and nuns take vows to avoid luxuries like soft beds, so it might not be much different from this.

Once I moved out of the hall and into my own room, an inmate, Rose, showed me how to fix the mattress. The single-size "mattress" is cotton batting covered in a thick plastic cover. Rose helped me stand the mattress up on end and shake the batting down toward one end of the mattress. To get the batting to stay at the end, she handed me a needle. Immediately I looked around to see if any guards or other inmates saw us. "It's not contraband because it is part of a sewing kit," Rose assured me. *Why is a needle considered contraband, and a sewing kit is not?*

After shaking the batting again, I used dental floss to sew the cover. I lost about six inches of length in my mattress (At five-foot-three, I can handle it.) Oh, but I could feel the difference.

Beds must be made by 7 a.m. Many inmates sleep on top of the "made" bed with just a blanket to cover themselves so they can continue sleeping. Bunkie does this, but it doesn't make any sense to me. I sleep between the sheets and make the bed when I get up. Sleeping on top of a made-up bed feels like one more adaptation to prison life that isn't worth it.

Besides, I get cold easily, so even though we all have two cotton blankets, I double up each blanket to cover myself. I also use towels rolled up or folded up, in a variety of configurations for support. One supports my back when I am facing out to avoid leaning up against the cold cinder-block wall. I use another towel roll between my knees. Even with all these adjustments, my bed is never cozy, but it's better.

I can't help but contemplate what would provide some comfort. Beyond material objects, simple things, like a comfortable place to sit, have a big impact on my mood.

JOURNAL: Everything here adds to my experience of overwhelm and wanting to escape. Looking for ways to be comfortable poses an ongoing challenge. There is no relaxing, no comfort, and safety is never a sure or lasting thing. Without comfort, there is no true rest, no relaxation. I *want* comfort. I know, Ralph says, "No wanting!" But even just for a few minutes? Can't I *want* comfort, even for a few minutes? No. No wanting.

A Buddhist might say that discomfort is an opportunity to right ourselves. Instead of backing away from discomfort, lean in. When the ground beneath us disappears, be alright with uncertainty, and relax in the midst of chaos. Today, I'm not feeling it.

Beyond comfort, the position of my body in my bunk is also important for a sense of safety. Feeling safe seems very close to comfort. Safety provides relaxation, while comfort provides support. *Not a lot of either going around.*

The night before Jera's first visit, I am awakened by a guard pushing on my hip, then my shoulder. I tense my whole body, making a fist with my hand atop my hip. I'm trying to wake up, nothing happens and the guard leaves. I'm extremely rattled and wake up shaking.

I tell Bunkie about it in the morning, and she says, "Oh yeah, guards can touch you when you are sleeping. If you haven't changed positions through a couple of counts, the guard needs to find out if you are still alive." One inmate tells me that she had trained herself to move around whenever she hears the guards go by. That doesn't make me feel any better.

All my life, safety education was about staying out of the way of potential threats. I remember being a student at St. John's College in Santa Fe. As a runner, I loved the challenge of hilly terrain. I took a new gal, Jane, out on some runs to show her some of the trails in the foothills behind the college. One day, we were running on a power-line trail—a clear swath under the power lines that ran through the pines and scrub oak.

We heard dirt bikes coming toward us. I said, "Quick, let's get off the trail and hide!" We did and they passed with no idea we were hiding near the trail. Once they passed and we got back on the trail, Jane asked why we did that. I was kind of surprised at the question.

"Protection," I replied. "We are women, the dirt bikers were probably men, and we are miles away from other people." *No brainer,* I thought.

Our survival instincts drive up all our prejudices and presuppositions, of course. Those bikers may have been friendly, but a concern for my safety says, "*Why risk it?*"

It's the same with our view of prison guards. We depersonalize them. They are always there on the periphery, but I see them as outside of "us."

It's kind of like living in a house with snakes on the loose. Even if you weren't afraid of them, you'd keep one eye on them, just in case.

Still, when a guard walks up to you, talks to you, or even looks at you, it feels invasive. I sleep with my back against the wall, whenever possible, keep a towel hanging down from the upper bunk to hide my face. Some guards don't mind; however, others make a big deal about it. One officer said we would get written up for having a towel up. Others just pull the towel down and leave it on the floor.

Inmates who had been down longer would let me know if the new guard on rotation was alright with us having a towel up or not. If not, I would put my pillow in front of my face. As a kid, it was never a big deal to have someone watch me sleep. Here, it's different. It's impossible to keep your guard up while sleeping. I want to shield my face for privacy and protection, even though most of the time, I know it's just an echo of privacy and protection.

I realize I am living a paradoxical power trip—guards dominate inmates and my role as "less than" must be perpetuated in order to feel safe.

JOURNAL:

Frequently I catch myself asking, "Why?" Not about the physical structure that surrounds me, but more about the rules and requirements. The question, "Why am I here?" comes when things are not well, not happy, and not simple. My next thought is, this is where I am. *Why* typically seems like a pointless question. This is where I am! This is a place in our world, and I am here.

Here, I'm always on guard and it's exhausting. Someone says to me, "You look tired. No, you look *exhausted*!" I just about burst into tears. There are times I don't know what it's going to take to get to the other side of this.

In a monastery, monks and nuns renounce freedom, comforts, and luxuries in service of discipline. It's a choice they make to nurture a spiritual life. But here, nothing feels like a choice. Prison restricts my freedom, movements, and access to basically everything. Here, the simplest of necessities seem like luxuries. Beyond losing our privacy and control, the guards and prison administrators take our dignity as well.

> JOURNAL: Buddhism says resisting change only brings sorrow and suffering. Instead of fighting change, I choose to reconsider how to live my life. I'm surrounded by change. I choose to put my attention on Spirit. Find my flow.

As I get the hang of prison life, it ingrains new habits in me. I'd prefer to develop habits that are good for me, like meditation and chanting. I like to sit or walk while I focus on my breath. I bring my awareness to being present in my body and my space. However, it's not as easy as it sounds. The trick is not to float away on one of the many distractions, like the nearby inmate's conversation or my thoughts of what my son might be experiencing right now.

Meditation takes many forms. As Buddhism spread across the world taking on different flavors, meditation has, too. Meditation, as well as many mindful practices, helps us remain focused and alert. In this way, we can be aware and relate to our experiences with equanimity, keeping us on the path of enlightenment.

I get caught up in just doing prison life. With all the distraction in prison, it would be easy not to practice. And even when there are moments to do nothing, nothing is what I want to do. At least, I don't want to be reminded of my overwhelming longing to be out of here. I miss my son. I miss my dog. I miss my life.

JOURNAL:

> I haven't done any meditation or any other mindful practice for several days. My head is abuzz with basic living conditions, rules, and being where I'm supposed to be.

The Buddha identifies our desire to have or not to have as the source of suffering. When I sit down to meditate, all these feelings come to the surface, and I don't want to feel them. But the whole point of meditation is to be present to everything, including what we feel and what we think. Contrary to popular belief, meditation is not doing nothing.

Curiously, prison helps me develop my practice by removing the distractions that I would have at home. I guess that's just what a monastery would do. I have very little to worry about when it comes to how I want to live my life; in here, that's been decided for me. However, the real challenge remains to live *present* in the present. That requires self-discipline.

JOURNAL:

> A Buddhist saying suggests, "Only dead fish go with the flow." It's a stable mind, with awareness, that meets the flow of thoughts or experiences, but does not get swept away by them.

My life here is undoubtedly a minimalist lifestyle. Our rooms have two waist-high metal lockers side by side, a bolted "desk" (about one foot wide and two feet in length), a steel bunk bed, and a plastic chair. There are two plastic footlockers under the bunk. Later, I find out that there are "good" and "bad" footlockers. The good ones are a little bigger.

To get a good footlocker, you befriend someone who is leaving and trade out your locker for theirs, leaving the bad footlocker for the new inmate. The metal locker holds only a few things: my food, dishes, books, and letters. The footlocker holds my clothes except for my jacket and my visiting shirts that hang on the end of my bunk.

In the beginning, I don't have very much stuff—only issued clothes. Do I *want* more stuff, or do I *need* more stuff? Do we all have an innate drive to collect stuff?

Getting set up with useful things that make life a little more agreeable takes some time. I often eat in my room. A plastic container used for preparing and eating is very important. Plastic containers are not sold in commissary. They are passed around throughout the population. Inmates covet a container that is minimally stained and warped from past microwave use.

Bunkie gets me a plastic knife. It's contraband, but so handy for cutting the contraband apple I have on rare occasions. I keep the knife separate from my other kitchen stuff, hidden in a t-shirt.

Then I have a plastic bowl, a plastic container for cooking (the lid also serves as a plate) a plastic mug, and a couple of plastic spoons and forks.

So many of our rules revolve around where we must be at a certain time. Because I was so anxious about being punctual, I bought a wristwatch that costs sixteen bucks. This one has an alarm and I even wear it at night so that it wakes me up in the morning. Set at 5:17 a.m., it gives me just enough time to get dressed and to be ready for breakfast.

For some reason, the current guards are always talking while doing their 4 a.m. rounds. Today, they're talking about buying a new car. Yesterday, the conversation was about the party they attended last Friday night. *I don't care about your party! I care about my sleep!*

Waking up before my alarm is annoying. Getting that last hour of sleep matters to me! I already must contend with lights on 24/7 and inmates snoring loudly. Now, I'm not going to be able to go back to sleep when they leave the building. *Ugh!*

Breakfast is called at around 5:30 a.m., and work starts at six sharp. Once dressed, I put my ID card and my pocket notes in my pants pocket. Now I'm ready.

Because we make such little money (I'm being paid a whopping twelve cents per hour in Water Ops), I find it so interesting to observe what inmates spend their money on. There is makeup on the commissary list, and I ask Bunkie, "Who buys the makeup? I mean, who needs seven-dollar mascara in prison?"

She laughs.

"I never wore makeup regularly on the outside," I exclaimed, "Why in the world would I use it in here?"

"It's the inmates in the drug rehab program that have to wear makeup."

"What?!"

"It's supposed to make them feel better about themselves," she says with a shrug.

"Aren't half the women in here in drug rehab?" I asked, "How can they afford it?"

"Yeah, most of us don't get it from the commissary. We get it underground. My supplier has a bag of makeup hidden outside. I can ask for the brands I want, and she has them smuggled in."

You guys are crazy! (I didn't say that out loud.)

Inmates in the drug rehabilitation program live in separate units, have more rules to follow on top of the regular prison rules, they attend classes that take priority over work, and from what Bunkie tells me, they must keep up appearances. I'm grateful my self-esteem is intact.

Our assigned clothes are basic army-green elastic waist pants, light green t-shirts, and black steel-toed boots. Everyone complains about the boots. The fit is sloppy, my feet move around, and there's no support. While I stand or walk, I feel every single rock through the soles. And by the end of the day, those boots feel like they weigh a ton, and my ankles are raw where the tops of my boots rub. The issued boots hurt my feet!

An inmate showed me how to put feminine pads around the ankles of my boots and told me to wear two pairs of socks, winter, or summer. With limited resources, we must be creative. Inmates joke that there are 101 uses for feminine pads, and I tend to agree. Feminine pads are available for free while tampons cost ten dollars a box. It's fun to try to come up with *one more way* to use pads.

We can buy Wolverine steel-toed boots to replace the issued boots, but they are close to a hundred dollars, so I started saving for them right away. Most of the inmates that work outside get the Wolverines, and if someone is leaving, more than one inmate will ask for the used Wolverines.

Tennis shoes are allowed after dinner and on the weekends. However, we must purchase them ourselves. Tennis shoes are one of the few things all inmates get as soon as possible. They cost about fifty dollars and we don't have any choices, one style, one brand. There are not a lot of options here. Used tennis shoes rotate through the camp. Somehow, Bunkie gets three pairs right away, but she has tiny feet. I'm thinking that certain sizes are rare, so only a few inmates can wear the old pairs. I purchase my own pair as soon as I can.

As spring becomes summer, I finally get some Wolverine boots. Unfortunately, that doesn't end my boot woes. I still wear two pairs of socks, and now I've developed a heat rash from my ankles to mid-calf. On 100-degree days, I can't wait to get back to my room to take off my boots and socks.

Even though there are some things you can purchase to replace the issued clothing (like the Wolverine boots), the issued cotton granny panties are all you get. As I work, they become soaked with sweat. When I have to go to the bathroom, getting those granny panties down is like taking off a wet swimsuit. I roll them down and roll them back up when I'm done peeing. It is truly one of the most unpleasant things I've had to endure.

I realize that the compulsion to achieve physical comfort takes up a lot of mental space. However, it's the emotional, inner life that feels ever so much more impactful. One day, I see a woman crying. Bunkie tells me that her two boys ran away from their foster home. I don't speak to this inmate, but I think about the emotional pain she must be going through. Sadly, there are many heart-wrenching stories. Stories that would make me cry, but I don't cry. I just hurt inside.

JOURNAL: There's an unspoken prison code: don't show your feelings; dry your tears quickly. I don't want to allow myself to be hardened. Buddhism is about cultivating compassion. Somehow, I must learn to feel things even if I don't express them outwardly.

The TV room is like a glass box—mostly windows—allowing guards to look in easily. It's a plain room with a TV bolted up high on one wall and hard plastic chairs stacked up. Just as with the showers, there are prison rules and inmate rules when it comes to what happens in the TV room. Prison rules: *nothing* is supposed to happen in the TV room, except watching TV. Nevertheless, I've heard stories of wild sexual encounters. The TV room is a place to escape.

As for inmate rules for the TV room, when I got there, we had a TV-room mama. If she was present, everyone defers to her. "What are we watching at 7 p.m.?" When she left, it was a free-for-all for a while. Inmates would come in and say, "We're not watching this, we are watching BET (Black Entertainment Television)." Sometimes an argument would ensue, but more often half the room would leave, and a bitch session would follow in the halls.

Eventually, the TV room would mellow out. Once, when there were four or five of us in the TV room, an inmate came in and began to change the station. Someone piped up and said, "Collin is watching this." *Nice!* The inmate sat herself down. Wow. I felt respected.

Sometimes, the mental escape of the TV room provided great relief for a little while. Movies on the weekend offered a considerable distraction. Three movies would play on rotation through the weekend. Never an R-rated movie. The schedule went up Friday afternoon, and if I wanted to see all three, I would organize my time accordingly.

As inmates, every minute inside counts toward "doing our time." So "pastimes" serve a dual purpose. They distract us even while we serve our time. However, some movies are not worth my *time*, like a Smurf movie. Nevertheless, the TV room is a way to burn up time. Just to sit in there and let my time pass.

JOURNAL:

I wrote to a friend, "I don't want to feel time on the inside. I just want it to fly by like sleeping when someone else is driving through some monotonous terrain. You wake up and you have traveled so far, and it feels like you have only been asleep for a short time."

Time on the inside feels so different than time on the outside. In here during a year, only a few things happen that are different from any random normal day. On the outside, there are so many different things that happen during a year that they blur together.

Some women count down each day to their out date. I do not. For me, it was fine to have the same day happen over and over until they run right into each other. I'm marking the bigger picture, the end of a week, end of a month, or another holiday down. I don't want to dwell on what I can't have, don't have, or what I am waiting for. I am *here*, and when the day is over, the week is over, or a whole month has passed, I am still *here*.

It's funny how I begin to see the value in the Buddhist admonition to "be present." Certain expressions always make me laugh: "Yep, that's going to take a minute." Or "Do you have a minute?" Ha! All we have is time! And a prisoner never says, "I need more time."

Entering prison, I had many good intentions of how I was going to make this time productive! In my mind, I had two years to learn something, discover my strength, come out a lean, mean, fighting machine. I also had friends asking me how I was going to use all my time. It felt like an assumption, "If *I* had two years, *I* would…" Of course, it doesn't really go like that.

I told myself I was going to learn Spanish. Bunkie speaks Spanish. Buenas noches y dulces suenos (good night and sweet dreams) stayed with me. Most everything else I learned would leave my brain after a few weeks.

I thought it might be a good idea to learn things that I could tell my workmate. Unfortunately, she knew formal Spanish, not the American household Spanish Bunkie was teaching me.

One day I asked Bunkie to teach me how to say hold on tight.

"Agarrate fuerte, why do you want to know that?" Bunkie asked, with a sly twinkle in her eye.

You know how I love driving the electric cart around as fast as it can go. Going around corners is great fun, but before my workmate got accustomed to my driving, she wasn't always holding on. As I turned left one day, she flew out." Bunkie and I had a good laugh.

After that, I would yell, "Agarrate fuerte!" as I took the corners. I would laugh, she would roll her eyes. That's about as far as my Spanish progressed.

At first, it seemed that creating my own structure and routines would take some of the sting out of everything they imposed upon me. I set up my own places for my daily activities: my bed, my place to sit outside where I meditate, and my spot for yoga. Nevertheless, there are times when all I want is *nothing*. No rules, no routine, no management of my existence. No thing.

'Nothing,' I'm learning, is a central idea in Buddhism and provides insight into the true nature of things. Buddhists talk of being in the world without holding onto mental constructions that tend to shape and skew our perceptions. Even our ideas of self, according to Buddhism, are mental constructs, and therefore subject to change. If we release our mental constructions, we find a new freedom to be in the world and see things as they truly are. Sometimes I really get that. Other times it's beyond my grasp.

POCKET NOTE:

Wonderland: the Zen of Alice. "Do you mean that you think you can find out the answer to it?" said the March Hare. "Exactly so," said Alice. "Then you should say what you mean," the March Hare went on. "I do," Alice hastily replied; "at least—I mean what I say—that's the same thing, you know." "Not the same thing a bit!" said the Hatter. "Why, you might just as well say that 'I see what I eat' is the same as 'I eat what I see!' You might as well say," added the March Hare, "that 'I like what I get' is the same as 'I get what I like'!" Zen practice is the practice of liking what you get.

(The source of this Pocket Note was an article about Lewis Carroll's *Alice's Adventures in Wonderland*.)

In a letter to a friend I wrote, "Being Buddhist is really, really good for me. I'm so happy that I have a *way* to deal. I read these Buddhist books and magazines, and they make sense to me. It's like, aha, I get it! Two people even say I look like a nun. Others comment on how open I am. This is not what I expected of myself."

I told Greta that practicing and learning Buddhism was the one thing here in prison that feels good. Buddhism invites me to move mentally, gets me unstuck, and helps me think in new ways. Ralph's advice is working, and I feel better than I had anticipated.

I prefer my workouts after work. After my work day, I look out my window to see who is out at the weight pile. I like working out when nobody else is out there. Almost every day I see two young women, they look quite harmless. After watching them a couple times, I decided to join them.

To break the ice, I offer suggestions on form and additional exercises for specific muscle groups. We meet up out at the weight pile most days. One day they bring a friend to work out with us. With my weight training background, I became their trainer.

For the remainder of my time, training became my thing; I always had a small group of women to train, my workout posse. I'd teach them how to use weights, I'd create different cardio drills, and make up interval training routines around the track. By the end of my sentence, I was teaching yoga classes as well.

Lucia, one of the gals that I met at the weight pile, was in my unit, but I had never talked with her before. When I met Lucia, she had only four months of her sentence remaining. She was a beautiful, serious young woman with two boys at home. She always wore her hair pulled back. Her friend, Julia, was a little more outgoing. She also had a couple children at home.

Eventually, I'd say hi to both Lucia and Julia when I passed them in the halls of our unit. I noticed them sitting together talking, then holding hands, and praying. They prayed a lot.

One day, Lucia and Julia came to my room. Julia said, "We would like to pray for your soul."

"Huh?" It took me a second to process what they were saying.

"Have you been saved?" Julia asked.

"What do you mean?" I replied.

Lucia chimed in, "Do you believe in God?"

"Oh! Yes. Well, I'm a Buddhist." Immediately I saw concern in their eyes. Then I added, "Buddhism doesn't have its own God, and it doesn't tell me not to believe in God either." That was good enough for them. Now they felt free to pray for me.

Lucia is my first friend in prison. Here a friend is not like a roommate or a pal you spend a lot of time with. A friend in here is like a friend at work that you see only at work. Except for our workouts, we see each other mostly in passing.

In Lucia, I recognize a younger me. I'd look at Lucia and think, *You look like I felt, many years ago.* When I was young, I took care of my siblings. The first time my mom left my one-year-old brother with me overnight, I remember getting up early and going outside as the sun was rising. I felt like I was going to faint—I was lightheaded, hadn't been eating well, and I had extremely low blood pressure. The cold kept me from fainting.

Standing in the early-morning sunshine, I was thinking that I didn't know what was going to happen next. *What challenges lay around the corner?* As I was growing up, chaos always meant another move, often to another state. Just when I got used to something, I'd be uprooted. If I liked anything, my bed, our house, a teacher at school—boom, it was gone.

My priority was to do a good job taking care of my little brother. But nobody knew how *I* was doing. Nobody even asked because I was there to take care of my brother, period.

Lucia, like so many of these women, was a teenage mother. At thirteen, she was married and had her first child. She told me that she was happy to have a reason to leave home. Though she never told me what her upbringing was like, what she said about her abusive husband, made me wonder about the extent of abuse she suffered as a child.

Just before Lucia was incarcerated, she experienced a miscarriage. After the miscarriage and before incarceration, her husband beat her so badly that she was hemorrhaging during the first few weeks of her sentence. She never talked to a doctor. Hearing that story just broke my heart.

I found out that most of these women came from very traumatic and abusive situations—not exactly a surprise. I heard over and over,

"Now it's time to take care of myself." I know this scenario isn't limited only to inmates, many women suffer and have no one to support or look after them.

> At what point do the burdens we carry start to adversely affect us? Unfortunately, the story I frequently hear from my fellow inmates is one full of burdens so heavy that they call prison "a retreat."

In here, we are looking for new ways to support ourselves. A few classes offered in here come from the outside, such as a personal trainer certification. A trainer friend of mine on the outside confirmed that she had this same certificate, but it cost her double what I could get it for in here.

A group of us signed up for the certification test. We received a manual to study for the test and an inmate formed a class to help us prepare. Because Lucia and Julia were in the class, I started studying with them. Much of the material was familiar to me because of my degrees in anatomy and nutrition. I ended up tutoring them and others preparing for the test.

Lucia opted to take the test early because she's leaving soon. I decided to take it with her. It was a bit of a crunch, but many years working out in gyms with personal trainers paid off. Lucia and I passed with flying colors!

During one of my initial prison interviews, the officer told me that once inmates found out that I was a nutritionist, I would have women asking me questions all the time. She was right. They also asked me about their bodies and health issues. "I hurt here," one would say, pointing to her lower abdomen, "What does that mean?" Knowing that most of these inmates had never finished high school, I looked for books to share with them.

There was a teacher who came from the outside once each week to collect papers, homework for any of the classes that came from the community college. One time, I asked him if he might be able to get anatomy or general health books sent in. I told him that I was a nutritionist and that I was trying to help these women out.

He whispered, "Willful neglect," as he shook his head.

"Woeful neglect?" I asked, "What's that?"

He wrote it down: *Willful neglect.* Then he said, "I got this. My partner is studying to be a midwife. I'd be happy to get some good books for you."

He got me a wonderful DK Anatomy book, a general health book, and *Prescription for Nutritional Healing* (Blach), which was great because I had one at home. I became the resident expert on a whole variety of general health and nutrition issues.

Lucia avoided the kitchen as much as I did, but for different reasons. We would go down together occasionally. One time, we hadn't even found our seats when she suddenly bolted from the room. Another time she got up and left in the middle of eating.

One day she looked like she was getting ready to leave, so I asked her, "What's going on?"

"You know who is here," she said, "and I feel like I'm going to explode or hit something."

"Let's get out of here then," I said as we left. We walked in silence for a bit. Then I asked her, "Are you still taking anxiety meds?"

"Yes," she replied, "They don't do much for me, but they make me tired and since my bunkie snores they help me get some sleep."

Trying to reassure her, I said, "You're definitively not the only inmate suffering from anxiety."

"No kidding," she said laughing. "I wonder why!"

"I'm curious if there might be other factors at play in how you're feeling." I paused to gauge her reaction, then I asked, "Can I ask you some questions?

"Go for it," she said sitting down on a bench.

"How long do you go between meals on a typical day?"

"It depends on what's going on that day, and also on how I feel." "Probably around four or five hours."

"If you aren't going to the dining hall except for dinner, what foods are you eating from commissary?" I ask, "Are you eating the mackerel or tuna regularly?"

"No, I eat crackers in the morning, sometimes popcorn instead of lunch." Lucia tells me.

"Are any of your family members diabetic—siblings or parents?"

"My aunt is. Actually, I think both of my mom's sisters are diabetic."

"I suspect there's a connection between your eating patterns and your anxiety. I'd like to recommend that you keep a food journal and make note of what you eat and when you eat it. Would you be willing to do it just for a week?"

"Sure, if you think it can help, although I'm not sure what good it will do. Food choices are so limited here."

"Don't I know it!" I agreed. "Mackerel and brown rice are my daily staples."

Once Lucia started eating tuna with her crackers in the morning, she noticed it made a difference in how she felt. We only had about a month to work on it before she was released. In that short time, as Lucia implemented my suggestions, she told me that she felt less anxious.

Before she left, Lucia beaded me a yellow cross, "Yellow because you like the sunshine," she said. I was so grateful. A little acknowledgment of who I am felt like a sprinkle of rain on parched desert ground.

The day Lucia left marked my sixth month inside. Feels like a season, experiences, people, learning about myself. My prayer for Lucia: "Change your world!"

Seven:
My Concrete Mat

*P*RISON IS SO NOISY! Inmates don't ever shut up! Falling asleep at night is challenging amid the perpetual cacophony of voices. Rather than being annoyed, I think, *Who invited all these irreverent, Spanish-speaking women into my bedroom?* That lightens the mood in my mind.

JOURNAL:

> Happiness comes from inner peace. Inner peace comes from mental training. Mental training takes the form of meditation. How to meditate, let me count the ways. Whether I am walking or working, when I shift my mindset or focus, I am meditating.

In prison, so many situations threaten to interfere with my inner peace. Some days, the chaos feels like it's all coming from my surrounding world. But other times I am aware that it has more to do with my inner turmoil. I want to have a peaceful center like a tornado but the noise, the people, and the place hinder me.

Even when I am present to my core, it's unsettled by my hyper-apprehensiveness. It's a sense of always being "on." Single moms, especially moms of young children, know this feeling well. I remember a time when my son was less than a year old and I got sick. I had this flu/cold sickness, and I could barely move. I couldn't just sleep in bed all day; I had a toddler to care for.

I created a safe space on the living room floor with toys and blankets, and gates up so that there was no way out. I lay down on the floor while

Jera played around me for the whole day. I had to be with him. I remember thinking, *He must know that I'm sick—he is being such a good boy!* The second thought was, *I can't wait for him to go to sleep for the night so that I can let myself go to sleep!*

I'm always "on" here, too, and there is no safe space to sleep. I want to carve out physical space, a safe place to relax. My goal is to be outside as much as possible. Mentally, I find more options outside.

I am always trying to find a place to sit where I can silently chant my prayers, read, and still hear the announcements. It's not like there are a whole lot of options: a few concrete tables, the benches on the unit's patio, the few plastic chairs that have been left out on the side of a building.

Out toward the running track, a concrete pad measuring one hundred feet by one hundred feet serves as our exercise area. The pad has a makeshift roof of deteriorating canvas for shade about twenty feet up. Bleachers on the side provide seating for the occasional volleyball or basketball game. There's an office, a bathroom with some lockers, and some weights. The bathroom sits back from the corner about fifteen feet, so it creates a small, isolated section of the pad. I settle in this corner of the pad. I call it "my concrete mat."

Against the bathroom wall sits an electric cart with a flat tire. Conveniently, that cart never gets fixed. It makes a decent place to sit. I lean against the wall with my feet up on the padded seat.

Sometimes, I start by putting three yoga mats down on the concrete and I just sit down. The only times we are allowed to have shoes and socks off is doing yoga or in bed! If I have the yoga mats out, I can take off my shoes and socks, *ahhh!* When it is hot and I'm wearing the black steel-toed boots all day, just a little fresh air on my feet makes all the difference. I don't know how inmates who stay inside all day can stand it.

Today as I head out to my concrete mat, I review my pocket notes and choose to work on fearlessness, daring, and being gentle with myself.

Buddha Behind Bars

> It takes four things to become enlightened,
> 1. egolessness (let go of territory) 2. faith (in three parts a. inspiration, b. knowledge, and c. follow through), 3. fearlessness (be daring and gentle—dare to look at your anger but be gentle with yourself) and 4. a sense of humor (stay connected to your wholeness).

Out on my concrete mat, I always assume someone is looking at me. It's a weird thought always in the back of my mind, no matter where I am. I only got used to it a little bit, or maybe I think I just get better at ignoring it. *Is that the same thing?* Even though outside is less crowded than inside, there are always inmates and/or guards around.

Yesterday, I was trying to get out of the wind and find a little warmth. I sat against a south-facing wall and missed my name being called over the loudspeakers. Apparently, they called for me four times. An inmate comes up yelling at me, "They are calling you!" Luckily, everybody knows everybody, and after your name is called a couple of times, inmates start looking for you.

My routine in the afternoons begins with loading up my mesh bag with a couple magazines, a book, and a yellow legal pad. Then I head out to find a place to sit for a few hours. I think about what my practice is, and it dawns on me: *Everything I do is my practice: yoga, sitting, being mindful in the moment.* I am thinking that it's just my way of being every day. I've read that the practice of Buddhism brings awareness, enlightenment, kindness, compassion, and love. I'm building my faith in this practice.

Buddha considered patience to be one of the highest virtues. Someone defined patience as letting go of the expectation that our circumstances match our desires. But I want my circumstances to change! *Sigh.*

Patience empowers us to accept things as they are. My patience practice starts with a pause. I slow down and put a little distance between emotional triggers and my reactions. Voilà! Patience. (Sometimes.)

I am reading about *virtuous cycles*, in the first book that Ralph sent me, *The Shape of Suffering* by Thanissaro Bhikkhu (Geoffrey DeGraff). He writes, "Patterns of behavior can be either desirable or undesirable," and he adds that these "can cause the feedback loops to form 'vicious' cycles, where they make the overall behavior progressively more undesirable." Other situations, he tells us, "can turn the same feedback loops into 'virtuous' cycles, where they make the overall behavior progressively more desirable." *I love the virtuous cycles!*

As I contemplate virtuous cycles, my mind conjures a memory from childhood of an old mill with its big water wheel. We went to the Salman Raspberry Ranch and Mill to pick raspberries in the summer. I vividly remember the old mill falling apart, the adobe bricks without their plaster, and the water wheel that no longer turns.

We would leap over the creek to the raspberry fields! It was beautiful! My sisters and I would explore and wonder about what it was like when the mill was working. *Were there horses here? What did the mill look like with the water flowing over the wheel, and the mill grinding the grain for flour?* We imagined so much life, movement, laughter, and energy.

I envision the virtuous cycle a bit like that water wheel. The water creates power to turn the mill by flowing or falling over the paddles mounted around the wheel. Like each paddle on the wheel, one positive thought, one calm moment, or one thing to be grateful for adds to the movement of the wheel. If you have a wheel with only a few paddles, the water flowing over them is creating very little energy. The more paddles on the wheel, the more energy gets created by the water.

There is an abundance of universal energy available. However, our experience of it waxes and wanes depending on the condition of the wheel. The water keeps flowing, but if I only practice occasionally, the wheel slows because there are only one or two paddles on the wheel. My own energy becomes stagnant.

As we create paddles (and fix broken ones) on the wheel, we can experience the flow of energy more and more. I add paddles by practicing gratitude. I fix paddles with every calm moment. As I "practice the virtuous cycle," I create momentum, I create flow. I see results.

JOURNAL: Vitality is always available. It's the energy of life.

I created a new pocket note saying, "One positive thought, one calm moment, or one thing to be grateful for." These are patterns of behavior I want to cultivate. I can try something different to change a pattern in either my thinking or behavior. When I set up a new framework in my mind, I can affect my behavior. I need only focus on one thing, just the next thing, to make this life better. Life could not help itself to be better when I have one positive thought, one calm moment, *or* one thing to be grateful for.

Upon reflection, this idea echoes my philosophy as a nutritional counsellor: the little choices add up to make all the difference.

Yoga is another paddle I'm adding to my virtuous wheel. I do a lot of yoga here in prison. In fact, this is the first time in my life that I have done yoga on a regular basis. I have taken a few classes here and there just as a form of exercise. I never learned the poses, the names of poses, or even that the practice of yoga involves much more than the poses.

My sister Dante sent me a five-day intensive course booklet by the yoga teacher Ana Forrest, and this became my yoga bible. At first, I look at the poses and wonder, *How do I get there?* My sister tells me that the booklet comes with cassette tapes. However, they are not allowed in. Then I hear about a new inmate that is leading some yoga classes. I go to her, show her my book, and ask her if she will work with me on the poses. She likes the Ana Forrest style, and we do yoga together for a few months.

I also ask my family to order a subscription to a yoga magazine for me so that I can continue to learn. After the first six months, I am doing yoga for about three hours at a time, an average of five days a week. I read that in the monasteries the monks sit for hours and even days at a time. *This time in my monastery may pay off after all!*

Even though we have jobs, as inmates, we don't run errands, go shopping, prepare our food, or go out to dinner, so we have time to fill. Somewhere along the way, instead of holding a pose for, say ten breaths, I use my stopwatch and hold poses for at least one minute. Holding a series of poses, each for a minute or more eats up a lot of time.

My yoga mats here are so thin and beat-up, I stack three to be comfortable on my concrete mat. I read something about micro-movements in yoga: a little turn here, a lift there, a little tension in one spot makes all the difference. *I love that—it lines up with virtuous cycles so well! How much can I do within a pose?* One positive thought: *Wow, my right arm can do this.* One calm moment: *breathe in and out.* One thing to be grateful for: *I am learning so much about my body.*

One day while I'm sitting on my yoga mats, reading a magazine with my feet bare, an inmate comes up to me and asks me what I'm doing. I put the soles of my feet together, dropping my knees to the side, and say, "Baddha Konasana."

She says she wants to learn yoga, so I show her some poses. The last pose I show her is *Downward Dog*. She says with a smirk, "My boyfriend calls this one, 'dessert.'" *Everybody brings their own bias.*

One afternoon I'm doing yoga and my boss, Mr. Thomas, is coming up the sidewalk. My brain kicks into overdrive. *Am I in trouble? Am I supposed to be somewhere? Do I stay on my mat or jump up?* He keeps walking by. He was just walking through our compound.

Now I'm his worker that does yoga. I wonder what that means to him. I work hard to keep myself "flat" with no other dimension than a hardworking inmate. Nothing to question, nothing to notice. As a woman, I've acted invisible to protect myself many times before.

103

When I step on my mats, I ask myself, *What do I need the most? What is best for me today?* I start facing the east, then the south, then west, and last the north. Shamans teach us to evoke a sacred space by creating a medicine wheel. This practice recognizes the four directions with prayers and or tangible representations of each direction. I appreciate that a sacred space can allow us to enter our inner world where healing can take place.

I've read something about how within sacred space we experience the lightness of our being, and we can commune with Spirit. I'm working on it. I want to get there, a sacred space. I remember the times before prison when I've watched the sunrise and asked for blessings from each direction.

When I face east, I am looking toward the camp. The concrete pad sits on high ground so if I'm out early on the weekends, the sun rises over the low horizon of our camp buildings. My unit is closest to me. The blinds to my room are shut because Bunkie is sleeping, as usual.

I am a little uncomfortable looking to the east because I know I am most likely facing whoever is watching me. I'm visible here to inmates watching from their room or from the TV rooms of two different units. *What a great way to get grounded: stop worrying about what others might be thinking, stop my mind chatter, and start concentrating on what my body is doing right now.*

Mindfulness of the body is attention from the inside out. The sensations of the body, give us a lot of information. Giving attention to the body keeps us from getting caught up in reactions, interpretations, and thoughts.

Buddhism regards the body and mind as one, or mutually dependent, (enmeshed) in contrast to other religious traditions that regard the body, mind, and spirit as separate entities. When we suppress or ignore our emotional and cognitive experiences, we tend to disconnect from the body. Conversely, when we distance ourselves from the physical manifestations of our experience, we lose touch with our inner life of emotions and thoughts.

Viewing our body as mundane and impure and our soul as pure and the essence of who we are, leaves us trapped in a prison of flesh and bone.

Buddha taught the Middle Way – a lifestyle free from the excesses of both sensual indulgence and asceticism.

POCKET NOTE:

> Body is nature, take care of it and it will take care of you.

I start my movement practice with some qigong moves, such as the Liver Cleanse Sequence. Supposedly when the liver is imbalanced, it manifests as anger, frustration, depression, and edginess. This one always seems appropriate here and I like it. In qigong, each organ has an associated healing sound. The liver's is 'shu.' Every exhale is shu. It ends with the affirmation "I am relaxed and flexible in my life. I am resilient!"

Facing south, I sit down on my mats to start some yoga poses. I come back to this view most often. The dirt slopes down slightly to the road just twenty to thirty feet away. Just a few feet away, a shorter variety of eucalyptus tree stands, only as tall as a tiny house. The small desert doves hang out here. *I love the doves!* There is a small flock that seemingly falls out of the tree and pecks at the dirt as if it is the richest, seed-abundant soil ever. Then the wind blows, and they all fly up disappearing into the tree.

Facing west, I view a field of dirt across the road. Beyond that, I see the officers' recreational buildings that are usually empty on the weekends. Looking between buildings, fences, and a few trees, I can see the horizon farthest away from camp. There are mountains over there, far, far away. One of the qigong flows I enjoy doing in the west is Beautiful Woman pose, sometimes adding the Snake Walk.

The Beautiful Woman pose is a standing flow, one knee comes up while the opposite arm stretches above my head, fingers spiraling back as if picking an apple. The hand on the same side of the raised knee stays beside my outer thigh with the flexed palm facing the ground. Slowly changing sides,

I feel the sensuality of the movement. The sensation of this pose stirs my sense of being a woman. For a moment, the inmate fades away.

Behind the officers' recreation center, there is another small field and then the men's prison. For a time, this gal stood over on the most western corner of the concrete mat, listening to her radio and just staring over to the men's prison. I asked Bunkie, "What is her deal?" She tells me that her man is over there in the men's prison. I kept wondering, *What are the chances that she could actually see that far, and see her man? Or be seen by her man?* Then I think about the energetics of it; *she is showing up for her man. Sweet.*

Starting my standing yoga poses, Warrior I, I'm facing west, and that feels good. My energy starts to build as I do the standing poses. It takes energy, and at the same time, I become aware of my energy reserves, which feels gratifying.

Facing the north is the hardest for me. North is the direction home. The longing to be home wells up like the awareness of hunger in my belly.

Just north of the concrete pad is the track and the shooting range. Beyond that stands a so-called mountain. Just a hill really. It goes up, there is a small saddle with a great saguaro cactus, and then the hill continues up even higher. I wonder what is on the other side. *What's the view like from up there? How far could I see if I was up there?*

Sounds of shooting fill the north. Some shots seem to come from the other side of the hill, although not as much as from our shooting range. Facing the track and the rest of the pad where other inmates are hanging out, I hear chatter. Between the noise and the people, it's a lot of distractions, all testing my practice. It is never just me on the pad.

I slow down with more qigong. The Flying Eagle. This flow moves the shoulders in every direction, and I scowl through the whole flow. *Ow, ow, ow.* I pause and stare north, wondering what my son is doing. *What is he thinking, feeling, right this minute? Is he hurting, craving anything, or satisfied and in high spirits?*

I remember some feng shui lore says to sleep with your head toward the north. So, I end with Savasana (Corpse Pose), head north, feet south.

I really appreciate Savasana. Although it looks easy, Savasana has been called the most difficult of the asanas. Obviously, it's not difficult to lay flat on your back, but I'm very curious how I can make it more than that. This is the time I allow my body to incorporate the good stuff I've done in my practice: the grounding and the energizing.

POCKET NOTE:

Buddhist practice offers awareness, gratitude, kindness, compassion, and love toward others and yourself!

JOURNAL:

Before prison, north was my metaphor for stillness and contemplation. Whenever I feel restless while waiting for something to happen or I want something to change, I summon the north into my being. I tell myself to be like a bear in hibernation. Be still and meditate in a moment of hibernation.

I worked with a spiritual teacher, Glen, before prison. I continued working with Glen while I was down. He had this visual language for getting to that deeper spiritual/energetic place, a place "under the sand." I would email him, and we'd set up a time to be meditating together, from afar.

During one of these meditations, I hear Glen ask me how he can help. I say, "Help me carry my sorrows."

He laughs, "Of course." Poof, he is Santa. Not wearing a red suit or anything, but he has a Santa Claus bag. A Santa Claus bag that can hold anything large or small while always looking the same size on the outside.

I see my sorrow all curled up in the fetal position that becomes big puffy clouds. He puts them in his bag. My sorrow over missing my son on Mother's Day becomes this big, rolling, wave-like cloud, and Glen puts it in his bag. Clouds that look torn, he puts in his bag. Clouds like baked marshmallows, he puts in his bag.

Then I ask, "Glen, what would you like from me?"

I get an image of Glen telling me, "Be solid."

My "solid" is a little fuzzy. My solid self is only a portion of my authentic self. Prison doesn't allow all of me to be manifest, to be solid.

This reminds me of how Diane Ackerman in *Dawn Light: Dancing with Cranes and Other Ways to Start the Day* says that dawn is the moment there is enough light so you can recognize a friend's face. I feel that I'm constantly in that space, that second right before dawn when faces can't quite be identified. *Who recognizes me as a friend, I wonder?*

With my practices, I feel I'm becoming more solid at my core, more concrete. I work to keep my energy flowing. I remember who I am, and my practice adds to my experience of the flow. This allows me to be as substantial as I can be.

I realize that my water wheel may still have broken or missing paddles. No matter. With each additional practice, I experience the flow of energy, like dipping into the soothing waters.

©2012 Jeane George Weigel, used with permission

Eight:
MOTHERING FROM PRISON

True detachment isn't a separation from life
but the absolute freedom within your mind to explore living.

—Ron W. Rathbun

J ERA'S WORLD WAS OFF-CENTER from mine from the start. He was a high-need child and had to be engaged every moment. When he was overwhelmed, screaming for hours, I held him until he came back to being comfortable in the world. Instead of trying to change him or fix him, I practiced being still inside myself. Practicing that over and over, I eventually embraced the stillness and that grew into patience.

When my siblings and I were young, my mother used to go away on frequent retreats by herself, leaving us at home. I think she was trying to find herself—beyond her role as a mother. In contrast, when I became a mother, I found strength in connecting to myself in this role. Motherhood had become a central truth of my being.

Jera was ten months old when his dad left. Just being a single mom is a lot of work. On top of that, Jera was not the type of baby who could just be set down and be left to amuse himself. I don't know how I got anything done. But I was committed to being there for him. I felt gratitude for the honor of being his mother. From the beginning of his life, it was always Jera and me. I have always felt that Jera and I were anchored in our relationship.

Being a single parent for a high-need child also had its upsides. I got to make all the decisions. I put a lot of effort into making sure that I covered every angle before making those decisions. I wanted everything to meet his every need: food, supplements, activities, and many different therapies. I sought out anything and everything to give Jera the tools to navigate life and make learning possible for him.

I never worried about how I would get through prison as much as I worried about how my son would get through this time without me. *What could I do*, I wondered, *to make sure my son does not feel like he is going to prison too*? I was so afraid he would feel abandoned—that he would resent me, or unconsciously feel guilty.

I'm so grateful for what we created before I went to prison. I feel lucky that Jera was fourteen years old when I went to prison. Many mothers lose their parental rights once they are incarcerated. Children might go to the father, grandparents, or foster care when their mother is incarcerated, especially if the children are young. Because we had so little contact with my son's father before I was imprisoned, it wasn't even a consideration that Jera would be staying with his father. He most certainly would not be.

The anticipation of my going to prison caused a huge amount of stress within my family. Jera's father being out of the picture didn't result in an outpouring of eagerness from my siblings to take my high-need teenager. What would be in Jera's best interest was only part of the picture. The needs of my siblings and their spouses and families had to be considered.

Two days before my mother died, she had said, "Maybe I should wait until next week to die." She thought she had one more thing she wanted to take care of. As if it was that simple. It seemed she was simply holding onto her responsibility as a parent and to a life *she* was living. Now it was my turn to let go.

I've had to let go of many responsibilities I knew that I could not handle from inside prison. Two aspects of letting go as Jera's mother really stung. One of those aspects was just asking for help. As a nutritionist, I've frequently heard people say how difficult it is to ask for help. The second painful aspect of letting go was relinquishing control. *Oh, Lord.*

I read a poem titled "What You Bring." If you release all expectations and let go of all those skills that usually work, then what is left are your superpowers. The superpowers come from your core, *how* you move forward when there is nothing left. Who you are when you are *emptied*, is what you bring.

Non-attachment presents one of the greatest challenges to new Buddhists, yet it's central to Buddhism's path to transcend suffering. Like many spiritual distinctions, practicing non-attachment leads through a space of paradox. The thought of detaching from things that matter most to us can leave us perplexed. For example, how can a mother ever be unattached to her child?

On the surface, non-attachment seems to conflict with all forms of loving and caring. However, non-attachment doesn't mean indifference. It accepts the present moment and creates the space to love unconditionally. Rather than constricting, non-attachment frees us to expand. No expectations, no limits to love.

This is another reason that I resonate with Buddhism. I love that I don't have to change everything today. I don't even have to change myself today. I can commit to a practice. Buddhism offers a practice of mindfulness for peacefulness. It is a learning process that starts by being curious, being willing to question, and finally leaning in to practice.

The dictionary reminds me that practice occurs in the actual application or use of an idea, belief, or method, as opposed to theories relating to it. When I practice accepting the present moment, it is momentary. As in meditation, I focus on coming back, come back to the breath, come back to the present moment. Life is full of distractions, and I practice, over and over, coming back to the present moment.

"Another crucial concept in Buddhism is dharma, which is the reality of the world and your life. Dharma changes constantly and is altered by the way you see and interact with the world, as well as the choices you make."—Lachlan Brown, *How to Practice Buddhism: A No-Nonsense Guide to Buddhist Beliefs*. This reminds me of Heraclitus's famous saying, "No person can step in the same river twice."

If I love my son unconditionally, I must let go of my ideas of what or who he is. I set aside my self-centered motivation for him to be any particular way. In the state of non-attachment, I can see who he is in the present. Only by accepting reality as it is, can I truly love unconditionally. That's my understanding of non-attachment so far. I don't always live it, but I keep coming back to it.

My sister Dante and I did not always see eye to eye. We didn't argue a lot; we just didn't communicate regularly. In the years before I went to prison, the tension grew between us. Normal conversations frequently seemed to deteriorate into arguments.

Before Kenge left, Dante seemed to avoid all contact with him. Then with the timing of Kenge's departure just before Dante and Chris's wedding, it left a dark cloud hanging over us. Dante and I never had the conversation, never discussed how she felt about Kenge or my relationship to him. I felt she disapproved of his life choices as well as my close relationship with Kenge.

I told my therapist that it felt like Dante thought she could do life better than me—probably parent better, too. My therapist found that interesting and said, "Sometimes the person who thinks that they can do it better than you is the very person you want doing the job because they are going to work very hard at it."

Turns out, she was right. Caring for a stressed-out fourteen-year-old was demanding. Dante and Chris certainly stepped up to the challenge. Through Dante's emails I could sense that this was stretching them, but they followed through with their role as Jera's foster parents, and I will forever be grateful.

Eventually, my whole family stepped up. In addition to Dante and Chris caring for Jera, my sister Greta and brother Mesa took care of Jera on all school breaks and during the two summers while I was inside. My dad offered financial assistance, paying for Jera's monthly expenses. Several friends also made financial contributions for Jera's support.

Of course, Jera had to make a lot of adjustments. Aunts and uncles are not the same as Mom. The new school was the hardest. He said, "There are a lot of jerks." The wrestling team is a huge deal in this small mining town. Jera would tell me how the wrestling guys are mean and hostile. One time, he told me that some students made the Spanish teacher cry. He said, "She was talking in Spanish and some guys started yelling, 'This is America—speak English!'"

It was difficult for Jera to get used to a new way of life. So many things he had to do were way outside his comfort zone, like moving from household to household. He traveled alone by bus from Dante's to Greta's. He had many new responsibilities including taking care of livestock, chopping and hauling wood for heat, and gardening.

We both were stripped away from our lives. We both are accommodating ourselves to our new environments. More than once, I heard women say prison wouldn't be so bad if we just had our loved ones with us. That could be a partner, child, or even a pet.

JOURNAL: How can I keep parenting when we're not together and we're both in strange new worlds? How can I create commonality with my son? I may have been torn away from my life, but I refuse to have my mothering taken from me.

In my first month down, I heard Kenny Chesney's "Somewhere with You" for the first time. I started singing my own version in my mind. *Somewhere with you, anywhere with you, my son, that's where I want to be.*

Jera had a music player with my music loaded on it. He liked listening to my songs to remind him of me. He would add his music to my collection. He found comfort and could relate to the type of songs that had lyrics about how tough life is.

On our phone calls, Jera always wanted to share new songs he found. One of his songs was "Colors" by Cross Fade. Jera said this song was about "shining out your best colors." He said that playing that song reminded himself to do his best. He said, "Mom, you always told me to utilize my white light."

Those phone calls were an important part of our connection. For me, they were a lifeline. Calls became my opportunity to find commonality with Jera. Or create it.

According to prison rules, I can buy six hundred minutes a month, more during the holidays/Christmas. A call lasts fifteen minutes, and that phone call costs $3.45. That allows for about four phone calls per week. Those fifteen minutes go by so fast! Once you make a call, you cannot make another call for thirty minutes.

I talk to my son twice a week and my dad once a week, and that would usually leave enough minutes to call one of my siblings, therapist, or a friend during the month. I would talk to Jera every day if I could.

I am determined to be fully present during each moment in my calls with Jera and notice everything. When Jera picked up the phone, it was like being warmed by the sun. I'd ask, "What have you been doing? How's school going?" It was so hard for me not to cry. We would talk about the weather, about Daphne, our dog, and about the animals on the ranch. *Oh, and how are you?*

Listening to my son's voice, I feel a flood of relief in my body. The human voice is so powerful. I am reminded of years past when Jera was beginning to talk. The way our brains are wired to tune in while listening to someone talk is marvelous. It's why a mother will always understand what her child is saying over a stranger who has yet to be accustomed to the speech patterns.

Science reveals that mothers are biologically wired to their children. When interacting, a baby and mother's brain waves sync up. And studies show mothers can identify their babies from sound and smell. No wonder hearing my son laugh *is* music to my whole body!

Our voices make up an essential part of the bond we experience with people throughout life and even beyond. I remember the first time I saw my aunt (my mother's sister) after my mother had passed away. Hearing her speak, I was on the verge of tears. She sounded like my mom. I didn't care what she was talking about. I wanted her to keep talking. I heard my mother's voice in hers and it was music to my ears.

My phone calls with Jera were short, but they made such an enormous difference in my world. We started to get into a comfortable groove with our biweekly calls. He tells me about doing his homework, the new things he was learning on the farm, his visits to Greta and Mesa. Jera would ask me what movie weekends were like. Which movies did I see? I told him bird stories.

He remembers me telling him that I wouldn't do things to get in trouble because I wanted to get home. And when things were not going great for Jera, I would tell him it would get better. With only fifteen minutes, my priorities are to listen and to say "I love you" as many times as I can.

It's almost a year into my sentence and I can't get hold of Jera. When nobody answers the phone, first I am annoyed—I must stand in line again and wait thirty minutes for a free phone. Then, if nobody picks up again, I'm filled with sadness, concern, and frustration.

Up to now, if Jera didn't answer the phone, it was always because he was at a friend's house or just physically not present at that moment. But now, I've been calling him many times each day and nobody has answered. This is so unusual and disturbing.

When I can't get through, something is wrong in my world! And I fear something is wrong in *his* world. There is nothing I can do except get back in line. *Please, please pick up the phone.*

After a few days of this, I email both Dante and Greta to find out what is happening. Greta emails me that she called Dante and Jera is fine.

That provides me some relief, but now I am left even more perplexed. If everything is okay, why hasn't anybody answered the phone? My thoughts cascade from worry to anxiety and depression. What is keeping them from answering the phone? I don't hear anything from Dante. It's now twelve days since I've talked to my son—I'm going crazy. I keep calling every day. I called nine times yesterday and no one answered. I'm sad and depressed.

Finally, on the fourteenth day, Jera picks up! I ask him what happened, and he says nothing happened. *What!?* I don't know what to make of this.

JOURNAL:

> I'm trying to wrap my head around the rabbit hole I just went down. Was I the only one suffering? Do they have any idea how precious my fifteen minutes of phone time with Jera is to me! Are they so immersed in their lives that they forgot about me? Am I expecting something extraordinary from Dante? Why didn't they pick up just once in the last fourteen days?

Not hearing from Jera for two weeks was traumatic for me. We finally had our fifteen-minute talk, but I felt like I was left hanging. *Will he pick up next time? Is this the new normal?* In the absence of any explanation at the time, I was left to process my own stuff: my thoughts, my emotions, my rabbit hole. At the time it was a deep, deep rabbit hole.

I went out to walk on the track. I find that walking is more conducive to processing and integrating than being in my room. Inside, I'm looking for a distraction from my thoughts. When I walk, I watch my thoughts arise and I encourage myself to expand, to allow myself to see where my thoughts want to go. Where will they take me?

I read this pocket note and start walking:

POCKET NOTE:

> I'm not lost until I lose my memory, and I commit to loving you as long as I can remember.

This is my parenting mantra! I wrote this pocket note after reflecting on a couple of experiences.

When my mom had cancer, we went to visit her family in California. An aunt of hers was renewing vows after fifty years of marriage. The vows said something about being committed to loving you for as long as I can remember. I thought that this was not about losing one's memory per se but any situation at all where you choose to keep another person in consideration.

I remember the ceremony Jera and I participated in together. This ceremony was about Jera and me committing to loving each other while we were separated. Jeff, my therapist who created the ceremony, told us that in order to love each other, we also had to treat ourselves with love. Part of loving each other has to do with committing to taking care of ourselves in a loving way. Jera and I committed to loving each other while being apart, out loud.

JOURNAL: I commit, wholeheartedly, to loving my son unconditionally! This will require a practice of loving myself unconditionally, too. I must care for myself in order to care for another.

I practice this with the Green Tara chant: OM TARE TUTTARE TURE SOHA. Ralph only gave me two chants before I went to prison. One of them, the Green Tara chant. It felt so profound and as time progressed, it had even more meaning.

Tara embodies the sacred feminine in Buddhism. The way I understood it from Ralph, connecting to Green Tara, through chanting and meditation, can lead to an enlightening personal experience. Particularly, the feminine experience.

JOURNAL:

"The Tara prayer (OM TARE TUTTARE TURE SOHA) recognizes our inherent perfection, the true nature of all living beings. We pray to Tara to remove all obstacles to listening to the teachings, obstacles to contemplating them, obstacles to meditating on them, so that the fruit of these teachings may be realized by ourselves and all beings. Tara represents the principle of pervasive love, pervasive compassion, the all-powerful principle of benefiting all beings without distinction. Prayer is what creates a receptivity in ourselves to the principles of truth available for all beings. When we pray we open ourselves...to the understanding of something greater, to cultivate qualities in ourselves. The first quality to be developed is Compassion, second Equanimity, third Love, and fourth Rejoicing. One method for cultivating equanimity is that every being—whether human, animal, Spirit, friend, or enemy—has been your own mother at some point in the cycle of rebirth."—Lama Tsering Everest

I practice the Tara prayer by chanting and visualizing. I visualize Green Tara as she embodies principles of fearlessness and courage. Then, as she would sit in meditation, I chant, asking that I incorporate her into me.

I know that chanting in many religions is a prayer, reaching out to the Divine essence. Ralph said that chanting is one of many tools to help one focus. Science points out that chanting sets up a vibrational quality in your mind and body that quickly brings you to a state of calm and relaxation.

I like chanting for the feel of the rhythm. Whenever I study or write, I like to listen to music for the same reason. I find that chanting calms me and gives me something to do when I feel like I can't escape feeling helpless. Chanting helps me come back to my center. From this centered place of self-awareness, I ask myself, *What are you upset or concerned about?*

As soon as I asked the question, I knew the answer: whoever cares for Jera, I envision them keeping me alive as Jera's parent the way I wanted to keep our mom alive for Mesa. Even though I am not present, I am still bound to Jera as a parent. *Why aren't they on the same page about this?*

When my mother died and my youngest brother, Mesa, came to live with me, it was a choice, not out of necessity. My stepfather at the time would have continued to care for Mesa. It was a decision that my sisters and I made together. It was so important to us that Mesa be raised with all the teachings of our mother, even though she had passed away. We concluded that no one was better equipped than us to pass along to Mesa who she was.

Am I asking too much of my siblings now?

Upon further reflection, it becomes obvious that my hopes, expectations, and desires are all attachments. Ha! Wasn't that what I agreed with Ralph about? That I shouldn't want anything while I'm here? And that means nothing!

I realize that letting go of these expectations and desires will bring greater peace and happiness. Yet, I still *want* to be alive in Jera's daily life even though I'm not present. I *want* whoever is taking care of my son while I am not around to carry the memory of me forward. I still want these things.

JOURNAL: Am I failing as a parent? "Wanting" probably indicates my failure as a Buddhist more than my parenting.

Parenting means so many things. Parenting causes a shift in our experience of our experiences. Of course, I know I am Jera's mother, but from here, I can't watch him as a mother carefully observes. From fourteen years of experience, I know how important routine is to Jera being balanced. I am aware of subtle changes in his mood that may indicate if he is struggling or just experiencing moods. I watch him experience life and it changes my experience. In a way, I'm co-parenting with very limited opportunities to connect with my son.

For me, pregnancy was a most profound experience of surrender. I surrender myself and sacrifice my needs and my wants, for this *being* called my child. It takes strength to parent a child. I could write a whole book on strength and parenting. So many moments of every day that I spent letting go of my exhaustion, frustration, irritability, to show up for my son.

There is no one way to be the perfect parent, I get that!

POCKET NOTE.

"There are a whole lot of ways to be perfect, and not one of them is attained through punishment!"
— Ursula K. LeGuin

JOURNAL:

Maybe I'm being too hard on myself? I must detach from my old notions of who I am when it comes to parenting. My identity before I came to prison has been shredded over and over again. Breathe and allow for the wonder in parenting, even from behind prison walls.

I know how difficult and extremely time-consuming it can be to care for Jera. During his stay with Dante and Chris, Jera was learning the way of life on the farm. Jera has benefited immensely by having Chris, as a patient, caring father figure in his life.

In each of Dante's letters and emails she seems close to being overwhelmed. But what then? What would happen if Dante and Chris decide Jera is too much for them? What would happen to Jera? Every part of me wants to say, *He's my son. I committed to parenting him. Give him to me.* Obviously that option doesn't exist.

Dante doesn't have my fourteen years of experience with Jera and I'm not sure she comprehends the struggles I went through. I had so many very, very difficult years with my son. I faced new challenges all the time with Jera. My commitment to being the best mother that I could be for Jera brought out the best in me. It was more than just parenting; this was my purpose. That demanded that I keep growing as a parent

I continue to practice finding peace within the present moment while reminding myself that Dante is doing the best she can. And I just can't thank her enough.

I get a fresh perspective of who my son is from the phone calls and the visits. Jera is empathetic, generous, sweet, confident, caring, and my family tells me he is continually striving to please everybody. He is working hard to make this situation workable. We are living "love in action." My parenting made this possible and he is making it happen.

JOURNAL: Jeff, Jera's therapist, says that the hand of the Divine is at work here. Jera is doing so well.

After that rough first semester, Jera is spending the summer with Greta and Mesa. It feels like a turning point for Jera. He seemed to grow in confidence and happiness.

Jera made a pact with Greta to complete a vision quest. A vision quest is a yearly commitment with a community of wonderful people. Spending a week together in spiritual questing. The first year is about stepping up and being a support person for others in the group who are going on the hill. Going out on the hill is about being in nature with no one around and fasting. The next year, spending one night out on the hill, progressing to two nights the following year. The goal being four nights on the hill, which we did together when I got out.

JOURNAL:

Jera seems to be discovering a sense of happiness within. For some people, it may take years to stretch into someone new. Then there are times when an event or situation forces you to re-evaluate who you want to be in the world. Maybe for Jera's growth, I needed to get out of the way. I'd call that radical non-attachment. Jera, I love you unconditionally!

Mothering can be challenging for so many reasons and being in prison is a huge challenge! Now, I live in close quarters with three hundred other women, many of them who have children on the outside. Most of the time, I would not know who has children except for the fact that intimate conversations are overheard in the phone room.

In the phone room, I see my fellow inmates at their most vulnerable. Our phone room has no privacy. Communication via phone and letters is always monitored. Somebody is always listening and/or watching you.

However, when *I'm* on the phone, it is *all* about me and my son. Even though I feel strong emotions, I am careful not to talk about feeling down or depressed in fear of being cut off or worse, being sent to the doctor for antidepressants.

The phone room has six phones in it with plastic chairs to sit in. Because there are two phones in the corner, it is impossible not to be touching the next person on the phone beside you. Therefore, one is called the "stand-up phone:" one person stands up not to be touching the person next to you. We wait our turn outside, sometimes in the burning heat and sometimes in the freezing cold. There is a cement bench out front and as you walk up, you call out "Last!" to see who is going to be in line before you. Then you are last until someone else comes and calls out, "Last!"

This is about the only place I see tears in prison, and it is heartbreaking! I'm sitting next to a woman while she is talking to her child, tears streaming down her face and trying not to sound like she's crying. "It's alright, baby," she says. Some women are really good at it. If I couldn't see her tears, I wouldn't know she was crying. On the other hand, when I cry, my voice breaks, and I can't breathe and I practice breathing. Still can't breathe and cry at the same time.

In the phone room, we hear stories: a husband is filing for divorce; a mother has lost parental rights; children are in all kinds of trouble. One time, a woman hears that her daughter has been raped, and immediately, the phone police disconnect her call. After waiting outside for thirty minutes, she tries to call her daughter back. They won't let the call go through. The officer on duty makes her wait until the next day to get permission to use a regular phone.

I'd see these women day in and day out on the phone. The pain is evident. I overheard phone conversations: women telling their children that they will change, be different, be there for their children just as soon as they get out.

I wonder, once on the outside, what stressor would cause one to slip up? The promises to our children and the knowledge inside yourself that you can be different, when does it all line up? With the limitations of prison, what gets us to the point that a change occurs? And, will it stick?

One time, a new young inmate came in pregnant, and she lost the baby. I heard someone say, "What is she crying about? I've lost a child too." All these women surrounding me have had hard lives. In prison, instead of "someone always is better than you," it's more like "someone always has had it worse than you." This seems like a fact. Most women in prison operate like *it's all about me*. It's understandable. For most inmates, prison is all about survival.

Where is the compassion? Both women deserve compassion. Is compassion absent? Or is it covered up? Buried by their wounds. Aren't they doing the best they can?

JOURNAL:

> How many kinds of compassion are there or is it that compassion can be understood differently from head, heart, or soul? Or is compassion so covered up with wounded baggage? Does compassion come naturally? Compassion buried. Compassion expressed. "The word usually translated as "compassion" is karuna, which is understood to mean active sympathy or a willingness to bear the pain of others."—Barbara O'Brien, *Buddhism and Compassion*. When are we willing to bear the pain of others?

The practice of compassion gives new meaning to my role as guide and teacher. Inmates come to me asking questions about many aspects of life as they might ask a therapist. I am careful to remind them that I have no psychology degree, or training as a therapist. I rely on my practical life experiences as well as my intuition. I enjoy having real conversations with my fellow inmates.

This one gal, Janet, has less than five years left on a fourteen-year sentence. She has four children. Each child she gave birth to while in prison. Before her current fourteen-year sentence started, she was in and out a lot. Every time she had a child, she gave it to her mother to parent.

"I've never actually been a mother," Janet tells me, "I birthed my kids; however, they were not mine. My mom is raising them."

I ask her, "What was it like when you were a kid? What do you remember about *your* mother?"

"I really don't remember my childhood," she tells me, "I don't remember what my mother was like. I don't even remember what I was like then."

Janet tells me that she wants to be a mother when she gets out, but she feels like the disconnect is enormous. Having given up her children, she never really had much practice being a mother.

As we continue to talk, Janet says, "I used to talk to a therapist. She was an inmate that was released right before you got here. It seems like you're filling her shoes now."

"I don't have any training when it comes to being a therapist." I said, "What I do is more like a meditation. Once I have an issue or person in mind, I observe and see what shows up."

"Oh, cool." She said, "Would you do that for me?"

"Sure," I replied. "Let's see what happens."

"What are the names of your three youngest children?"

"Joaquin, Luke, and Jacob."

"I have each of them in my mind. Now I mentally ask, 'What do you want your mother to know?' and we wait for a response."

Janet says, "They're teens by now. I suspect they are angry with me for being in prison."

"Right." I held up my hand to have her wait for a moment.

"I see Luke," I told her. "He's on the hill in front of us, arms crossed, looking defensive. He doesn't want you to put any expectations on him."

Tears come to my eyes as I sense the conflict in him. I sense he's longing to be held by his mother and he has a strong attitude of self-protection.

Janet asks, "Why are you crying?"

"Your son wants to be strong in front of you. He doesn't want you to see him cry, but I feel his sadness and aching. These are his tears."

"Ohhhh." Janet says slowly.

"When you are present with him remember this time," I tell her. "Don't look for the right words. You don't have to do anything. Just allow yourself to release all your assumptions about what he feels. Let go of any concern for what you should do, or not do as a parent."

She teared up. She let out a sigh, and I saw the tension in her face and shoulders melt away. "That's amazing, but what about Joaquin and Jacob? I'm so afraid I've failed them, and they will never forgive me."

"I think Luke speaks for all of them," I said. "They are afraid of you, as well. You're as much a mystery to them as they are to you. And that's okay. You don't have to plan how to mother. You just must be present. And as a Buddhist would say, "Stay in the moment. What is, is."

"After fifteen years down," Janet said, "I don't know what to expect out there. About anything, much less about mothering. Even though I've talked to them on the phone, I don't really know them."

"I understand that." I replied. "Allow yourself some freedom about what it means to be a mother. As parents, we think we know our children. Of course, we know something about them. But thinking we know everything about them leads to expectations and blind spots. Kids, like all of us, want to be seen for who they are, not who we think they are. We all want to be loved unconditionally. Like any relationship, parenting always needs to evolve."

"Cool!" she almost shouts. "Gotta go to lunch." And just like that, she was back in her tough, prison character.

One day, I go to the TV room and only two other women are present, Wendy and Alicia. I like playing Scrabble® with Wendy because she's smart and she challenges me, and not many inmates can do that. I don't know Alicia, except that she is from Española, New Mexico. I spent some years growing up near Española. Wendy knows Alicia from previous jail time—not her first merry-go-round, as they say here in prison.

Alicia is in her twenties and leaving soon. They're talking when I walk in. Wendy asks Alicia, "What are you going to do when you get out?"

Alicia laughs, "Things are going to be different *this* time."

Wendy's tone gets serious, "You were a heroin user. You going to shoot up when you get out?"

Alicia nods and softly says, "The first chance I get."

"I want you to write a will," Wendy says. "Write the things you would say to the people you love if you were dying. Then I want you to pin it to the inside of your coat, have it with you every time you use."

Alicia remains quiet for a moment and then blurts out, "I'm not going to do that."

Wendy cries and my eyes well up. "If you can't write it down, you should at least make a point to call someone you love and tell them goodbye."

"I've made it this far," Alicia says lightheartedly. "C'mon, let's get in line for dinner."

I kept imagining Alicia out of prison going through her day. By then, prison seems so far away, and death is not even a thought. She's thinking, *Hey, just a little break. Just a little bit to take the edge off. I deserve a break.*

JOURNAL:

Wendy's conversation with Alicia really sticks with me. I want to ask all the women here: can any of us recognize the tipping point (that one risk too many)? If we could, would anyone pin a will to the inside of her coat? But none of us can see the tipping point. We fool ourselves into thinking we can and pinning the will into the coat would acknowledge the risk we are taking.

Is it just the young that think they are invulnerable? They don't think in terms of risks. They're going to live forever. As an adult, is it experience, or dumb luck (all those times you've survived risks that could have gone awry), that grants us permission to be risk-takers? Or is it denial? Or is it that we don't want to become trapped underneath the fear of taking risks?

We all have had experiences and looked back thinking, *Whoa, I survived— unscathed*, and we're afraid, ashamed, or too damn foolish to look deeper.

The Buddha said there are no good or bad emotions. Emotions are a fundamental part of who we are. I read somewhere that with mindful practice, negative or difficult emotions can give us useful information about how our emotions rule us. *What is my relationship to my emotions? Am I ashamed of my anger? Do I love feeling happy and hate feeling sad?*

It's a challenge for me to acknowledge all emotions as they arise without judgement. The Buddhist answer to such judgment is compassion. Compassion towards oneself, and the object of one's emotion, will neutralize the negative, and even allow positive emotions to arise.

POCKET NOTE:

"the way of one who is grounded in eternity and moving in the field of time. The field of time is the field of sorrow. 'All life is sorrowful.' 'you realize the eternal within yourself. 'You participate with joy in the sorrows of the world.' — A Joseph Campbell Companion: Reflections on the Art of Living, p 120

JOURNAL:

"When you see yourself in the mirror, that is the mortal. The eternal is that which you are…If you can hold to that still place within yourself while engaged in the field, your performance will be masterly." — *A Joseph Campbell Companion: Reflections on the Art of Living,* p 198. To me, the still point Campbell writes about is the sacred space of the eternal 'I am.'

Being grounded in the eternal, we can live, breathe, laugh, and cry in this time, in this world, and that is our participation in this life.

Today I feel sorrow in my heart being separated from my son. This, of course, is nothing new. However I took it on today as a focus of my practice. Today, I work on my sorrow: I recognize that there is a still point within me. This is the place where I can be one with what is eternal and at the same time participate with joy in the sorrows of the world. Or in my case, the enormous sorrows carried by these women all around me.

JOURNAL:

Avalokiteshvara—the goddess of compassion. Kuan Yin is one of four female aspects. I assume everyone is compassionate at their core, but the garbage, the barriers that prevent us from experiencing compassion, make me wonder at times if compassion is ever going to be expressed, or will it be drowned by a lifetime of baggage. Remove the garbage and uncover the compassion. Restore ourselves, then compassion is restored.

Because I am in prison, it's not like anybody can call me up and let me know what is going on in their world. I knew Jera was going on a trip with Mesa, and I wouldn't be able to talk to him for a week. But a few days later, I get an email from my sister Greta, telling me to call Jera at my friend Vida's, in Fort Collins. Jera has something to tell me.

Vida doesn't answer right away, so I call Greta. Nervously, I say to Greta, "I can't get hold of Vida yet, please tell me what's going on?"

"Don't worry," Greta assures me, "Jera is fine; however, he got bit by a rattlesnake."

"Oh my god," I blurt out, "how did that happen?" I'm thinking, *He's been bit by a rattlesnake and I'm not there!* I want to scream or cry...or both.

"It happened on the drive with Mesa," Greta continues calmly, "Mesa took him to the hospital and now he's resting with Vida. We decided it was best for him not to continue the trip."

My chest is tight, so many questions running through my head. "It sounds very scary," I said.

"Jera wants to tell you all about it. They know you will be calling, so don't worry they will answer the phone!"

I get off the phone to save my minutes. I call again and Vida picks up, whew!

"Oh, great it's you!" Vida says, "Here's Jera."

I say, "Oh, thank you!" Jera gets on and I ask, "How are you doing?" Immediately I start to cry.

"I'm okay. Don't worry. My whole leg looks like one huge, swollen bruise, all yellow, black, and blue! I can barely bend it, so it's kind of difficult to move around and go to the bathroom and stuff."

"Does it still hurt?"

"Mostly only when I move around. It's getting better."

"Did they give you anything to put on it?"

"Well, Vida put pineapple slices all over my leg I guess to get the toxins out. She said it looked almost gangrene. The first day she had me soak in a bath with Epsom salts."

"That sounds right. Tell me how it happened."

"We were driving through Wyoming. Mesa and the whole family, and all their gear. I was sitting in the back area with all the luggage."

"Sounds cramped."

"Oh, it was. So, when we finally got to a rest stop, I jumped out to stretch my legs. There was this hill with a bunch of big rocks. I was hopping from rock to rock, and about halfway up, I stood on one rock and yelled back to the others, 'This is my mountain!' and suddenly I felt a sting."

"Oh, my God, did you *hear* the snake or see it?"

"Well, I heard it as I felt it, and then I saw it, too. And as I turned to run away it struck again but this time it barely grazed me."

"So, then they rushed you to the hospital?"

"Yes. In the car, I was feeling like I was outside my body, watching and wondering what was going to happen next. I wasn't in a lot of pain. I felt tingling in my leg, and I was just sort of observing my body's response to the venom."

"Did they put pressure or use a tourniquet?"

"None of those home remedies are helpful and they can end up causing more harm than good. Incisions and sucking the venom out is sort of a wives' tale. Even ice packs don't help with bites."

"How did you learn so much about snake bites?" I said laughing.

I learned it in the hospital. They were all very friendly.

"Did it bleed a lot?"

"A fair amount, but it's important to let the wound bleed."

"Were you scared?"

"Not really. And I wanted to stay as still as possible. Mesa told me to keep my breathing steady to stay calm. He told me that panic just speeds up your pulse which spreads the venom faster around the body."

"When we got to the hospital, they treated me with anti-venom, but they didn't have much on hand. So, they took me to another hospital to get more anti-venom."

"How long did you stay in the hospital?"

"Just one night and then they released me. Then we went to Vida's place."

"I'm so glad you're okay. My minutes are almost up; I'll call you again in a couple days. I love you and I wish I was there for you."

I'm sure he could hear the strain in my voice, still trying to hold back tears. Jera said, "It's alright if you call me every day, not for me. I'm fine, but for you."

We hung up, and immediately I cried intensely. I felt so helpless! I know I couldn't do anything or change anything. But not being there in person, even just to hold his hand, makes me feel like curling up in a ball, face to the wall.

I had to get control of my emotions and the best way to focus my mind is to do some research. So, I decided to read up on snake bites and recovery. I couldn't Google, but I do have some books. I came up with a list of vitamins Jera could take to help his body deal with the snake bite: calcium and magnesium to calm the nervous system, extra vitamin C to help his immune system deal with the venom, a vitamin B complex, vitamin E, and zinc.

I called back the next day. When Vida answered I said, "Thank you, thank you, Vida."

"No problem, Collin. I tried to think what you would do. I called your veterinarian friend. She reassured me that we were doing all the right things."

"Who thought of pineapple slices for a snake bite?"

"I Googled snake bites and that came up, so, I decided to try it."

"I'm so grateful for you. I so appreciate you looking after Jera."

"We're doing everything we can to make him comfortable. We got him all set up on the couch. We're feeding him healthy and adding in a little comfort food. He loves his mac and cheese."

"Thank you so much for going the extra mile. Knowing you are there for Jera eases my mind. I knew he would be in good hands with your medical background."

"I know how much you want to be here yourself for Jera. I just tried to think of what you would do if you were here."

"I have so much respect for you, Vida. It means the world to me. I just want to be included in Jera's caregiving even though I can't be there."

I gave her the list of supplements and Vida went out right away and got everything I told her.

POCKET NOTE:

"We are able to be pierced to the heart...while never forgetting the beauty of the world and goodness of being alive."

I excerpted that pocket note from Pema Chödrön's *Taking the Leap: Freeing Ourselves from Old Habits and Fears:* "There comes a time when we are able to be pierced to the heart by our own suffering and the suffering of others, and by our own regrets, without it dragging us down. We can hold the sadness of life in our hearts while never forgetting the beauty of the world, and the goodness of being alive."

That is my goal: never forgetting the beauty of the world, the goodness of being alive, and the gratitude of being mother to my beloved son. *We are breathing the same air that circles this planet, we see the same sun, we see the same moon, there is oneness.*

About a year into my sentence, Jera tells me a story:

One day, out in the wild, a fire is burning everything in its path—all the trees and all the grass. Every animal is running away from the fire, except the hummingbird. The tiny hummingbird flaps its wings so fast and flies from the fire to the river and back to the fire. The hummingbird fills up its tiny beak with water, then takes the water to the fire.

The other animals stop and watch the hummingbird. The elephant, who could carry so much more water than the hummingbird, asks, "Why are you doing this? You are so small and can only carry a tiny bit of water. You can't even hope to put out the fire."

The hummingbird replied, "I'm doing the best that I can."

Jera says to me, "That's what you and I are doing Mom: the best that we can."

Jera's capacity to blow me away makes me so proud and so delighted. We are the ones we have been waiting for!

Poem sent by Greta:

WHAT YOU BRING

This morning hangs
Like unfurled, shuddering wings on the edge
And wishes itself back in the safety,
The nest, the warm arms,
The closed eyes and bliss of the black space
In which to simply be and rest.
But knowing, even while turning in retreat,
That the heaven husk, emptied,
Already floats on the storm away.
Behind now nothing.
Ahead everything.
Swirling, churning,
Awake, aware, alive, messy, unknown.
Never in all time would such a step take place
With retreat an option.
But in the moment is courage born.
In knowing the forward step is not your choice.
But what you are, what you bring, is.

—Anna Edmonson

Nine:
THE DIRT AND THE SKY

EARLY IN MY INCARCERATION, I was talking to my sister Greta. She was preparing to bring Jera for his first visit. She asked me, "What kind of restaurants are in the area?" *Ahh, if only we could go out for dinner sometime!*

"I don't get out much," I said, laughing. She was mortified.

My family and friends on the outside often forget how limited my scope of experience is here in prison. At moments, even I am struck by the strange realization that my entire existence takes place within a circle barely one mile wide.

Let me give you a guided tour of my little world. As you drive onto the property, over a cattle guard, a flag waves out front of a small cinderblock building on your right. That's the office and visitors' area. Most of the women's compound is hidden behind this first building. The rest of the women's prison camp consists of a series of connected buildings and our recreational spaces.

An assortment of spaces and buildings extend a half-mile radius around the women's compound. We call these areas "Land's Out."

A hundred yards past the women's prison, you'll come to a Y in the road. If you stay to the right, you end up at the men's medium security facility.

There are orange trees on a small triangle of green at the Y in the road. The first time I saw oranges, I thought, *Fresh oranges?* Right away, the inmate I was with (we are never alone) tells me, "Don't eat the oranges. These are not the kind you can eat."

135

Really? They look like regular oranges. What are they going to taste like? I was told they taste terrible and yet I always wanted to try one for myself.

Whose idea was that anyway? Planting orange trees just to look at the oranges. Yes, if this was my spread, the oranges would be edible, and they would be delicious!

I would have lots of edible fruit trees, oranges, the best apples, and apricots—my favorite. Now when I see the oranges by the side of the road, I imagine them succulent, just waiting for me.

Oranges are not served very often. Instead, they regularly serve terrible, bland, mealy, red apples. Oranges and bananas are a treat. Seeing oranges on the trees feels like yet another metaphor for life out of reach.

As you stay to the left past the Y and before you reach the warehouses, you come to the men's prison yard on the right.

Beyond the fence to the left is open land with scrub or shrubland. Within the fence the ground consists of mostly dirt. The women who work Lands Out have the job of making sure the dirt looks good. Every day, a whole crew of women go out there and clean up the dirt. They weed and rake dirt, day after day after day.

There are designs in the dirt everywhere. Next to the road, you'll see rocks formed into images and symbols. The women have made some cool arrangements: a lizard, a medicine wheel, and a Kokopelli (the Hopi figure with a flute). That one always gets me–the Kokopelli figure is a sort of muse to remind us to recognize joy and spread joy in the world. *Ahh.*

At the corner of the men's yard is a mound of dirt, a small hill, with a shade canopy at the top. A paved road, just wide enough for a truck to drive up, allows guards to watch the yard. On the side of the mound, women have sculpted an ant carrying a big, lumpy bag on its back. We refer to the mound as "Ant Hill." I suspect the humor of this name was lost on many of my fellow inmates: *We* are the ants with bags of rocks on our backs.

On the left past Ant Hill stand the warehouses. Behind the warehouses, five ponds appear like an oasis surrounded by a smattering of palm trees. The man-made ponds function as part of the water treatment system. The first pond smells foul. The other ponds don't smell, and I always enjoy watching the breeze on the water.

I would love to make the ponds a place for inmates to walk around. I'd have a few picnic tables around the ponds. However, most inmates never see this area, only the women working at Water Ops or other Land's Out facilities.

After the warehouses past the men's prison on the right, we come to a few dirt lots. Now, we are at the farthest from the women's prison, and past the fences lies open range land. From here, the road circles the men's facility where a guard in a truck slowly and continuously patrols the perimeter.

One of my recycling jobs involves transporting shredded paper to the designated dumpsters. We have about six dumpsters. For a while, they were all behind the kitchen, but then they had us move them way out to the dirt lot on the very edge of the prison property. This lot is on the far side of the men's prison. Every time the dumpsters are full of shredded paper, we must get in the bins and stomp around to mash down the paper.

One time, I'm inside a bin walking back and forth in shredded paper while my work partner is doing the same in the other bin. I said, "I bet this is softer than my bed. Let's lie down and test it out." We each lay down in a dumpster three-quarters full of shredded paper. It is *way* softer than my bed!

Lying there, I notice the top of the dumpster forms a window to the outside. Looking up, I see only sky, I hear only quiet. Out there isn't prison. For a moment. I taste freedom as if all it would take is one step and I would be out. Unfortunately, we could not stay there very long because the patrolling officer would get suspicious if he didn't see us.

The dirt and the sky are constantly in a state of revision, modification, and transformation. Even the weather here adds to the sense of constant change. In April, the day starts out at 40 degrees, reaches the 70s by lunchtime, and 90 degrees in the afternoon. In June, it's up to 110 degrees and above. The heat on the breeze feels like I'm standing too close to a camp-fire. I instinctually turn away, but in this situation, it doesn't help at all. There's nowhere to turn.

One day, we had a dust storm, a wild experience! It looked like a rain-storm coming in, but it was red dust making our eyes gritty. We are put in lockdown to stare out the window at the red haze. I sit and wonder, *Where did this come from?* The next day, I talk to Greta, and she tells me that they heard about it. Called a "haboob," it reached two miles high and fifty miles wide!

In prison, so many things seem unchangeable: same clothes, same steel-toed boots, same rules. At the same time, little changes occur regu-larly: inmates are released, new inmates arrive, and guards rotate around the prison. And today, the acacia tree is blooming—a subtle, but magnifi-cent change, with its yellow fluffy puff balls. What a beautiful color.

JOURNAL: The Buddhist idea of impermanence reminds me that change is inevitable, continuous, and unavoidable. When we don't recognize that things are impermanent, we "want." Bud-dhism says we cling or crave things, people, even feelings. Im-permanence means more than things arising and passing. Even as they are present, they are changing in nature. When I go with the flow, I'm truly embracing that state of impermanence.

Beyond the outermost fence of the compound, wild burros roam free. I rarely see them, but often I hear them bray. Next to the lot where the paper dumpsters sit lies an overgrown junkyard. Known as "the Bone-yard," this plot is home to rolls of fencing, old washing machines, and old defunct desks and chairs. Two huge, green, metal recycling dumpsters sit in front of the Boneyard gate where crows and ravens love to scavenge.

Despite its ugly contents, the Boneyard is my favorite area. It's remote, and it has the best views.

Because of its isolation, the Boneyard offers the perfect place to eat our contraband food. I stop the cart, turn off the radio, and we sit eating an orange in peace. Back on the compound the orange peels and even the smell of oranges could give us away.

These sweet, fragrant oranges were appropriated from the kitchen, not the orange trees on property. We found several ways to lay our hands on contraband food. My friend that works in the officer lounge lets us know occasionally when she's hidden food in the trash for us. During the holidays, for example, it's easy to sneak out a few cookies still in their decorative tins.

I also love the quietness of the Boneyard. My work partner shares my yearning for silence, so we never talk much here. It almost feels like sacred ground.

JOURNAL:
My perception shapes my experience, and my participation shapes my point of view. The Boneyard (a junkyard) transforms into a sacred space. As I listen to the sounds of nature, listen to the bones, the bones of creation, what is waiting to be revealed?

Way in the back of the Boneyard, in a shady spot under a large bush, a small old wooden spool and a couple stumps become a lovely makeshift table and chairs. *I wish I could come out here by myself and make this my private oasis.*

JOURNAL:
I'm constantly reminded of the Buddhist insight that life and its environment are one, intertwined. Life doesn't exist without an environment. And life can profoundly affect its surroundings. Therefore, it's the living things within the surroundings that brings the environment to life.

The entire compound is filled with examples of living things shaping the environment and bringing it to life. Our two patches of green lawn thrive out here in the desert only with great care. One area of lawn lies between paths as they come together in front of the kitchen and the other lawn fills the middle of the oval track. As tempting as it may be to lay down or walk barefoot in the green grass, it is absolutely forbidden.

Even the concrete walkways and manicured dirt tell a story of the play between life and environment. Every time I walk to the phones, I pretend I'm walking past a Japanese rock garden. I've given it life, and it gives me peace and serenity.

Few places inside the compound foster tranquility quite like the Boneyard. But with the right attention and perspective, I can steal moments of stillness and serenity, such as listening to the leaves of the eucalyptus trees whispering sweetly in the breeze.

A couple varieties of eucalyptus surround the compound. Some tall ones line the path from my unit to the kitchen. Out back, next to the recreation area, I like to sit by one short, squat eucalyptus tree.

Moments of tranquility inside the compound are quickly disrupted by activity and noise. I've managed to adjust to the constant background noise inside the prison building: women chattering, carts moving, toilets flushing, and even the intercom. But I don't think I'll ever get used to the sounds of gunfire.

Yes, there's a shooting range just over the fence from our athletic field. When I wrote to a friend that part of my job is working on the shooting range, picking up shells, she wrote back, "I can't believe that they let you shoot guns." *Yeah, right.* Obviously, the range isn't here for prisoner's recreational use. SWAT, DEA, police, and undoubtedly others use the shooting range as a training area.

My recycling job entails going into the range in the early mornings with Marcia, my workmate, to pick up shells. They collect shells into buckets at the range. We pick up the buckets to take to our fifty-gallon recycling drums. Pouring shells into those drums is the loudest noise ever!

As I pour the bucket of shells into the big drums, I don't have enough hands. Hands to pour the shells and hands to cover my ears.

The range is split into several sections for different types of training scenarios. The one closest to our track, range number five, is for long-range shooting and is used the most.

Next to the shooting range sits a house without a roof. Trainees storm into the house as instructors look down from the scaffolding. Another section has pop-up targets where they have competitions. And a dirt lot with doors and partial walls propped up provide barriers for the trainees to bust through.

Sometimes, guys show up in green and brown camouflage, sometimes they wear all black, and sometimes, big fat guys drive up in big fat trucks and just shoot all day long.

One guy who comes on Sundays and shoots on the number five range for upward of five hours at a time. He'll show up at 9 a.m., pause for lunch in his truck, and then keep shooting for another couple hours. The whole time he is out there, I can't walk on the track. I always feel like going over there and asking why. Aren't there better things to be doing on a Sunday? Most of the time, he comes alone. A few times, I've seen a young boy with him, maybe around ten years old? *Why? Maybe this is his form of meditation?*

At first, I assumed I would get used to the sound of gunfire. But at times, it becomes so wearing, so unnerving, so disquieting. Some days, it goes on and on, and the sound feels painful in my head. I don't get used to it and we don't have any way to escape the piercing sounds of gunfire.

This reminds of a bear back home in Colorado that got rescued from a small concrete cage next to a shooting range. In addition to his inhumane confinement, the gunfire contributed to his stress. With all caged animals, it is considered humane to keep predators and prey from sensing each other. Housing cats and mice in the same room causes undue stress. Likewise, this shooting range seems inhumane next door to our prison.

141

Because I spend most of my time outside either working or hanging out on my spot of concrete slab out back, I spend a lot of time looking out behind our compound. One of the training sessions the men do is a grueling loop. First, they shoot. Then they run over to the obstacle course where they climb over a tall wall, run over to a high bar to do pull-ups, flip a tire, push a car down the length of our track, and finally, run up the hill behind us.

I know a few women (myself included) who would love the challenge if given the opportunity. There are so many times that I look up toward the hill and I want to climb up there. An obstacle course, a hill to climb, something physical to conquer. To get to the top just see what is beyond this hill.

The tire mysteriously shows up at our track one day. This tire stands as high as my chest when on its tread. Flipping that tire becomes our next preoccupation and not an easy task. Squat, push with the legs, don't try to do all the lifting and pushing with the arms. Then try again. One of the inmates says, "This is tiring!" We all groan at the pun and keep lifting. I pushed too hard, hurt myself, and had to stop tire flipping for a few weeks.

Despite all my efforts to practice mindfulness and find peace, occasionally, my own wants and needs crash to front and center, especially when I'm feeling low. Today, I feel like a two-year-old having a temper tantrum.

This place! I want to stomp off to my room, slam the door, and not talk to anybody! *If only I had my own room and a door to slam!* The monotony of annoyances taxes my brain. Being woken up morning after morning by guards talking or women tromping by at 5 a.m. The toilet flushing over and over, never alone, just wanting to plop down somewhere comfortable and not move.

Add to this the seemingly endless, unsettling sound of gunfire. Loud noises produce stress in the body, the flight-and-fight response. I'm so tired of it.

What's going on here? I'm so grouchy! Someone cut in front of me in the shower line. When I finally get to shower, I realize that I am so flipping mad. I don't say anything, what's the point?

JOURNAL:

> Impermanence can be such a helpful idea in times of stress: "this too shall pass."

Oh, I'm sick. I feel like a ton of bricks fell on me. *No wonder I'm so grumpy!* My guess is that it's a bacterial infection. I take vitamins and I look for an opportunity to be alone. It's been raining for a couple days, and I haven't been able to enjoy any of my quiet places.

Now that I've been down for a while, I do whatever I can to be by myself regularly, even for just a few moments. Like lying in a dumpster, looking up at the sky, soaking in the sensations of quiet, the vast light, and the color blue. I seek to make the moments of my life sacred.

JOURNAL:

> The landscape surrounding me could be my chrysalis! The dirt and the sky are the smooth inner membrane of my transformation house. Like the caterpillar that turns into soup within the chrysalis before molding itself into a butterfly, I shape and mold my insides to make them my own.

I remember the day it dawned on me that my surroundings were like a chrysalis. I had to laugh. *This is one noisy chrysalis!* And though the dirt and the sky may be like a smooth inner lining, this chrysalis abounds with prickly things, like cactus and thorny trees. From the window in my room, I look down on prickly mesquite trees. Even the acacia with its yellow ball-shaped flowers, has sharp thorns.

143

The interior landscape of the prison adds other sorts of prickly chaos to my chrysalis: rattlesnakes and scorpions! We wear steel-toed boots to protect us from rattlesnakes. However, it is the scorpions that rattle me. Did you know that scorpions like to nest up high in trees or up in roof tops? Even though the first floor is occasionally visited by rattlesnakes, it is the second floor, where I live, where it is always "The Season of the Baby Scorpions!"

Walking down the hall to the bathroom, I'd detect movement out of the corner of my eye just inches from my foot. There's a baby scorpion keeping pace with me. They blend in so well with the linoleum!

I remind myself, *I'm a Buddhist abstaining from killing any living being!* I call out, "There's a scorpion in the hall! Would someone please take it outside?" Lucky for me, there was always a willing inmate around, and with her shoe—whack! So much for a long and healthy life! *Poor scorpions.*

One spring day, a woman brought me a tiny lizard, maybe two inches long. There are a lot of lizards running about, but I'm not familiar with the different species. There were rumors that Gila monsters were in the area, so we called all the baby lizards, Gilas. I later read that Gilas are one of only two venomous lizards in the world, and then I realized these were definitely not baby Gilas.

With rattle snakes, scorpions, and Gila monsters, there are plenty of reasons to look down. I try to remind myself to look up. Then the sky becomes a door to the outside. When I am walking around the track, I'd think of myself up off the ground, walking among the sunsets, like walking among the most beautiful field of every kind of flower imaginable.

JOURNAL:

Just as the landscape that surrounds me extends beyond the area it occupies, my own boundaries shift with my shifting perspective. The sky becomes a metaphor for impermanence and for a boundless boundary. I'm looking for the inside of me to be bigger than the outside: expansive and unrestricted.

I read a lot and I often ask myself, *How can I use my mind, my mindfulness practices to improve myself?* However, invariably this seems to lead me to ask, *What expectations and limitations can I release to better be my authentic self?* It's a never-ending meditation, like the sky never-ending and always changing.

POCKET NOTE:

"Bringing absolute love into human form involves learning to hold the impossibility of ourselves and others in a way that the sky holds clouds—with gentle spaciousness and equanimity." — John Welwood, from Perfect Love, Imperfect Relationships: Healing the Wound of the Heart

Something that comes up for me is how hard I've been on myself. Being Buddhist about my suffering, I recognize that suffering is not part of my identity. It's the raw material of this life's experience. I am not the suffering. I am the *story. Am I learning about the impossibility of myself?*

JOURNAL:

Being here in the present moment, I see myself as separate from my suffering. I feel that when I acknowledge my suffering in the moment, it ceases to be a part of my "Being," and some deep letting go happens. For the moment, I live in a prison-shaped chrysalis in which a Haboob (sandstorm) constantly blows. I'm learning how to keep my eyes from getting too gritty. And my window to the outside, the sky, is inside of me. Within me, there is so much room to expand beyond my suffering.

I can wholeheartedly savor the beautiful sunsets and still yearn to hug my son. Both of these are true for me at the same time.

My brother Mesa wrote this to me: "I love and remember you; may you feel the warmth and prayers we are all sending. Surrounding you with our arms, our songs, our love. We eagerly await you, our arms and hearts open, to return home, Love always."

I've never felt so connected to people so far away. Truly, love transcends time and space.

I hope my relationships with the people I love will benefit from my time on the inside. From this time inside of myself.

Greta sent me this poem:

CHRYSALIS MOUNTAIN

The mountain stands us still
and blows us a thick cover of stars.
What we are ready for
is not   what we expected.
We learn to see sideways
We grow antennae.
The crystal night enfolds us.

While we are rapt in stillness,
our DNA   changes.
We go to our heart's mountain
to stand still   within change.
We spin   everywhere
a vast change.

©2010 Susa Silvermarie, Reprinted from
We'Moon 2012 Calendar

Ten:
THE SHAPE OF MY SUFFERING—
TURNING FIFTY IN PRISON

W*HY DO I HAVE to have a birthday this year?*

It makes me so mad! I never imagined that I'd turn fifty in prison.

The tangled web of meaning around this milestone of turning fifty has so many significant implications: cultural, physical, and emotional. I want to think of it as crossing a threshold to a new beginning. How can I feel that here?

This birthday, this year, in this situation, creates the perfect storm. Can I embrace being fifty on my own? The Buddha said that when a change occurs inside oneself, everything outside changes. I'm clearly still wrestling with this one.

When my mom was in her early forties, she was looking forward to turning fifty. She'd say things like, "I hope I have grandkids to play with when I'm fifty," and "When I'm fifty, I'll pass on my knowledge by teaching people how to be better therapists," and "When I'm fifty, I'll have so much to celebrate!"

It was not meant to be, however. She got cancer at forty-six and died the following year. She would have been fifty-two by the time the first grandchild was born. Ever since my mom passed away, I wanted to turn fifty in a grand way to honor her and make her proud.

I thought I would have so many reasons to celebrate turning fifty, but in prison it doesn't feel like a true celebration. Yet here I am and every day I'm getting closer to fifty. *Damn!*

In the midst of this stress, I found a perfect passage from *The Shape of Suffering*. (It took me months to read this book. I could only read a little bit at a time, then a lot of meditating and contemplating.) Immediately, I made this new passage into a pocket note to contemplate further:

POCKET NOTE:

"He has no uncertainty or doubt that mere stress, when arising, is arising; stress, when passing away, is passing away."

Here's the shape of *my* suffering as my birthday approaches: I feel like the stress is arising, arising, and arising some more. The Buddhist word for suffering, *dukkha*, has many related meanings such as dissatisfaction, unfulfillment, and stress! I couldn't be more dukkha at the thought of this impending birthday!

JOURNAL:

Dukkha = Suffering, dissatisfaction, unfulfillment, stress. Stress arises from not getting the support, appreciation, and success that we are looking for. Stress will always be there, but we don't have to suffer from it. The more we learn, the easier it gets. (So, they say.)

I don't want to turn fifty in prison! I'm suffering about this. I don't want a birthday this year!

One day while I'm walking the track, I recognize the source of my dread: *I don't want to be a fifty-year-old woman!* In the eyes of the media, my American culture, a woman over fifty has no sex appeal. *So, what is left?* Am I leaving behind being desirable and attractive? Will I become invisible and ignored? Will menopause make me a crazed monster that no one will want anything to do with?

In prison, I have consciously set aside my sexuality. However, when I get back into the world I fully intend to live as a vital, sensual fifty-year-old woman. It follows that I must consciously reject society's sexual objectification being seen and seeing myself as an object rather than a person.

I've read that when women internalize this sexual objectification, it disconnects them from their own bodies. This disconnection robs them of feeling love, connection, joy, and happiness, and it gives rise to substance abuse, eating disorders, appearance anxiety, and depression. *Hell no, that's not going to happen to me!*

Women inmates often express that they feel safe here in prison for the first time in their lives. This paradox goes to show just how terribly unfriendly the world is to women.

I'm writing an essay on gender, crime, and justice for a Gender in Society class I'm taking through the local community college. I'm reading about the difference gender makes when it comes to arrests, prosecution, and incarceration. The statistics on violent crimes perpetrated against these women prior to incarceration are disturbing. And simply heartbreaking. My textbook devotes six pages to rape and an additional nine pages to violence against women. Just a few pages in and I'm appalled, and I can't stop crying. I have to put it down and come back to it later. It is too familiar, too close to home.

I take a break to color in my mandala coloring book. Because I can't draw for crap, my artful expression is more suited for coloring books. Coloring is easy and gives my mind a break.

Back to writing my paper, my emotions stir up quickly, *Why are we, as women, treated in such an inhumane way?* There are no answers, no excuses, and no logical explanations. The suffering inflicted by rape can never be shed easily. I feel such a pain in my heart, so much sadness, and I'm so angry!

The textbook says fifty percent of incarcerated women have experienced abuse before incarceration. I'm skeptical, so I decide to get some data. I conduct my own study, asking "Have you personally experienced violence, sexual or otherwise, before incarceration?" To get a random sample, I choose to ask all twenty women on my floor first (not just "friends"). My random sample included ages nineteen to fifty-four years old, Hispanic, Asian, white, and Native American.

Only two out of twenty inmates responded with a no! That's only one in ten women who have *not* experienced violence toward her person! I was hoping that this was skewed somehow, and so I went downstairs and kept asking. Consistently, I found nine out of ten women in this prison have experienced some act of violence.

Most of the women did not tell me their stories. They would often answer, "Yes" or simply nod. Those who said more reported mostly sexual assaults, with answers like, "My mom's boyfriend raped me when I was ten years old."

I think about all these women who have lived with abuse without any support, healing process, or resources. Many turned to drugs as a means of escape, and some wound up here. The system addresses the drug problem of these women; however, it is superficial and misses the core issues.

I suspect it's not that much different for women outside. The statistics say one out of every three women has suffered sexual abuse, but that doesn't include the women who have experienced non-sexual violence. These are often not reported. And other forms of violence can be just as crippling. Violence is perpetrated against people based on race, religion, gender expression, sexual orientation, and even weight and body shape.

Learning about this abuse and violence leaves me feeling overwhelmingly disheartened. *How did we all end up here?* Such unique individuals here, walking this road with me. *What happened?*

I've been aware of the prevalence of rape and violence against women for a very long time. It's not new to me. When I was about twenty years old and going to school at the local community college in California, my professor stated the common statistic that one-third of women have been sexually abused. To see if the statistics held up in our class, he had us write a yes or no on a piece of paper. Our class result was just a tad higher than the national statistic.

After that, I often thought, *For every ten women I know, at least three have been sexually abused in some way.* I started asking women I knew if they had ever been sexually abused and I found the numbers were always higher than three in ten. More like three in five.

These numbers are astounding, and yet I wonder, how many people have checked in with their circles of friends? This affects everyone. Our mothers, our sisters, our neighbors! The implications are staggering; it explains why women are in prison and imprisoned in other ways, such as drugs. I can imagine so many ways that women may feel imprisoned: drug addictions, abusive relationships, being a single mother, or even just trying to survive with low-paying jobs.

Unfortunately, I'm included in these statistics, as is one of my sisters. Sadly, our stories are typical. I was sexually molested when I was twelve years old by a family friend. I was embarrassed and ashamed, wondering if it was my fault, wondering if I could have done anything to prevent it from happening. I didn't tell anybody for years.

I was in college when my sister was raped. A high school classmate of hers broke into our house one night when she was by herself. I stayed with her the next day and that was the first time I told anyone about what had happened to me. She had to suffer court proceedings watching this young man lie and deny his actions. He never showed any remorse, and he received a very light sentence. Both of my sisters transferred to a new school.

Many years later when my mother got cancer, the anger I had toward the man who molested me still dominated my mind and emotions. I struggled to process the experience of my mom having cancer while this other issue still took center stage. Fortunately, with the help of a particularly competent therapist, I began to process and release the sexual abuse trauma.

I was lucky to have access to resources throughout my life to assist and guide my processes of healing. Most of these inmates do not have the resources for improving their situation and for transforming themselves. Though violence against women is one of the most widespread violations of human rights worldwide, this is shockingly evident in prison.

How do we heal this? I wonder. I remember a Buddhist quote, "Healing does not mean the damage never existed. It means that the damage no longer controls our lives." *Right on, but there's so much work to do.* I write to my friends and loved ones, "What are we going to do about this?"

As I continue to read, I discover that the United States is the most rape-prone country in the whole world, even though there are other countries where women officially have fewer rights than the women of this country. *Why, why, why?* A quote from the textbook struck me: "In cultures where there is more equality between men and women there is less rape," but, wait for it… "when women are valued for having wisdom and skills rather than just seen for their sexuality—*that* puts them in partnership with men." *Yes, that is key!*

Both men and women push men into what I call, the "Act Like a Man" box. This model for a man demands that he control his body, his feelings, and, by all means necessary, dominate his relationships. The women's corresponding box is labeled, "You Are for Sex."

These thoughts reflect unconscious biases that are prevalent in our culture. I want to be more aware when they appear. Then I want to tell myself, "Stop, breathe, and jump out of the box." I want to shout, "Everybody, wake up! Tell a woman she is valued for her skills, her wisdom. Tell her to jump out of the box!"

I can't shake the thought that most of these women have been physically and/or sexually abused before their prison time. As I sit, reading, I hear women laugh. More than once, women have told me that they have laughed more in prison than ever before. *How is that?* The fact that some women feel safer in prison than in their lives outside absolutely amazes me—and at the same time, I get it.

Living with three hundred inmates immerses me into the suffering of women. I see beautiful, scarred women. Suffering is all around us; you don't know until you look and listen. Ignoring suffering also blinds us to the beauty that is present. The suffering of all these women, both those in prison and those outside, helps me put my own suffering in perspective.

Journal:
> Wisdom comes through understood experience. Challenges are not the source of suffering. Dukkha arises because we don't like the way things are. We don't have to like the way they are, but we can accept and appreciate the way they teach us something. We can have gratitude for every teaching and then we won't feel as stressed.

There is an element of intention in all suffering. There is an origin, a cause, to the suffering: I want what I don't have. Recognizing this dissatisfaction opens the possibility that suffering can be ended by changing our intentions—or abandoning them entirely—which is precisely the point of Buddha's teaching.

I can see the inner me is not creating all the stress, mostly reacting to it. Early on in my prison sentence, I was stressed about every little thing. *What was that over the intercom? What time is it? Where am I supposed to be? I can't sleep, my stomach hurts, my feet hurt, my hands hurt.* I was stressed all the time. My mind was always worried. My body was always tense, I felt filled up with anxiety.

One day, breathing in, breathing out, I have a vision of all my feelings outside my body instead of inside my body. I see that "I," the core of who I am, is not as dukkha as I thought. For all the physical discomfort, hard bed, and tension of not knowing what is around the corner, I realize all this stress isn't defining my moment-to-moment being.

JOURNAL: Everything is dependent on something else to exist. Who I am is ever-changing. According to Buddhism, self is a transitory experience just like sounds, sensations, thoughts, and feelings. The Buddhist idea of "no self" may be better understood as "no unchanging self." Still, I feel like there is another self, the "I" at my core. My inner Tara, as I refer to it, has an innate purpose of being Collin in this world. It's my Collin-ness.

In the present moment, the message for me is to be on a spiritual path, not ignoring my human nature. That means my Buddhist prayers, meditation, Qigong, yoga, and gathering new information through reading and listening. I'm reminded of Mesa's Native American teaching to "walk every day in dialogue with spirit." I'm expanding into a new view of what it means for me to be fifty years old.

Of course, I realize that I'm a vibrant woman, sexuality is still present, but dormant only by choice while I'm in prison. "Women over fifty don't have sex" is merely a myth.

Celebrations in here have a different feel to them. A little subdued, but also, they feel a bit rebellious, like inmates are trying to infuse this experience with personality. Nobody asks how old you are. Inmates celebrate birthdays by saying "Happy Birthday," making cards, making cakes, and having "eating parties." Eating parties are the prison equivalent of a potluck.

As my birthday approached, I realized nobody planned an eating party for me. I kind of wanted one, but I knew it wouldn't happen. I was rarely invited to eating parties. But that's not new to me: even on the inside I continue to be something of an outsider.

It makes me wonder, *Am I'm too serious or intimidating?* But obviously, I'm approachable—I get asked a lot of questions. They mostly ask health-related questions, "I've been having this throat and lungs thing; is it an allergy?" "Does coffee make you poop?" "What's this bump on my side?" "What should I eat?" These questions lead me to assume that word has spread about my background in nutrition and physiology.

Inmates ask me other types of questions, too. "Do you know how to write? Will you help me with my essay?" "What does narcissistic mean?" "What does perceptive mean?" I have gradually realized that among the inmates, I'm embraced as a wise woman. *It feels good to be asked to offer my wisdom.*

A woman last week had terrible pain in her belly and after seeing the prison doctor finds out she has an ovarian cyst. She comes to me, and I show her what's going on in her body with my cool, illustrated anatomy book.

Just this morning, a newbie (I don't even know her name) came up to me and said, "I've had eleven surgeries on my knees. I saw the doctor and he told me to do these exercises. What do you think?" Turns out, her bunkie referred her to me.

I encouraged her to be gentle with herself, start with the easiest exercises. I recommended that she purchase the vitamin C from commissary. I explained that we don't have a lot of choices, but even adding vitamin C can benefit the body. She said, "That makes sense; I think I'll try that."

Offering support to these women feels like I'm nurturing a community here. Maybe I'm not such an outsider after all. (I still can't wait to get out of here.) I feel so very sad that there are women who want to come back to prison, who know they will be back.

There are beautiful women here, scarred and damaged women, and I'm sure they all have skills, wisdom gained from the life they've lived. And it's not just women on the inside who are beautiful and scarred, but outside as well.

We need an open heart to have open eyes. Emotion must flow. "Sadness feels alive and fluid." It's an essential part of living a full life, while "depression feels dead and stuck" and gets in the way of living. Emotions give us information—they are useful. Allowing emotions to move through us allows for integration instead of cementing a belief from the moment to fix us in a pattern. (quotes are from The Mindfulness Solution by Ronald Siegel, MD)

If we value each other, if we value women, if we value women becoming equals to men, that changes everything. I decide to write a letter to everyone, listing what I value about each person. There are so many things I value about myself as well.

I'm so grateful for all the wonderful human beings in my life. I'm not appalled about being fifty anymore. Let us live! I love you. I love you. I love you all!

The night before my birthday, an inmate in my unit found out that her fourteen-year-old daughter had just been raped. I felt pain in my heart and wept.

I'm not afraid of being fifty! I breathe your air, I feel your sadness, your anger; breathe in. Breathe out.

I received ten books and lots of birthday cards. I do not feel alone—I feel cared for. After the months it took to buy the necessities (boots, tennis shoes, ankle socks, and of course French vanilla creamer!), I finally got myself a radio! A birthday present to myself, the radio is only about three inches square and half an inch thick. It picks up only a half dozen local channels.

The first time I noticed a woman with her right hand over her heart and a faraway look in her eyes, I wondered if maybe she was silently saying a prayer. *Why not? I'm in a monastery.* Then I learned that the radio was commonly carried in their bras, and they were just changing channels. I continued to imagine that they were saying prayers. It's a good reminder for me to say my prayers as I walk around the track, listening to my radio.

My boss allows us to have our birthdays off. Because this year my birthday fell on a Wednesday, which is usually a busy workday, I took Monday off. I slept till 7. That's late here! I had my earplugs in, and a blanket folded up over my head. I worked on my greeting cards all morning.

For lunch I had my usual brown rice, vegetable flakes, pizza seasoning, mackerel, and a packet of cream cheese. Yummy! I enjoyed an afternoon of yoga, and had popcorn for dinner. I made a chocolate volcano cake yesterday and shared it with some friends. It may have been the circumstance, but it turned out to be my best chocolate volcano cake yet!

Chocolate Volcano Cake

1 ½ bar dark chocolate, melted with some French vanilla
    creamer and a little water.

1 package of caramels, melted with some French vanilla
    creamer and a little water.

1 package chocolate chip cookies, crushed-up fine, with
    some crushed Mini Spooners (those little rolled up
    wheat cereal)

Mix the crushed cookies and cereal with some
French vanilla creamer, packet of hot cocoa mix, and the
can of 7-Up®.[1]

In your big microwave bowl, layer some cake batter,
put the chocolate mix in the center, and add the remaining cake batter around the sides and over the top.

Cook for about twenty minutes in the microwave,
taking it out every five minutes to check on it.

Once it is cooked through, let it cool. Then dump it
upside down on the lid.

Cover with the caramel mixture and serve warm.

---

1   7-up is a registered trademark of Keurig Dr. Pepper Corp.

Greta sent me this poem:

UNFOLDING

How long will it take
to become snow the lattice
of water frozen into flower?
How long to become rock
solid unn oticed support
for the feet? How long
to be tree rooted for centuries?
To simply breathe and see
a snare for the tangle it is
at that moment To not
constantly wind back
what has lost its way
but to sit with
pain gardenia a handful
of pebbles scattered
each stone unturned its own
universe shifted by wind
or water The moon as
simply a moon each
fist unfolds to
finally hold
emptiness

—Claire Blotter

Eleven:
WHO AM I TO YOU?

IT'S THE DAY OF JERA'S FIRST VISIT! Ah, I'm so excited. I'm also stressed out. Last night, I awoke to a guard pushing on my shoulder—checking for signs of life.

I'm up early, showered, and dressed in my "visitor" clothes. When we receive visitors, we are required to wear buttoned-up, short-sleeved shirts instead of our normal green t-shirt. I'm restless and must be outside, pacing. I'm uneasy about being in the room with real, normal people and guards watching me. *Can I be an inmate and the Collin my family recognizes?*

There are a lot of visitor rules. Our visitors' dress code includes no tank tops, halter tops, backless outfits, mini-skirts, mini-dresses, sleeveless shirts, see-through blouses, pants, skirts or dresses, jackets, or open-toed shoes. If it is in the opinion of the staff that you are inappropriately and/or provocatively dressed, they will not let you in to visit. One time, my niece was denied entrance because she was wearing leggings. She had to go back to the hotel and change. No purses, wallets, phones, electronic equipment allowed.

Once my visitors are allowed in, an officer will call my name on the intercom, and then I can go into the visiting room. My emotions are all over the place. *What if I cry the whole visit?*

Ms. Shanice is the guard on duty when I have my first visit with Jera. She's Black with an obvious wig and very long fingernails. Her fake fingernails are long and painted, not plain, but fancy, with different colors, sparkles, and embellishments. When she walks into our unit, she pulls a pair of white gloves from her black utility belt. As she puts on her white

160

gloves, her expression and posture suggest she's preparing to pick up dog poop. She looks at inmates disdainfully and snaps at us like reckless children, "Come here!"

I'm pacing up and down the walkway past the door with one-way glass. I'm nervous about how Jera will see me. I don't want him to see me as a stranger. In one of our phone conversations, I told Jera about becoming a Buddhist, and his reaction was, "Mom, you don't need to change!"

Like other prisoners, I've worried about how my status as an inmate would affect other people's perceptions of me. And now I'm wondering how my new Buddhism might do the same, at least for Jera. I want to act "normal" for him so he doesn't worry about me.

The door from the outside is directly opposite this door, so when the outside door opens, I can see silhouettes of everybody waiting to go into the visitors' room. Longing to see a familiar face, finally, I recognize the shadow on the other side of the one-way glass: the familiar stance, the unmistakable walk of my brother Mesa.

Greta and Mesa have brought Jera to me! This is an enormous gift, such a blessing. I'm talking to myself as I go into the room and sign in. *Breathe, don't cry, breathe, don't cry.*

I want to be with my family! I see Jera! He has grown since I left; he's as tall as I am now.

We are all a little tense, and I am trying so hard not to cry. We settle down on the small plastic chairs at a child-sized plastic table. I don't blink—I don't think I'm breathing. I feel so much nervous tension in my body as if my family might disappear, poof up in smoke, unless I'm physically holding them to the ground.

Jera and I are sitting side by side. I have my arm around Jera's shoulders. As we're talking, I don't know how to be present. I feel like I'm listening to this conversation going on between Collin and family while my inmate self is hypervigilant. *Where are the guards? Am I following the rules?*

There are so many things I want to say, and I don't know where to start. "Let's get snacks from the vending machines."

"Yes," says Jera eagerly. "So, mom, what do you do every day?"

"It's kinda boring." "I get up super early, eat breakfast super early, and start work in the dark."

The whole visitation setup has absolutely no dignity. One wall has all the vending machines. Visitors are not allowed to bring purses, wallets, or even paper money. They must keep their change in clear plastic bags.

Inmates cannot touch money. We can't even touch the vending machines. This was the only time we saw money in prison. You don't think about it until you see visitors with plastic bags filled with coins. It feels weird not to deal with currency at all.

I teach him the love handshake, which is just a slap, shake, thumbs up and touching, and then swivel fingers up to make a heart. We practice it and laugh. He thinks it is awesome and ends up showing all his friends back home.

About thirty minutes into our visit, I tense up as I see Ms. Shanice get up and walk towards us. She walks up and says, "Is this your son?"

"Yes"

"I thought so, but you are too close. He's going to have to move across from you. And try not to touch each other." *She doesn't want me to get too close to my son? What is she thinking? What am I going to do?*

I feel like falling on the ground crying. I tell myself, *Breathe.* I want to beg her to leave us alone, let me be with my son!

Jera pipes up quickly, "It's alright mom, I can switch chairs with Greta."

Greta gets up, and immediately says, "Don't worry, Collin, we got this."

Jera reassures me, "It's alright, Mom. It's alright."

We decide to play a game. We find Connect Four and checkers. All the games are very old, worn out, and missing pieces, but we make it work. I start to relax a little.

We eat non-stop—this is what all the inmates do. The vending machines have drinks and food we never get to eat. While Greta is wondering how in the world will she find something gluten-free and healthy in a vending machine, Jera and I treat the vending machines like a buffet.

We try just about everything. Pizza bites, potato chips, candy, ice cream, pizza, cookies, soda, ramen (only Jera eats ramen), popcorn, burritos, and burgers (we only tried burgers once—frozen vending machine burgers are yucky). Finally, Greta chooses popcorn. It's no wonder inmates consistently say that their stomachs hurt after visiting, mine included, but every bite is worth it.

Eating feels good. Eating is such a familial ritual. I have wonderful holiday memories, like the year we put pomegranate seeds in the green bean dish or the first time my sister made chocolate pecan pie. Instantly it became a mandatory Thanksgiving dessert. For a moment, eating pizza bites with my son feels like I'm out of prison.

We go out to the adjoining patio for pictures. I've paid in advance at the commissary for pictures. As one of her jobs, an inmate takes pictures, and days later, when they are printed off, she gives them to me.

After the pictures, we hang out on the patio. I point out the different types of trees and where I've seen the wild pigs.

I like hearing all the family stories, what everyone has been doing— even the boring stuff. Time flies by, hours seem like minutes. Too soon, it's time for them to leave. I want to make it a quick exit, so we hug quickly, and I get teary. I'm so happy that I got to see everybody!

I don't watch them go out; I breathe to maintain my composure.

I must sign out to be released back into the general population. Ms. Shanice makes me wait, just stand there and wait for twenty minutes or so. Our way out back to the compound is through a bathroom, one door into the visiting room and the other door outside to our compound. When Ms. Shanice is ready, she comes into the bathroom with me, puts on her white gloves, and says, "Strip search."

I think I might just lose it. I thought she was just making me wait to escort me back to the compound. *Stay calm. Be calm. I can get through this!* I undress, my bare skin in the cold air, bare feet on the concrete, turn around, bend over, spread my cheeks, and cough. *Please just leave me alone! Let me go!*

Whatever feeling of being normal and free I enjoyed for our brief visit, evaporated in one cold moment. I go back to my bunk and do my best to block out the fact that I'm in prison. Sometimes, it feels so good to go unconscious, stare at the wall, and transport myself out from this place.

The next time I talk to Greta, she tells me that Jera stayed at the hotel pool for a long time after seeing me. She felt that he needed to cry. For all of them, seeing me as an inmate was not easy.

The visit did give Jera and me the connection that makes this reality more tolerable. That connection we get in person reminds us of who we are. I'm not just an inmate, or a Buddhist, living far, far away from Jera. Now, with less that is unfamiliar, we have a little normal back.

I know these visits are not easy for my family. The time, logistics, and emotions. When I see my family, especially my son, I'm reminded of who I was on the outside. What can be conveyed in person is a truth of mind, body, and spirit. Despite the brevity of our visits and the pain of seeing them leave each time, being with them is like a mini vacation from prison. After our first visit, my apprehension decreases.

After the first visit, Greta and Mesa alternate bringing Jera down to visit me in Arizona. Greta comes with her family, bringing Jera while Mesa comes with Jera by himself.

All visitors must be approved. It takes a month or so to send the paperwork out and have potential visitors fill it out, and then prison administrators approve them for visits. Visiting is only on the weekends.

The visiting room is used for more than our family visitations, like meetings and religious services. Religious services are held in the visiting room because the chapel building has black mold.

The whole time I'm inside, the chapel just sits empty and closed up. There are a couple chairs behind the chapel where inmates sneak off to even though it is off-limits. When I go there, it is only for fifteen or twenty minutes at a time because I can't hear the intercom.

Occasionally our camp director calls an assembly. The visiting room isn't big enough for all of us, so they call us down one unit at a time. One assembly was all about our dress code. One time they called us down for mandatory DNA swabs. Today the assembly is about violence.

"Bunkie," I ask, "Why are we having an assembly about violence? I haven't seen any violence since I arrived."

"Remember that newbie that arrived about a week ago," Bunkie says, "The one with the really short hair? She threw a punch at her coworker, and they took her to the county jail. She won't be allowed to come back here."

I replied, "Oh, so they want to remind us not to throw punches?" We laughed.

At the assembly, this one incident turns into a lecture that amounts to "Fighting will not be tolerated." Good to know; at least violence is not something I'm constantly worried about.

One time I saw a flyer announcing, "Buddhist service on Mondays." I was so excited. There is a Buddhist service—no, really, we Buddhists have a *time slot!*

For all the traditional religions, someone regularly comes in to lead a service. But there isn't anyone for Buddhism. It would be so nice to listen to what a monk would have to say. I wonder where my practice would go with that interaction.

Buddhist time in the visiting room is on Monday evenings, from five o'clock to seven o'clock. This does conflict with mail call. If I'm anticipating a letter, waiting for mail trumps the Buddhist hours. Sometimes, I ask Bunkie to pick up my letter, depending on the guard on duty.

During my first Buddhist service, there were four inmates present. Only two call themselves Buddhists. Nothing about the Buddhist service is organized. A gal named Robin led the group. She tells me that there are only a few Buddhists in camp. She says, "We do some meditating." That didn't last more than a few weeks.

Robin was all about fitness, so we did yoga a few times. Robin asks if I have anything that I'd like to do. I said, "We could chant." She didn't like the chanting, so eventually, she only came once every few months. I always felt that the other women that came just wanted to see what being Buddhist meant.

There was one time that this Native woman came, and I led a guided meditation. Afterward, she told us about this "vision" she had in her meditation. In it, she was flying over mountains as an eagle, flying over trees on a blanket of rainbow colors, to the sun. She told us that the eagle is the messenger to Great Spirit and the rainbow is a bridge between the human and spiritual worlds.

The following week, I saw her in the dining hall. As I walked by, she beckoned me over. I told her, "I appreciated what you shared with us at the Buddhist meeting."

"Thank you. I'd like to sing you this Lakota song I'm working on."

"Sure." I sat down to listen.

She sang words I did not understand, but it was beautiful all the same.

I don't think I had another interaction with her. That's what it's like more times than not—a couple interactions and then the fellow inmate fades into the background of prison.

I love going to Buddhist hours, but there are times it doesn't work out. If I've worked in over 100-degree heat all day, I probably don't want to be outside anymore, even for Buddhist hours. Still, for the most part, I love the times I can go in the visiting area for Buddhist hours, it is a rare moment to have some time to myself. I am so grateful.

The times when nobody shows up for Buddhist hours, I am all by myself in the visiting room or on the patio. Sometimes, a guard comes by; however, I am never questioned or told to leave. I have this feeling that they consciously left me alone. *So odd.* Sometimes I chant, sometimes I

WHO AM I TO YOU?

do a few yoga poses; most of the time I just sit, meditate, or observe, and think. It is very peaceful.

I like being on the patio, it's practically private! I put my yoga mat under the acacia trees with the yellow puffballs growing over the back wall. The walls around the patio are the closest to the "outside" property fence—and the wild pigs, Javelinas, who frequent this area. I loved seeing the wild pigs, especially a mom and her babies. The flag clanking in the wind reminds me of my wind chime back home. The sun is setting, and nobody is talking—this is as good as it gets.

I am still in alert mode, aware of the tension coursing through my body and mind. However, I sense the peace. I feel the mindfulness of the practice like a breeze on my skin. I notice moments of clarity and feeling conscious amid the daily sensation of slogging through the mud of prison life.

When I leave the Buddhist space, I walk out with a little bit of peace, like lint on my sleeve. I look around myself and think, *Wrap that peace around me and stand tall.* I bring this feeling with me—this feeling of being me. At least until the next guard passes by or I must stand up for count.

It was quite surprising when one day, a friend encouraged me to come along to meet a visiting Buddhist who came in to talk to us few Buddhists. The visiting room happens to be unavailable, so with our yoga mats, we head to the weight pile. It is evening, a beautiful sunset is happening, Greg, a sort of scruffy man in his mid-thirties, doesn't look like he has a clue. He tells us, "I don't have a talk prepared." He laughs and asks, "Do you have any questions about Buddhism?"

Robin asks a bold question right off the bat, "It's so easy in here to get angry or sad, but nobody is going to show any emotion and we don't talk about it either. How can we deal with these intense emotions?

Greg seemed to go off on a tangent, "I recently broke up with my girlfriend of three years and I can say I've had plenty of intense emotions. Sometimes I'm mad at her and at other times, I'm very sad. I think we must start by just being aware of those emotions."

As he goes on describing his emotional issues, I'm thinking, *In here, our problems are so much more intense! A husband leaving his wife while she is locked up in here creates extreme fallout, no house or family to come home to. Just being aware of our emotions isn't enough.*

Greg continues, "I've tried to talk to her, but we just fight. I meditate, but sometimes the intense emotions just come right back up. When it gets overwhelming, I go to my meditation center to talk to my mentor, or to my friends to get a fresh perspective."

This is lame, I'm thinking. *I can't go anywhere, it'd be so nice if someone, a Buddhist monk or nun, perhaps, came to visit us on a regular basis. The Christians get priests and services. Even the Jehovah's Witnesses come to visit.*

I can't help but wonder, *What was Greg thinking when he volunteered to come to a women's prison? Know your audience, right? We are inmates and our relationships are not like those on the outside.* I'm feeling exasperated and disappointed.

JOURNAL:

Maybe I can't really be a Buddhist in prison. Buddhists consider the sangha (the community of Buddhists practicing together) to be essential. Buddhism teaches that without the support of other people our spiritual progress is greatly hindered. I've taken the vows and I'm doing the work—prayer, meditation, and self-reflection—everything Ralph taught me. Maybe that will have to do for now. Maybe I'll find community when I get out.

We had a brief taste of community each time we celebrated the annual Buddhist festival of Vesak. All the inmates with "Buddhist" on their paperwork are allowed to participate. We got a day off and a special dinner.

Robin has done this before, and she told me that we could ask for special "Buddhist food." What did I want? Vegetables! The inmate cook came in before dinner and helped us prepare our meal. We made a big stir-fry and a fruit salad for dessert. It was delicious.

Once we ate as much as we possibly could, we all went our separate ways. I went to do some yoga and to meditate. That was my daily practice, but it seemed to take on a special significance that day.

Vesak calls Buddhists to recommit to our practice and to the principles of Buddhism. This celebration commemorates the Buddha's birth, enlightenment, his death, and his passing into Nirvana. We celebrate Vesak on the full moon during the month of May, which varies from year-to-year. I got to celebrate it twice while I was down.

As significant as holidays and Buddhist hours may be, visiting with my son and family matter the most. Visits were precious to me. *Every minute* felt precious. I felt all my longing to be out of prison, crystallized when I couldn't have those visiting moments.

Greta, her husband, Joe, and my niece Isa, were bringing Jera for a visit. I was always early when I knew I was having a visit. As the time approached for visitors to check in, I would pace. Without being able to check in with my family, monthly phone minutes being at a premium, I just have to wait.

Visitors check in between 7:30 and 8, or after lockdown. Lockdown happens at 10:30 for an hour before lunchtime. Visiting hours always end at 3 p.m., in time for our dinner and afternoon lockdown at 4:30 p.m.

As it neared 8 a.m., I still don't see my family. I am getting very nervous. *Did something happen on the way from New Mexico to Arizona? Car trouble?*

Then I see them. Whew! Now I wait for my name to be called so that I can go into the visiting room.

No call.

They are leaving! No! Why? They should know all the rules, dress code— why are they leaving?

I go get in the phone line, anxious to call Greta. "Why did you guys leave?" I ask.

169

"We were just a couple minutes late and the guard turned us away. We will come back this afternoon after lockdown."

I sigh, "Okay. I can't wait to see you all!"

A punitive mindset pervades the prison staff. They don't consider all the effort most of these visitors go through to get here. They are traveling long distances. This seems like such an easy opportunity for them to be lenient.

I am so sad and hurt! I haven't seen them for months and now I'll only get to see them for a few hours. Sitting on my bunk, uncomfortable in my visiting clothes, not wanting anybody to see me. Inmates always want something to talk about. I wonder, *Why were they late? It feels like a personal affront.* Our visiting time will go by so fast. I sit there, waiting and crying.

Visiting is always allowed on Saturday and Sunday, but because my family has a day of drive time, they always leave on Sunday. My one day of visiting is cut short. I can't help wondering, *If it was me, I would be early every time. I would have been doing everything to make sure everybody was ready hours before the visit.*

Of course, I am overjoyed to see Jera! However, I can still feel the tension around them being late. Greta mentions that she was waiting for everyone to be ready and then they missed the turnoff, causing them to be late. Everybody apologizes and we act like we have all the time in the world. I needed my walking meditation around the track to process the chaos within myself.

JOURNAL:

Part of my suffering was annoyance that we lost that precious time. Part of it is a false expectation that others treat me like I would have treated them. But who's to blame? I don't know if Isa was taking a long time getting ready. She has a reputation for rushing at the last minute. Driving on the highway and missing the turnoff might have added several miles to the drive. I don't know what caused their delay. I'm just upset.

Continuing down my rabbit hole, I reasoned that if I had caused that breakdown for my sister in prison, I would have been asking, "How can I make it right?" Any adult could step up and take responsibility. Since visiting hours are available both Saturday and Sunday, I would have offered to return on Sunday. But my sister didn't think that way. Maybe because of the long drive or any of a number of other reasons, she didn't even consider that as an option? *Ugh!*

Then I remember what the Buddha said: "Peace begins when expectations end." *Is this really about me?* Is it about who I am for her, or is it just about my expectations? In these moments of stress I have been making a habit to read a Buddhist article or text. This crisis seems to be the epitome of suffering so far. In that moment I knew the perfect text to read was the Four Noble Truths.

JOURNAL:

The Four Noble Truths. 1) *Dukkha* (suffering) is real and universal. 2) *Samudaya*: there is cause to the suffering: the desire to have and control things. 3) *Nirodha*: suffering can cease. Non-attachment allows the mind to experience freedom. 4) *Magga*: there is a path, a practice for the end of suffering—the Eightfold Path.

I'm so grateful for all the times my family visited. Each visit was like a precious vacation. It meant so much to be with them. It was like being in my life again for a few minutes.

Many friends told me they would come to visit me, but only one friend made it. On the day Nancy visits, I'm very excited and a little nervous. I wonder what she will think when she sees me in my prison uniform. I wonder what we will talk about.

She looks so happy to see me and I find myself more relaxed than I expected. I share with her the story of making a cake for another inmate, Bertilla. I tell her about asking Bertilla's friends to share with

Bertilla what they appreciate and value about her. I ask Nancy if she thinks I've changed. She says, "You are still you—it's just that you are in prison."

As we eat from the vending machines, Nancy confides in me. She shares experiences of pain and suffering. I realize I was conscious of her pain at times; however, we had kept our lives to ourselves. Never had that conversation. It's interesting to know that in this circumstance we can share on this intimate level.

There is a flyer on the bulletin board in our unit by the Prisoner Visitation and Support—a nationwide alternative ministry to prisoners. I decide to write them, and eventually, I have a visitor. Mary Ann started visiting after I was down about eight months. Those visits with Mary Ann were fun and relaxing, with unedited conversation.

Our first visit, I cried. I was realizing how much I kept myself in check and how much I held in. Oh, to talk to someone for even a few minutes about life, not prison life. Mary Ann shared her birthday with Georgia O'Keeffe. She says, "Lucky me." Her husband was dead. They had both been professors as well as having a love for travel. She said her house was filled with things from those travels. Her niece was living with her to help get her house ready for sale.

I didn't talk about being in prison, I talked about my life outside. I told her about my son, my nutrition business, things I liked to do, like hiking. She would tell me what foods or supplements her niece was into and then I'd give her nutrition suggestions or food preparation ideas. She started taking notes and having more nutrition questions the next visit.

She would send me a beautiful card a week before our visit to remind me of her visit. I didn't need reminding. I enjoyed just having that relaxed moment just to talk.

Most inmates don't have visitors regularly. Some inmates never want visitors. It's a constant reminder that the outside world is moving forward without us. I'm stuck in a state of suspended animation, within my chrysalis. The visitor situation can create sensory and emotional overload:

smells of microwaved food, families chattering, kids crying, emotional interactions between inmates and visitors, and guards constantly hovering and pacing.

Over time, I feel the gap widening between the inside of prison and the outside of prison. It gets harder and harder for me to even write letters. There is an inmate version of myself that I must maintain. I know that all of us would be different people if we were free. In the presence of people who know me, especially my beloved child, I expand. Being with him is touching the other side, a taste of freedom.

Greta's poems keep reminding me of beauty and just another way to look at the universe.

THE WAY IN

Sometimes the way to milk and honey is through the body.
Sometimes the way in is a song.
But there are three ways in the world: dangerous, wounding and beauty.
To enter stone, be water.
To rise through hard earth, be plant
Desiring sunlight, believing in water.
To enter fire, be dry.
To enter Life, be food.

—Linda Hogan

"The Way In" is used by permission from Rounding the Human Corners, (Coffee House Press, 2008).
Copyright ©2008 by Linda Hogan.

Twelve:
WORK: LOVE IN PRACTICE

EVERYBODY HAS A JOB IN PRISON. Inmates run almost every department of the prison, including the Food Service, Recreation, Commissary, the bathrooms, and Education. The Facilities Department employs inmates in an assortment of maintenance-related shops including the Electrical Shop, HVAC Shop, Maintenance Shop, and Landscaping/Grounds Crew. Also, a factory within the prison employs inmates putting parts together for the military.

I've read that Buddhism holds work in high regard. Work within a practice can help create balance between inner and outer mindfulness, between stillness and activity, and between personal practice and practicing within a community. Buddhism emphasizes the importance of acting with skillful intentions to get good results. Actions have results, and those results are a product of intention.

Much of my practice involves asking questions: What's my intention? Why am I doing this? Will this lead to suffering, or not? In this way I develop discernment.

There are "good" jobs and "bad" jobs. Bunkie tells me the easiest jobs, like cleaning the bathroom on our floor every morning, only pays about twelve dollars per month while working in a "shop" like the Electrical shop pays about twenty-five dollars per month.

A few jobs with increased responsibility, like Recycling, pay about seventy-five dollars per month. Recycling has more responsibility because inmates are dealing with trash that might come from offices, and they travel between the compound and the warehouses.

Bunkie told me that Water Ops offers a certification that we can take with us. *Maybe get a job at a water treatment plant when I get out?* Bunkie points out the Water Ops boss, and one day I see him go into the main office. I take a risk and follow him in.

Suddenly, I'm standing in front of the prison director, Ms. Juanita, and a group of officers. As always, she has a disapproving expression on her face as she sees me walking in. I turn and ask the Water Ops boss, Mr. Roger, if I can work in his department. I tell him I have had lots of science classes. The officers burst out laughing. One says, "What you did outside does not help you here." Then, they tell me to leave. A week later, I got the job in Water Ops.

When I tell Bunkie that I'm going to be working in Water Ops, she suggests that I get a good water jug. Many women faint here because they're not used to the Arizona heat and don't drink enough water. We can buy these crappy water bottles, but they are cheap plastic and break all the time. I can't fathom why they don't issue a good water jug to anyone working outside.

One day, an inmate who lives on my floor gave me a good water jug. I was surprised, but happy. She said that she doesn't need it as she works inside. I thanked her profusely. It's a classic old brand of great quality. This jug makes me happy and remains my pride and joy throughout my stay.

Another inmate gave me work gloves. Inmates pass around items that might have been available to purchase at one point but were later discontinued. It is odd to me that we inmates are outfitting each other.

So, I am ready for my first day at Water Ops, leaving the compound in the dark with my water jug and gloves. It was weird to leave the compound in the darkness. I'm thinking, *I just leave? Where exactly am I going? I only know the general direction of the water treatment plant.* It's too far to see from our compound even in the daylight. It's just some warehouse-like buildings in the distance. Bunkie has pointed out some inmates that work at Water Ops, so I look for them and follow them off our compound grounds through the darkness.

When we arrive, we stop by Mr. Roger's office and check in. I watch and listen, learning the routine. An inmate tests the water from the tap. Then we leave the boss in his office and walk over to a warehouse. The women are cranking up the Spanish music, making coffee and talking non-stop. I sit down.

No one talks to me. I am on the outside—no comprehension of the conversation and thinking I should have brought some hot chocolate. Once the sun is up, it's time to go to work. The boss comes to get us and tells us what we are to do for the day: weeding!

It turns out that most of our time working at Water Ops will consist of weeding and pruning. We prune the palm trees around the ponds on a regular basis. Every time Mr. Roger says cut down more, I internally question it. *Why? Leave the trees alone!*

Mr. Roger seems like a good guy. Monday mornings someone always says to him, "What did you do this weekend?" Of course, nobody asks us that question. Every inmate will have the same answer: "Same thing I did last weekend." I amuse myself imagining what I could say. *I did an extra hour of yoga. I read a whole book. I washed my hair. The usual.*

Another entertaining question: "Do you have time for...?" *Eh, about a year. Ha-ha.*

One day, he said something about playing Scrabble. I like Scrabble, so I ask if he knew this good Scrabble word, "frowzy." He seemed intrigued and said, "Let me write that one down." I could not find many inmates to play Scrabble with. Many inmates speak English as a second language and most inmates have little education and limited vocabulary. Which means that I often play with inmates looking in the dictionary for a few minutes to find words like "easy."

Now I'm settling into a routine of spending my days at Water Ops, pulling weeds, and learning more about my fellow inmates.

Jen is the first person to approach me in Water Ops. She's a younger woman with blond hair. She's the only white girl in Water Ops and doesn't speak Spanish. Jen is the boss's favorite, and she has more "privileges" like driving the truck. She drives around the property and can go out by herself on the weekends to check things, fix things, or turn off the water if there is a problem with one of the sprinklers.

In my first week, Jen takes me with her in the truck. Being in the truck feels good. Jen listens to country music, not my thing, but a reprieve from all the Spanish music! I'm on one of those short drives in the white truck with Jen, thinking of Jera and how much I want to be with him wherever he is! Kenny Chesney comes on singing, "Somewhere with You." *Oh, this is my song!* With limited choices for music, country music becomes my music for my stay.

Inmates seem to change a bit as they near the end of their sentence. I imagine they start thinking about what their life on the outside is going to look like and maybe dread walking back into their old lives. It's not unusual for an inmate to screw up in her last month, 'catching' a new sentence, as we would say.

I've talked to several women who have said that prison changed them for the better. The big question is, "Will it stick when they get outside?" How much of a shift "inside" does it take to change life back on the "outside?" In my view, all newly released inmates are like recovering addicts (whether or not they were previous drug users). We are all trying to create a new life.

Jen will be getting out in a couple of months. I am a little surprised one day when she talks about her nervousness to see her son after being in prison for the last five years.

"I'm nervous about getting out," Jen says. "What if my son doesn't remember me? He was only two when I left. He was fussy back then. He would have big outbursts over anything."

"Wow," I said, "I don't think I knew you had a son."

"Yeah, I was a teen mom, and I don't talk about him much," she replied.

"Well, he sounds similar to my son." I tell her. "He would totally melt down at the smallest interruptions to his routine."

Jen continued, "What if he wants nothing to do with me? He's been living with my mom for the last five years. What if he doesn't want to come live with me?"

It is an unwritten prison rule that inmates rarely share details about their lives. I'm a little surprised that Jen is sharing so much with me. I listen to Jen and try to offer advice.

I tried to reassure her. "Maybe he doesn't know you, but you will be there. And that's all you have to do is be there. Every day that you show him how excited you are to be his mom, he will be more excited to be your son."

"You think?" she said with a quizzical look. We got out of the truck to get back to work. That was typical of conversations in prison, brief but sometimes intense.

A few weeks later we are called to an assembly. Two officers told us that someone in the women's camp was dispensing contraband to the men's camp. They had footage of someone throwing a boot, filled with contraband, over the fences into the men's yard. I thought, *That had to be quite a throw!* She had to clear two fences, each at least twelve feet high with razor wire on top. These two fences are separated by a road width. The officers said that if the person stopped, they wouldn't pursue the matter further.

Neither Bunkie nor I have any idea who was throwing the contraband. It must be one of the inmates who works in a Lands Out job. And it must be someone with a great throwing arm.

Generally, I am oblivious of the happenings of the compound. I leave at 7 a.m. and don't return until the afternoon. Bunkie, always aware of changes and the goings-on of the compound, keeps me informed. When I notice that I haven't seen someone for a while, I ask Bunkie, "What happened to so-and-so?" She always seems to know.

One day, Jen didn't show up for work. When I got back to my room, Bunkie gave me the news: Jen was the one throwing contraband over the fences. I was stunned. I said, "Even with the warning, she didn't stop?!" Bunkie told me how the drama played out.

Jen was taken to the main office for questioning by Ms. Juanita while officers carried out a full shakedown of her room. Turns out, they did not have proof she was guilty, and the officers did not find anything in her room to implicate her. However, Jen confessed her guilt *and* told the officers that she had a picture of the man in her bible.

Jen had only one week before her release, and she blew it! Everybody said that she would catch a new five-year sentence or more.

The next workday, nobody said anything. I heard that Mr. Roger was devastated and that he felt betrayed. Apparently, he felt like he knew her, but then she was just another inmate, out to use anybody for her gain. He never let us know how he felt. Of course, I never brought it up. I felt it was best to keep my head down and do my work. But Mr. Roger was a changed man, he wasn't quite as friendly.

For days, I wondered where Jen was coming from. This was not the only time I observed an inmate choose to break the rules and not leave prison. Why did prison look like a better option than the outside world? Unfortunately, I can think of a few reasons.

JOURNAL:

Does the outside world, the world as Jen knew it before prison, look too daunting? Or was it more about who she was and who she is now? How many times in her life had Jen felt used? Was Jen being herself? Was she someone just out for herself? Was she terrified to be free? Does prison change one's perception of self? Did she like herself better as an inmate? Did she think that this was the best version of herself?

Maybe prison has made me a simplified version of myself? Parts of myself are left uninhabited. In some sense, life is simpler in prison. Everything I do is precisely spelled out. But...I'm finding more pieces of myself. So, the question becomes: who will I be when I get out?

Dolores was another woman working Water Ops with me. For a Mexican woman, she is big (not fat), at least five foot seven, with muscles. Without Jen around, I start hanging with her at work. She had told me she wanted to get the water certification; she wanted something for all her time spent inside.

Mr. Roger would give her jobs like, replace a part in the machine that continuously measures the water being used throughout the facility. Dolores would have me help her out and we would figure it out. Neither of us is familiar with any of the gauges, valves, meters, and other equipment we had to work with. We'd just go back and forth between ourselves saying "Why don't we take this out, see what happens to that?" We fixed stuff. We worked well together.

I liked working with Dolores because she was real, straight up, and she said things I thought were amusing. She said that her skin never looked so good. "You know, here we take better care of ourselves." She had been a drug user, but now she was clean and was taking care of herself.

In sharp contrast to Dolores's glowing health, I am suffering here. I have no healthy food and none of the supplements I had been taking before coming in. My body hurts. Just within two months of being inside, I noticed that my "healthy" is wearing off. I hit a low at about three months in. I get up in the morning, my hands and feet aching and incredibly tender.

I tiptoe down the hall, and every step feels like I'm walking on small rocks to the bathroom. I can barely turn the bathroom stall handle; my fingers don't want to grasp a single thing. It hurts to try to hold anything; the pressure of squeezing my fingers together is agonizing. And I keep going.

The water treatment plant serves the men's prison as well as ours. The first pond is the most noxious, as water pours in directly from both facilities. Water comes down pipes and then flows through a large grinder. The grinder must be checked and cleaned daily, quite an unpleasant job. Then all that nasty water goes through big grates and out to the pond.

At Water Ops, most of my days are spent picking up trash and pulling weeds. The trash consists mainly of tiny bits of plastic that float in the water and get washed ashore. The grinder chops up everything into these tiny, bandage-sized bits.

The wind blows the scraps of plastic up the banks of the ponds and then they get stuck in the desert tumbleweeds against the fence. With about ten women and only three rakes—how are we supposed to clean this up? I am looking down, thinking *Sometimes, it is in the details!* I sat down on the ground and started picking up these scraps of trash and putting them in trash bags, one scrap at a time.

Some of the gals are bitchin' about the work saying things like, "This is bullsh*!" and "This is a waste of my time." But I figure, *I'm going to be here in prison for more than a year. Does it matter what I'm doing?* I think, *What are you complaining about really? What else are you doing with your time?* If it takes three hours for ten women to clean up twenty feet of dirt, they can afford it. We are only getting paid about twelve cents per hour.

JOURNAL:

"Practice most often refers to a specific activity such as meditation or chanting, that one does every day. Making that effort is Buddhism."—*The Practice of Buddhism* by Barbara O'Brien. Buddhism, or being a Buddhist sounds easy if it is all about making an effort, instead of a list of rules that I must follow to be a Buddhist.

When I am weeding or picking up trash, I think of all those sayings: *It's not the goal but the journey that is important* or *How do you eat an elephant? One bite at a time.* This is my practice; I live one moment at a time.

I don't get angry if they want me to pick up trash one tiny piece at a time. It's not really *my* time—it's *their* time. They decide what I am supposed to do while I'm here.

For me, whatever they have me doing is an opportunity to practice being in the present. I get their work done and I do my inner work as well. This is what my Buddhist practice looks like here. It's my version of the Zen Buddhist saying, "Chop wood, carry water."

One day after Mr. Roger lays out the plan for the day, one inmate huffs as she gets up to leave. As Dolores and I take off, she says to me, "The other inmates don't like you because you work too hard and make everyone else look bad."

"Oh, well. It's my job and I'm here to do my work," I replied with a shrug. That was the end of that conversation.

Truth is, I am careful about my work. I care about it. I've always had a strong work ethic. As the oldest of five kids, I got it at a young age. I remember sitting for a neighbor baby when I was ten. My mom said, "You must realize that these people left the life of their precious baby in your hands." *Whoa! This is critical*, I realized, *any mistake could mean disaster*.

Another time, one of my chores was milking the goats. I got delayed one morning, and Mom told me that the goats would be in pain if I left them un-milked. She always impressed upon me the importance of doing good work; bad work yields bad outcomes. I've brought that attitude into everything.

Buddhists use the term 'work meditation' to refer to a period of work with the same status as sitting or walking mediation. It's an opportunity to practice mindfulness in action. Like all meditation, it's a practice of observation, while releasing attitudes, beliefs, and feelings that interfere with having a meaningful awareness of the task at hand, no matter how tedious, trivial, or gross it might be.

Work mediation is not new to me. It's who I am. Now, through my Buddhist practice I will add even more mindfulness to my work.

Still, to inmates I look like a kiss-ass worker. In my world, I am focused on my practice. In their world, I'm just working too hard. *Eh, so be it.*

I enjoy my walk to and from work. I look out past the fences wondering if I'll see a wild donkey today. Spring comes early to Arizona. As the mornings get lighter earlier, there are more and more weeds growing on the banks of the ponds.

One specific weed was abundant and difficult to uproot. It stays low to the ground and has a thick root, like dandelions. I suspect it was the common mallow weed. I pulled so many of these weeds! I even develop a technique that works, a twist and then pull.

In addition to our hands, we use a hoe and a weed whacker to destroy the weeds. The weed whacker works best on flat land and with weeds that grow upright. And there are always a few women who run to the weed whackers instead of pulling up weeds with their hands. It is nice to stand upright once in a while, but the vibrations of the gasoline powered weed whacker numb the nerves in my hands and forearms.

When I get off work, it feels so good to go to my room and take off my boots and relax. I feel like saying some cliche like "Honey, I'm home. Is dinner ready?" I imagine flopping down on a comfy couch, watching some TV, and being served dinner. That cracks me up. Back to reality: I feel intense pain everywhere. And my hands are numb. I feel that my body has used up all its reserves.

And I'm developing a heat rash right from the top of my boots encircling my calf. I'm so uncomfortable. I shower and try to cool down. The rash calms down until I'm weeding again the next day. One day, I get the same type of rash on one wrist above my glove. I figure out that I'm allergic to a particular weed.

Is the $27.87 I make for a month's work worth all this physical pain?! I'm starting to wonder how I'm going to make it in here. I even started dreaming about the weeds. These weeds have taken over my life!

I learned a meditation a long time ago I call "Being in the River." Imagine your body in a river. Imagine the water flowing through your body. Let everything negative float away in the current and hold only the positive ions that float into your body. Relax. You're giving and receiving with no effort. Just let it flow.

Before prison, I experienced grace and ease with this meditation. I was in a pure river, so easy to stretch out, my molecules filtering out the heavy waste and feeding myself with the abundant nutrients. However, here in prison, the river is polluted. I'm stretched ever so thin to allow all the extra toxic debris to pass through. I feel that I must allow more river to pass through me to find the rare nutrients to sustain myself.

I've discovered a Buddhist meditation to assist with bodily pain and discomfort. Buddhists call this form of meditation *metta*. It consists of cultivating lovingkindness by speaking and thinking thoughts of compassion toward yourself and others.

Start by paying attention to your breath and repeat to yourself, "May I be truly happy and free from suffering." Continue being mindful of your breathing, feel your inhales and your exhales. Don't try to control it or change it.

Continue mindful breath and add awareness of the pain or discomfort in your body. Mentally label the location, for example, neck, shoulders, or back. Notice the sensations: burning, aching, contracted. Notice the location and extent of the pain or discomfort. How much space does it occupy?

The next step is to notice your emotional reactions that come up. Notice the difference between physical sensations and emotional reaction. When one has a friendly, interested attitude towards these, it can lead to a dialog which may offer insights. End with a few minutes of mindful breathing.

One day, an inmate, Linda, asks me to sit down with her. She says she can talk to someone about getting me a recycling job. The recycling job is a good job! One reason is that there are only two inmates working together. There is more responsibility, so the pay is better. And my favorite thing is that once the work is done, you go to your unit. There is no sitting around a warehouse doing nothing. I am so ready to leave Water Ops!

The way the recycling job works is that when someone leaves the position, the person already there is the higher-paid, bossy one. The bossy one will pick who she wants to work with and submit her preference to the recycling boss—Mr. Thomas. He checks out the inmate and decides if she will get the job.

Linda arranges for me to talk to Betty, the inmate who is working recycling at the time. I am on my best behavior; I want this job. Linda told me that Betty was not known as the easiest inmate to get along with; however, she only has a few more months before her release. Therefore, if I make it work for a few months, I will be the bossy one, get paid more, and will have a say in who works with me.

I get the job! Working recycling gives me one of the top salaries, about seventy-five to ninety-five dollars per month. Sure beats what I was making in Water Ops. Recycling is my job for the remainder of my stay.

My new boss, Mr. Thomas, is ex-military, like most guards, and gives orders like a military officer. In addition to running the recycling operation, Mr. Thomas oversees the shooting ranges. He gave me a pair of Smith & Wesson sunglasses and earplugs, the good kind. Earplugs are common with all the snoring going on at night.

My job description includes collecting trash in big trash carts, baling cardboard, and driving a forklift. I like driving the forklift. I move the dumpsters about and load pallets, twenty high on a flatbed trailer. We also build targets for the shooting training camps and whatever else Mr. Thomas can think of.

Betty isn't so difficult to work with. She wants everything done just so, without any input from me. That's okay, I can do it her way and learn as I go. Only a month in and Betty irritated Mr. Thomas with her questioning and backtalk, and he fires her. Don't question the boss. Another valuable lesson learned.

I've only been working recycling for a month and now I get to be the bossy one. I also have the chance to handpick the inmates I will invite to work with me. I choose Marcia, a small woman from South America. I know she was transferred from another prison to finish out her last couple years down. She is probably near my age, and I want someone who will work. She turns out to be a great work partner.

Marcia is my work partner in recycling for over a year, the remainder of my stay. She speaks formal Spanish—not like most of the Spanish spoken here in prison. She is married to an East Indian man. She's also a Jehovah's Witness, though I didn't know this for a long time.

One day, we're told to take the covers off law books. They are updating the men's library and getting rid of boxes and boxes of old law books. We have thirteen pallets of law books! This ends up taking days. As we trash the covers and recycle the pages, we fill up all the dumpsters. Then we wait for the dumpsters to be hauled away and emptied.

Later, we have a whole pallet of buckets of chocolate to throw away. Each bucket is thirty pounds of chocolate. Think of carry-on luggage and having to throw it up in the overhead bin on an airplane. Even though the best-by date was three years ago, we still want to taste it. It's chocolate!

The nectar of life is in my hands, but unreachable—we can't get the lids off! We throw those buckets on the ground and against the wall as hard as we can hoping the lids will fly off. We throw big rocks on top of the buckets, trying to crack the lids. We can't get one single lid off! Thirty pounds is not a lot; however, my shoulders are sore the next day. And not one taste of chocolate!

Another time, Marcia and I found a huge scorpion at the bottom of a dumpster. It was in a corner and slipped out through a crack. We did not want to find it in the dumpster again tomorrow, so we decided to track it down. I got on the forklift and moved the dumpster, telling Marcia to keep a lookout for it. And there it was, the biggest scorpion I've ever seen.

I said, "I can't kill the scorpion because I am a Buddhist, and we should try to move it. Maybe we could put it in a box and carry it to the edge of our boundary line?"

Marcia said, "No, I want to take care of it." She picks up a huge rock, holding it with both hands, and throws it at the scorpion. She misses. I yell. Unfortunately, she did eventually kill it while I looked on from atop the forklift.

From then on, we were very observant while jumping in the dumpsters, and I am grateful for my steel-toed boots. As the weather warms up into the hundreds, we must be careful, drink more water, and wear gloves. We constantly get in and out of the big blue-green steel trash dumpsters. They get very hot. I burned myself on the dumpster edge a couple of times.

We also must be careful when we bale cardboard. One person stands in the huge wire cage of cardboard. That person hands cardboard to the person at the baler. Once there is no more room for any more cardboard, we wire it up. Then with the forklift, we make a wall of cardboard bales.

One time when Marcia and I were baling cardboard, a man drove up to deliver wire for the baling machine. We are not supposed to be even talking to this outsider, but he is making this delivery, so we say hi. While he takes out the wire from the back of his truck, he drops his sunglasses. Both Marcia and I apologize for not being able to pick them up. He kind of laughs. I feel well-trained.

In the desert, summer is hot, but the winters are so cold. It's my second winter. We are working in the very dark early-morning hours. It seems like the wind is always blowing as I watch the eastern sky for any light and wait for the sun to rise at around 7:30 a.m.

I'm wearing long underwear, two pairs of socks, and two beanies—one on my head, and the other had conveniently become unstitched at the top so I could pull it down to cover my neck. It's a trick I learned from an inmate. My jacket is lightly quilted and not very warm. This winter, I have been assigned one, yay! And it fits; it's not an extra-large hand-me-down. It has been so cold that some water pipes froze, which I hear is quite a rare occurrence here in Arizona.

Even though it is cold, it's mostly cold in the mornings. I don't wear my coat 24/7. If I'm going to dinner, I leave it in my room. The coat is bulky and hard to fit in the limited space of my locker. I hang it up on the end of my bunk, like all other inmates.

One day when I get back from eating, I notice my coat is missing. Someone stole my coat! I have no clue who stole it. I can't stop thinking, *Inmates stealing from inmates is a crying shame. Come on, really?*

The next day, I go down to the laundry to ask for another coat. The guard on duty says no. I was already assigned a coat. Therefore, I can't have another coat. *Seriously?* I asked him if he would talk to my boss, Mr. Thomas, seeing as I work outside every day and I kind of need a coat.

Why is it so complicated? Someone probably stole my coat because every year there are never enough coats to go around. Therefore, once the assigned coats are given out, the rest of the inmates are on their own. When I come back to my room later in the day, Bunkie has a medium size coat for me. I'm surprised and she tells me someone gave me their coat. Someone I don't even know. Once again, an inmate helps another inmate. Cool.

The next day, I hear my name on the intercom and go meet Mr. Thomas in the main office. When I got there, he was bristling mad.

"Who do you think you are?" he says as he walks out the door. "Follow me."

He's a least a foot taller than I am, and I'm practically running to keep up with him while he yells at me. "You think you can use my name to get what you want? Never use my name again. You have some attitude!"

I said nothing. Typical of interactions with prison staff, we weren't having a conversation. This classic, one-way communication was just a prison officer asserting dominance.

We go to the laundry and Mr. Thomas is talking and laughing with the guard like they are longtime pals. I hang back, so I don't hear everything they are saying. Then the guard hands Mr. Thomas a coat and he throws it to me saying, "Now you have a coat. Get back to work!"

"Thank you." Now I have a 2X coat, and I'm astounded at how pissed off I am.

I am so upset. I go to work and as I drive the forklift around, anger and frustration are just boiling up in me. As I drive between buildings, I let out a couple of screams. The forklift is so loud no one can hear me. My logical brain is going over and over the "conversation." *I have an attitude? I think I can get what I want?* I must never forget that I'm just another inmate. But I guess I thought I was human too.

JOURNAL:

> Why the heck am I so pissed off? I have been working for Mr. Thomas for almost a year and I don't think that I've ever "had an attitude." It can't be me—why am I so pissed off at him? I hear myself asking, "Why the heck did Mr. Thomas have to be such a dick?" Why did he make this choice?

The next morning, I wear the 2X jacket over my medium jacket and I'm finally warm! Now I wear two jackets to work every morning.

189

Dream 10.13.11 I'm running on a path that I've run on before (in my dreams). It's in the forest, the ground is brown and soft. The trees are tall pines, and the ground has bounce. As I'm running, I realize if I sing, I can go faster. This is what it feels like to be in the zone. If I stay in my joy, life is better. Ha, who knew?

When I am called down to the office for my twice-yearly interview, my case manager asks me about my *participation*. They are big on "participation" in here. For him, participation equals showing up for classes. He wants to know if I'm taking any classes in addition to the required ones. I tell him "I'm not."

"That's not good," he replies. I wonder what he says to the women that sleep all day and stay in their rooms. And what about the women always hanging with someone, looking like they can't stand to be alone? Somehow, taking classes shows them that we are participating, "growing as a person."

Participation? I work a job. I am doing yoga. I'm reading all the time. I think of participation more as being awake and aware. I notice I'm beginning to think in Buddhist concepts. Even Buddhist words come to mind more readily. I'm learning more on my own than I have in any of these classes.

However, the funniest part of all this is that nobody teaches the classes! There are no teachers! Sometimes, an inmate will step up to teach a class, but I have yet to meet a teacher.

Besides "parenting" and other mandatory classes, my case manager wants to know what I'm taking for "personal growth." "How about a card-making class?" he asks. The card-making class coordinator is stressful to be around. Her nervous energy makes me see how reasonable it would be for her to self-medicate. I found out later she was in for drug charges. I did want to learn how to make custom envelopes for handmade cards, but I just asked someone who has been down for a while, and she was more than happy to show me how.

There is also a computer class offered. I thought this could be a useful class to take until I talked to someone in the class. I asked someone in the class what she was learning, "Oh, we learned how to turn on the computer." *What?! You're not learning web design? Now that would be handy.*

Turns out that there is a nutrition class taught by an inmate I know, Martha. She also teaches the "Fitness Trainer Certificate," which I'm taking. When I found out that the certificate, which is a national certificate, is half price to us inmates, I signed up. Everybody knows me as educated, with nutritional information. Martha comes to me the night before each class she teaches and has me go over her education plan with her. She also asks me to be a guest speaker.

For the Fitness Trainer Certificate, a workbook is sent in, which I go over with Martha before she teaches. I also tutor a couple other women who all take the training. When I took the test, I passed with flying colors, only one wrong answer on the whole test!

Then there is the mandatory, parenting class. Sophia says, "I don't even have kids. I'm at the beginning of a ten-year sentence. What am I going to learn about parenting now that will make any difference later?" If only we learned something valuable in that class!

Parenting class with no teacher means that we watch videos. Many of the videos have nothing or little to do with parenting. An *Oprah* episode on the worst child abuse cases. A VHS movie on newborn care and *1, 2, 3 Magic—Getting Your Child to Do What You Want Them to Do.* How about *The Longest Yard?* And we watched a couple of lame Christian movies. You know, "Spare the rod, spoil the child," "The father should be the disciplinary figure while the mother cooks and cleans and picks up after the kids." I just shake my head and think, *The parody of it all.*

We watch a movie made in the seventies; I forgot the name. A man in a suit is teaching an informal class. He says, "Men are visual people, they see a good-looking woman walk by and they can't help themselves, they have to look, whereas women are not stimulated by the visual." The room erupts in laughter, hoots, and hollers. Remember, seventy-five percent are lesbians (according to the statistics)!

From that point on, in class or out on the compound, I frequently see inmates point and shout out, "Look, there goes a woman!" Other inmates would loudly hoot back and whistle! I must endure this class two times per week for twelve weeks! I keep thinking, *Oh my gosh, seriously?!*

Buddhism teaches us to be present. In some ways, I'm practicing Buddhism ironically as an escape from my present reality.

Surprisingly, Buddhism still works in spite of my motives. Concentration is a key part of the Buddhist path. Being in a state of concentration is simply being. It's being present, being nothing, being one with emptiness, and being in luminous awareness. The practice of attention gets stitched together from short intervals—distraction provides the occasion to practice mindfulness. And mindfulness evolves into concentration.

With all the distractions here, prison may be the perfect place to practice.

Most of my days are spent pulling weeds. That's a perfect metaphor for my practice. The boss yells at me and pisses me off—pull the weed of anger. Officers laugh at my request—pull the weed of a bruised ego. Try to glean a parenting lesson out of *The Longest Yard*—hmm, some things you just have to let go.

They're *all* weeds. Pull them and let them go. And then I'm free again. I'm present. That's the real work.

I love my practice.

Thirteen:
HUNGER ARISES WITHOUT FAIL

"EVERY CHALLENGE IS A NEW OPPORTUNITY." *How many times have I heard that one?* I can't count the number of times I've faced a new challenge here in prison by thinking in the most positive tone, and without irony, *Ah, another opportunity for growth!*

Faced with absurdities and indignities like strip searches and senseless rules and procedures, I often call to mind the Serenity Prayer: "God grant me the serenity to accept the things I cannot change, the courage to change the things I can, and the wisdom to know the difference." It has a surprisingly Buddhist feel to it, though I'm told it was made popular by Alcoholics Anonymous and adapted from a prayer of a Christian theologian (Reinhold Niebuhr).

In prison, our most irksome, unsettling challenges arise from the everyday basics of life, like eating, sleeping, and hygiene. Personally, matters of food and hunger threaten my budding, Buddhist serenity most of all. I have dramatically adapted my hunger and my eating habits to the demands of prison life, and still, I find myself railing against numerous rules and limitations here that make healthy eating impossible.

I often wonder, *Do the authorities neglect nutrition as part of the punishment? Is it willful neglect? Is it the careless fallout of budget considerations? Or is it just ignorance?*

The failed dietary system in prison may simply reflect the overall neglect of nutrition in our wider culture. As a holistic nutritionist, I advocate a new health paradigm and a new relationship with food. Holistic nutrition views food as more than fuel. It encourages conscious eating of healthy foods to promote vibrant physical and mental health. Good nutrition supports a strong immune system and helps to prevent disease.

I'm very passionate about food as medicine. The right foods can alleviate pain, anxiety, and depression. Having a passionate relationship with the foods we eat, enables us to live intensely, and to enjoy our lives to the fullest. My slogan on my business cards captures this philosophy: "Don't Diet, Live It!"

Most inmates share neither my enthusiasm, nor my angst about food; except for an occasional complaint about small portion sizes, nutrition doesn't seem to appear on most inmates' radars. My training and experience have certainly amplified my personal desire for nutritious food. In addition to my nutritional education, my Buddhist practice undoubtedly heightened my awareness of hunger and the ways hunger impacts how I feel, both physically and mentally.

Nevertheless, it seems you would have to be blind not to see the connection between such a poor diet and the physical and mental health of this population. Obesity offers the first clue. Like the "freshman 15" (the fifteen pounds a college freshman predictably gains), an inmate can reasonably expect to gain forty to eighty pounds in prison.

The predominant factor contributing to obesity seems to be behavioral: most inmates spend nearly all their commissary money on cookies and candy. No doubt, the imposed weekly limit of 15 packages of cookies per inmate is less about diet management than inventory management.

Inmates justify their obvious weight gains in various ways. One says, "I'm not getting out any time soon, so who cares what I look like?" Bunkie says she will take diet pills when she gets out. Whether the issue of eating pertains to looks, health, or even hunger, most inmates respond with some version of "I don't care!"

Stress undoubtedly contributes to weight gains in prison, but the significant constraints prisoners experience around food and nutrition are appalling. The limited variety of foods options available in both the cafeteria and commissary are further constrained by a lack of access to refrigeration and cooking facilities (we share one microwave per floor). Additionally, unnecessary rules and our highly regimented schedules— frequently modified at the whim of the guards on duty—create additional strain on appetites and dietary habits.

Despite my nutritional training and my commitment to being as healthy as possible, food persisted as a sore spot for me during my time inside. I was constantly reminded of the effects of poor nutrition on my behaviors and my baseline level of health. Prison affects every aspect of how I would normally approach food.

JOURNAL:

> I am suffering about food every day. The Buddha said the path to enlightenment begins by recognizing that life entails suffering (the first of the Noble Truths). In the face of limited food options, the constraints imposed by the facilities, and the rules and regimen of prison life, I must discover ways to bring mindfulness to my consumption of food.

Before I came to prison, I ate a predominantly vegetarian diet, even though I wasn't a Buddhist. Buddhist vows include "refraining from killing any sentient being—animals." This doesn't mean that all Buddhists are vegetarian. Historically, monks depended largely on the generosity of lay people for their food. And receiving gracefully has an equally important place. Therefore if someone offered them meat, they would likely receive it and eat it thankfully. The act of eating meat is distinct from the act of killing it.

Monks view food as nourishment and maintenance of the body. It's more about eating for balance than eating what you desire. In prison, most of what I desire is off limits, but that just makes the balance part even more challenging. That's another connection between prison and a monastery because the opportunities to indulge the senses here in prison are quite restricted. Still, there are days I get exasperated by my limited food options.

At home, I have a say in what to eat and when. I shop for food I need and want, and then I carefully prepare the food to eat. In prison, I only get to shop once per week for a very limited number of food items. I imagine this is one way that a prison and a monastery may be similar. Prisoners and monks don't get to go to a supermarket.

JOURNAL:

In prison, my options for gratifying my hunger are severely limited. I read that Monks often rely on alms (donations) for their food. Monks see food as a gift, something that is received, not appropriated. Monks receive whatever is given with gratitude and they bless the community with prayers and teachings. In this way, they live in a symbiotic relationship with their community.

The weekday breakfast menu never changes: corn flakes with milk and a piece of fruit (typically an apple). For a long time, I didn't go to breakfast at all. Commissary oatmeal became my weekday routine. Eating the same staples day after day, I had to get creative to avoid getting bored or going crazy. *How many ways can I make oatmeal appealing?*

I separated the trail mix I bought at the commissary. It's the only product with whole nuts and dried fruit. There are some dried cranberries and only five to seven almonds in a whole bag of trail mix. I give away the yogurt peanuts to whomever walked by at the time, until Bunkie got mad. She wanted them for herself. "Okay, you can have my yogurt-covered peanuts."

I soak my almonds overnight to activate them, to make them come alive, and add them to my oatmeal. Just three at a time to make them last. Maybe a few dried cranberries if I'm feeling brazen. Ordinarily, it's oatmeal with a few pieces of pineapple because that's what I have the most of.

Soaking those three almonds brings back a piece of who I am at home. This is one way of taking "care" of my hunger. I eat so much oatmeal that coming up with alternatives is a must. Sometimes I eat brown rice, granola, honey, cinnamon, and vanilla creamer all cooked up together instead of oatmeal.

The main ingredient of the trail mix was dried pineapple which I make into pineapple upside-down cake.

Pineapple Upside-Down Cake Recipe:

Dried pineapple from trail mix
1 can of 7-Up®[1]
A handful of caramels
Package of sugar-free shortbread cookies

Soak the dried pineapple, separated from the trail mix, for a few hours.

Crush the package of sugar-free shortbread cookies.

Drain the pineapple to get rid of that sugary water. (Don't give it to someone to drink, ugh.)

Put the pineapple in the bottom of your big plastic cooking bowl.

Melt the caramels and pour over the pineapple.

Mix the crushed-up cookies with the whole can of 7-Up® and pour on top of the pineapple.

Microwave for 10 minutes.

Dump it out onto the lid and dive in.

---

1 7-up is a registered trademark of Keurig Dr. Pepper Corp.

Eating pineapple upside-down cake is especially pleasant while enjoying hot chocolate with a peppermint tea bag in it, or as I call it, "comfort in a cup." With all the food constraints we endure, anything I can do to alleviate the sense of oppression helps. When I pay attention to my food, I feel better.

Eventually, I am getting sick of oatmeal and start eating more granola from the commissary. Our granola is not what I am familiar with on the outside. Our granola consists of predominantly rolled wheat and a small amount of rolled oats. I assume wheat is cheaper than oats. With no refrigeration in our rooms, I tried dried milk for a while until I read an article that said the freeze-drying process makes the cholesterol particles unsafe for human consumption.

One early morning as I'm driving our golf cart to pick up trash, I notice a semi hauling a gigantic milk tank at the warehouse. *Mmmm, and the guy hanging around looks like a convict.* We rarely see a man that isn't a guard or a prison official. Outside prison, I'm not so inclined to check men out. In here though, any new man is like, "Oh look—a man!" In a women's prison, men are a bit of a curiosity. *I kind of just want to see what they look like.*

I mention the incident to Bunkie, and she confirms that our milk comes from another prison where they have an inmate-run dairy on site. That means our milk comes straight from a dairy! Compared to the seconds and thirds we consume regularly, I'd say that's pretty good.

Now my best breakfasts consist of granola and bananas in the dining room. Granola is also becoming my favorite dessert or dinner. I mix a little peanut butter in some granola and pour Hershey's®[1] chocolate syrup on it. *Hershey's® chocolate syrup makes everything better!* Breakfast in the dining room is the only time any fruit is served. An apple, an orange, a banana, or a grapefruit. I've never eaten so much grapefruit. The red apples are terrible, hard, dry, tasteless. *Why are they called Red Delicious?*

Today, there are green apples, Granny Smith apples. *Oh, now we're talking!* I can make apple crisp. At home, I'd make apple crisp by peeling the Granny Smith apples and chopping them up. Then I'd mix them with cinnamon, a little lemon juice, sweetener, and my secret ingredient:

---

1   Hershey's is a registered trademark of The Hershey Company.

a splash of almond extract. Then I mix the oats, with a little gluten-free flour, butter, cinnamon, and sweetener. Finally, I put the oat mixture over the apples and bake until the apples are nice and soft.

At home, I have a friend who loves my apple crisp so much that I make it especially for her. I can just hear her, "Shut the front door! You made apple crisp; I'm coming right over!" Then she cusses continually while eating it and I just laugh at her enthusiasm.

I find a way to take some of these Granny Smith apples to my room to make apple crisp. Here, I make do with cinnamon and granola on top of the apples. I must be sneaky when making it. I don't want the smell wafting into the building from the microwave. I nervously wait for it to be done. A guard could walk in, and I'd be busted. Once cooked, I take my plastic bowl of apple crisp and find a place outside to eat it. Today, I eat my apple crisp one delicious bite at a time, and watch a beautiful sunset. Pure bliss.

We get Granny Smith apples only a few times a year. There are so few things to enjoy. I am not very interested in sharing my apple crisp. To me, apple crisp is pure delight. I don't want to share it with someone who sees it as cooked apples. I want the shared experience of amazement, *Wow a green apple is simply a beautiful thing.* I miss the enjoyment of sharing a meal with a sense of wonder and awe.

Weekends are a little different than weekdays. Breakfast and work each start an hour later. I work every other weekend picking up camp trash. This means that I can sleep until 6:30 a.m. Of course, the guards are coming off their Friday and Saturday late-night events while we are waiting for breakfast. So, once again, they're late opening the kitchen.

About a year into my sentence, it's winter again in Arizona. I start going to breakfast on the weekends. Every weekend morning, the menu consists of bran cereal, and a flat coffee cake. The coffee cake never tastes great but it's something to eat alongside the coffee that I'm drinking. I refuse to even try the bran cereal. It truly looks fake, like small pieces of cardboard, except the time we get some with raisins. Then it looks like pieces of cardboard with mouse poop.

I daydream that I am having coffee and cake at a coffee shop. *Do monasteries have coffee shops? I bet they have awesome vegan coffee cake.* Sometimes, inmates working the kitchen ask me if I am done, pushing me out, and I say no. *No, I'm not done* as I stare out the window, sip my coffee, and eat flat coffee cake.

It isn't that I'm preventing anyone else from eating breakfast; there is plenty of room for other women to sit. It's not that breakfast hour is over; the inmates working the kitchen just get pushy. I find myself very resistant to being hurried. Especially by inmates and while I'm eating. I want minutes—not hours—to enjoy something, anything. The fact that there might be something to enjoy, let me at least look for the possibility of appreciation.

Sadly, my days in the coffee shop are limited. I've been having weekend breakfast for a few months now. I am feeling anxious, bouts of depression, and hypoglycemic-like shakes. I want to go to bed after dinner instead of going out to the track. When I get on my bed, I face the wall. I stare at the wall, willing myself to be elsewhere. I feel this staggering longing to be anywhere but here!

JOURNAL:

I feel like I'm going through a mutinous phase. *I want off this ship!* My mindset of living in a Buddhist monastery has morphed into one of living on a ship lost at sea. The ship metaphor fits the conditions: the deprivation, the hopelessness, the fragile mental state of the "crew," the rule-of-law authoritarianism, and the crew's incessant devotion to its subversion.

I know I am off balance, and I can't live like this. I must figure out what is going on with me. I can't talk to anyone, phones are being monitored, and a prison doctor would put me on who-knows-what medication. I'm thinking, *Maybe this is the effect of diabetes or menopause?* Time to get off this ship and get back to the monastery!

This whole "coffee-shop mutiny" episode reminds me of an old Native American parable that sounds surprisingly Buddhist to me:

An old Cherokee is teaching his grandson about life. "A fight is going on inside me," he said to the boy. "It is a terrible fight, and it is between two wolves. One is evil—he is anger, envy, sorrow, regret, greed, arrogance, self-pity, guilt, resentment, inferiority, lies, false pride, superiority, and ego."

He continued, "The other is good—he is joy, peace, love, hope, serenity, humility, kindness, benevolence, empathy, generosity, truth, compassion, and faith. The same fight is going on inside you—and inside every other person, too."

The grandson thought about it for a minute and then asked his grandfather, "Which wolf will win?"

The old Cherokee simply replied, "The one you feed."

The Shape of Suffering delves deeply into the effects of food on both body and mind. It gets me thinking, *Like the wolves, we must feed what we want to persist.* What is the "food" for mindfulness? The food for persistence? The food for serenity? The food for concentration? The food for equanimity? And in the same vein, how do you starve ill will? Or what must be curbed to prevent restlessness from arising? To avert anxiety, laziness, or uncertainty?

My nutritionist brain kicks in, and I realize I need to be more mindful of what I eat. *Hello*, I'm having coffee and coffee cake to create "a better experience." Truth be told, it's just an escape. *I want the fantasy!* Neither coffee nor coffee cake are nutritionally sound choices. The first thing to go, then, must be my weekend mornings at the coffee shop. I'm back to eating oatmeal on the weekends and slowly I start to feel better.

JOURNAL: Buddhism doesn't teach denial of the senses but discourages over-indulging the senses. Therefore, eating can serve as another mindful practice and meditation.

One morning, I'm just about to eat my oatmeal when the fire alarm goes off. The fire alarm is very loud and there are also lights flashing in the halls. When the fire alarm goes off, we must stay in our rooms unless a guard comes to get us. The alarm is deafening! I put my earplugs in and eat my oatmeal. As the sound of chewing echoes in my head, I'm thinking, *Now, this is me mindfully eating my oatmeal!*

Weekdays, it's five hours between breakfast and lunch. After five hours of work, I'm starving! My nutritional options and opportunities are further constrained by logistics: a challenging schedule and limited facilities.

JOURNAL:

> Hunger arises and falls away. Through the lens of Buddhism's idea of impermanence, all experience is subject to change. Not only shall hunger arise and pass away, but the nature of my experience also changes. This moment is transient! It's not about the hunger. It's about my participation in relation to the hunger. This too is mutable. It seems obvious and yet so easy to overlook.

When I work in recycling, I often get the chance to go to my room for a snack around 10 a.m. This at least allows me a choice not to eat whatever is on my tray at lunch, just because I am hungry.

One day, over six months since I arrived, I was waiting in line trying to figure out what is for lunch. All the inmates were waiting in a line that wrapped around the building. They were staring at all the inmates eating inside. I see something green on the tray. I can't figure out what it is, so I listen in to the inmates in line trying to find out what the green stuff is. Nobody seems to have a clue. It's not until they hand me my tray, I realize it is a tiny salad! The one and only salad I ever saw during my time in prison. *Why don't we have more vegetables? Ugh!*

I make most of my lunches in my room now. By the end of my stay, I ate only one or two meals per week in the dining room. In the morning, I set up my freeze-dried brown rice soaking in water with the freeze-dried veggies, a new condiment, and a dash of soy sauce. When I get back to my room, I cook it in the microwave, add a pack of mackerel, a pack of imitation cream cheese, and Sriracha hot sauce. This is my staple meal, besides oatmeal.

JOURNAL:
Buddhism teaches that freedom comes from the elimi-nation of desire. I'm noticing this connection between content-ment and freedom. My practice is all about increasing content-ment with my mackerel and brown rice.

In prison there is a lot of time spent waiting in lines, waiting for meals, waiting for mail, waiting to go to sleep. I hate waiting in lines and avoid them whenever possible. The lines for meals usually take anywhere from half an hour to an hour to get food. At lunch, there are two lines, one for the general population and the other for the women that work factory jobs. The factory workers line always goes first so they can get back to work. As a benefit of working the recycling job I get to go in the factory worker line. But even this advantage doesn't improve the cuisine. The mo-notony of menu items is dismal.

The menu is fixed on certain days of the week. Wednesday, for exam-ple, is hamburger day—I only try the hamburgers the first Wednesday I am in prison. They are so terrible I never eat another hamburger again. It is the same with the fish. When fish is served, I'm not eating it.

Thursday is chicken day, Cajun, Mexican, or BBQ. It's the same chick-en leg baked with different spices. Chicken is always served with collard greens. Collard greens from a can with chicken grease from those baked chicken legs and vinegar. *Good God, that stuff is terrible!* And I want to eat collards! I am always looking for a vegetable to eat.

Fridays are either Mexican or Italian. The Mexican is the best. Chicken fajitas are not bad except for the fact that they put black pepper on everything, and I can't stand black pepper. The Italian lasagna and spaghetti are terrible! That's as far as the Italian cuisine goes.

We have two dinner times, early dinner at 3 and late dinner at 4:30 after lockdown. Dinner at 3 p.m. is called "short line." To go to short line, we must be in our uniform "greens." We can dress casually for late dinner. I'll go to the short line instead of late dinner when leftovers from lunch are promising. However, most of the time I eat in my room, and at dinner time I go do yoga.

If there is any healthy, good food on the menu, Bunkie informs me. She says, "*You* want to go eat today! Frozen orange juice cups, like the ones from McDonald's with the foil lid!" Yes, even orange juice is a once-a-year kind of thing. I jump up and head for the dining room.

I think that being here brings out my hunter/gatherer instincts. One time, we had baked yams—real yams, not canned sweet potatoes, just straight-up baked yams, and cantaloupe! I couldn't believe my luck that lunch was filled with beta carotene! It was Thursday, so there was also the chicken, which I just can't stomach anymore. Cantaloupe and yams, perfect.

I cross my fingers, hoping for the rest of the afternoon that leftover yams will be served at short line. Because yams are a possibility, I'm going to get in line early. *Yams again!* I eat as much as I possibly can.

Occasionally, a new cook brings some welcome variety to the otherwise predictable menu. The cooks change regularly because the cook is always an inmate, and they are always coming and going. Unfortunately, the basic staples remain the same. Cooks rotate, but Wednesday always remains hamburger day.

One day, we got a new inmate, a white gal. After a few days, I hear that her name was Cordon Blue. *What?* She's white, I'm not expecting a Spanish name, but Cordon Blue? When I talk to Bunkie about it, she tells me that Cordon Blue is going to be our new cook because she was trained as a chef. *Oooo, that's promising.*

Bunkie doesn't know her real name and I hypothesize how she got that nickname. She probably told her bunkie that she trained at a Le Cordon Bleu culinary school. After that everyone knew her as Cordon Blue. I never did learn her real name.

A few special moments feel a bit more satisfying than the usual routines. Sundays, we have brunch—*yay*—the only day of the week that we have eggs. We still have breakfast at 6:30 a.m. But after lockdown at 11 a.m., we have brunch.

Holiday brunches are pretty good, but Mother's Day was the best! This meal was a real memorable highlight of my time in prison. Huevos rancheros, black beans, a corn tortilla, and a piece of chocolate cake from Walmart! I know it came from Walmart because I took all those Walmart boxes out of the trash to be recycled.

The cake boxes were marked as 'thirds.' I don't know exactly what "thirds" means. 'Seconds' usually refers to fruit and veggies that don't look perfect—smaller, some marks, or even sometimes underripe or overripe. "Thirds" typically get discarded or, in a case like apples, processed into cider. So, if food such as a cake is marked thirds, does it qualify as food or waste?

For the big holidays, Thanksgiving, and Christmas, we were allowed to bring a bowl to dinner to take food back to our room. I'd fill my bowl with sweet potatoes and later make sweet potato pie with a cookie crust. Remember, we had no refrigeration, so food rots fast, but this does not keep women from taking tons of food and saving it forever!

Someone gave me some turkey days after Thanksgiving. I could smell that it had spoiled rotten. *It smells terrible!* Bunkie says, "It doesn't smell bad, let me eat it." I have this realization: *she can't smell!* She told me once how much she loved perfume. However, she had to have her husband pick it out for her because she can't smell. She said that she never let him know that she couldn't smell the perfume.

Bunkie takes the turkey and microwaves it saying, "That will kill anything." Now it smells even worse! Before you know it, three women are hanging out with Bunkie at the microwave, eating this foul-smelling turkey! I'm thinking, *Can anyone smell around here?*

Back in my research scientist days, working in a lab that studied taste, I learned some cool things about taste and smell. With the loss of smell, there is automatically a loss of taste. It's the flavor of food that is made up of hundreds or even thousands of chemicals that are smelled, not tasted.

I have heard that people who have snorted cocaine may lose their sense of smell. Bunkie is not a drug user though. Perhaps the reason Bunkie can't smell is because she mixes ammonia and bleach when cleaning her house. Mixing bleach and ammonia causes the release of toxic vapors called chloramines. She told me once that she fired a cleaning lady because this person would *not* mix ammonia and bleach.

I remember a hands-on, learning activity about smell and taste, the jellybean test. You start with the gourmet jellybeans, the ones with all the crazy flavors like buttered popcorn, licorice, or bubble gum. The person taking the test closes their nose with one hand, with eyes closed – picks a jellybean and puts it in their mouth. Then with eyes open, chewing on the jellybean, tries to guess what flavor it is. Before it's all gone, open your nose and the flavor will come flooding to you. If only I could get my hands on some jellybeans, I'd love to try it here in prison.

In prison, there are rules about everything. Food is no exception.

I bought hot cocoa and it comes in a bag that is not resealable. I had an empty creamer container that seemed perfect to protect my cocoa from bugs and moisture. However, I was told by an inmate that I would get in big trouble if I did that. *Why?* Bunkie explained that this "original container rule" was intended to prevent us from hiding contraband.

Contraband is defined as any goods that are illegal to possess or goods that are prohibited from being traded. In prison, almost anything can be contraband. Even approved property such as magazines counts as contraband when they exceed allowable quantities. Contraband can also be any altered item such as a t-shirt with the sleeves cut off.

Not surprisingly, food is, by far, the most common form of contraband. If it is not sold at the commissary, it is contraband. Take a banana from breakfast to your room, that's contraband.

Prison rules are rarely explained by the authorities. I stored my cocoa in the creamer container anyway. *Some rules are meant to be broken.*

When my friend, Nancy, came to visit me, we talked about Buddhism and veganism. Nancy shared with me her challenges in following a strictly vegan diet. I told her about how Buddhism seeks harmony over strict rule-following. We had a good laugh about my rule-bending attempts to find harmony in prison.

When the new year rolls around, we got new food items in the commissary—mostly stuff I wouldn't even try, like beef and cheddar on a stick and more cookies. However, corn tortillas were a welcome surprise and our only gluten-free option. So, here's what you do: sprinkle a tiny bit of imitation mozzarella cheese on a corn tortilla and then pop it in the microwave until crispy. Prepare a tuna pack with lemon juice, a bit of chopped pickle, and hot sauce. Then put the tuna on the crispy tortilla and eat it.

I wish we could buy vegetables at the commissary; even canned ones would be better than nothing. Oh right, no cans, no refrigeration. *Why not vegetables in foil pouches?*

After commissary, everybody is eating and making weird food dishes. It's evening in the TV room, the evening after commissary and inmates are passing around their little concoctions. This is where I first experienced a saltine cracker with a little peanut butter and a piece of pickle on top—*not as bad as expected, but not my favorite.*

Some of the food that inmates make for inmates can be extremely unhealthy, but it tastes good. For example, a potato log is for special occasions, like birthdays. I never actually made one, but I watched others make it.

POTATO LOG RECIPE:

INGREDIENTS:

Potato chips – small bags, BBQ, Onion, Jalapeño and of
course Hot Wings flavored potato chips.

Packs of chicken

Soya Goya (Mexican spices, salt, cumin, etc.)

Cream cheese (non-refrigerated imitation cheese)

Shredded cheese (non-refrigerated imitation cheese)

Pickled jalapeño's

Start by crushing up your potato chips, in their
respective bags.

Drain the liquid from the chicken packs into a cup.

Add spices and a little water to the liquid from the
chicken pack.

Add shredded cheese to the chicken.

Mix the cream cheese with the pickled jalapeños.

Add the liquid from the chicken pack, with spices,
to the crushed potato chips, to make a thick, goopy
paste.

Open a plastic bag and lay flat. Spread the chip
mixture out, making a flat, thick slab. Spread the cream
cheese mixture on that, then the chicken, and finally
more cheese. Roll the whole thing up, tucking the plastic
all around it, and pop it in the microwave until heated
all the way through. There are many variations, like adding pepperoni or turkey sausage to the chicken mixture.

There is something indulgent about it even though it is truly terrible. I ate them a couple of times; however, every time I ate potato log, my stomach would hurt for hours, so much it was not worth it!

Also, after commissary, inmates are hyper and loud, staying up all hours talking, fueled no doubt by another concoction: coffee balls. Instant coffee, peanut butter, and sugar all mixed up together. Inmates covet coffee balls; rarely will someone give you a coffee ball. Even half of one can make me feel the caffeine buzz.

I don't use that much coffee. I went through only two bags of instant coffee my whole stay. I don't care for the coffee balls, but I enjoy iced coffee in the summer. The iced coffee is awesome if you know how to make it. I had to learn the right way to make it from a friend. Sometimes, I'd just ask her to make my iced coffee because getting the right blend of instant coffee and vanilla creamer is more difficult than you think.

Iced coffee helps me through the tedium of parenting class. Women drinking iced coffee, laughing their heads off, make the two and a half hours go by quickly. There are a couple of inmates that talk about opening a drive-through coffee shop and selling prison iced coffee when they get out.

One day as I am walking through my unit, I see a couple of women eating together. These are the Spanish-speaking women, no English. I notice they are eating nopales!

I am familiar with nopales (cactus pads or leaves). I've eaten nopales swimming in a delicious cream sauce next to scrambled eggs. It's really good! They taste a little like green beans or green bell peppers. And they are nutritious and a good source of fiber and minerals. I've never prepared them myself though.

I ask Bunkie, "Do you think I could get those women to make me some nopales? I'll pay them."

"Yes, Anna will prepare nopales for you."

Anna only speaks Spanish; therefore, Bunkie is the go-between. Bunkie tells me how much it will cost me to have nopales. I'm over the moon! I mix nopales with my instant brown rice, pack of imitation cream cheese, and hot sauce—oh the pleasure of variety. I wish this was a regular thing; however, it is a rare occurrence.

Eventually, Anna lets me watch her prepare it, so I can learn how. In prison, recipes get passed down verbally inmate to inmate. Nothing ever gets written down. You hear a rumor that so-and-so makes the best ice coffee, so you go ask that person for her recipe. Usually, I ask for a demonstration, and I'd make mental notes.

Cactus pads are better young and now the plants are disappearing. Somehow, a guard finds out we are eating the cactus. Before I know it, I see the women working in Lands Out cutting down all the cactus in and near our compound. *What's up with that? Why is eating cactus pads a bad thing? Who's making these decisions and why? It seems just spiteful.*

JOURNAL:

Shenpa is a Tibetan word meaning "the urge, the hook, that triggers our habitual tendency to close down." Any pain or tightening in the body triggers us to reach for relief. To get unhooked, we begin by recognizing that moment of unease and learn to relax in that moment.

Hunger arises without fail. Feeding my hunger doesn't mean that it won't return. Impermanence is inescapable (which is a good thing). It's only because of impermanence that a seed becomes a tree. I know I will feel hunger in my body again and again.

However, Buddhist practice isn't the way to cope with or overcome impermanence. It is the way to fully embrace, appreciate, and live it! Hunger is an opportunity to practice, an opportunity to choose my experience. I can take action toward fullness, contentment, being satiated, or fueled for well-being, and for life.

This is different from knowing the sun will rise tomorrow. My hunger always gives me another opportunity to feel different, even if it is only a tiny, tiny bit different. The hunger is not wrong, it's not a misshapen sin. This applies to all my needs: physical needs, feelings of safety, and a need to feel of value and to count for something. Hunger doesn't trap me—it's my frame of reference. Hunger in all its forms moves me through my environment.

JOURNAL:
The Shape of Suffering says, "One's attachment to food derives from one's attachment to one's identity as a being." From a Buddhist perspective, food may be metaphoric. What will quench my hunger? Prison lets me inquire into what hunger and satisfaction really mean to me. Food is primal. It touches our essential nature.

All hunger is not the same. One sort of hunger is simply my body saying that I need fuel. The other kind of hunger comes from all the places inside me that are dissatisfied. Even though prison defines my food options, I still have choice; I can eat mackerel as a healthy choice, or cookies to satisfy my longing for sweetness in my life.

JOURNAL:
No matter what your food options are, how you address your hunger gets to the core of who you are. What is it about who I think I am that shapes the food experiences I desire? Does being a nutritionist foster a desire for more nutritious foods?

The inevitability of hunger and the stress I feel around food eventually becomes a regular reminder of my spiritual journey. My hunger is an invitation to discernment. Hunger could even become a sort of prayer bell for me, inviting me to ask, "Am I hungry for a specific food or hungry for a particular experience of consuming food?"

Monks ritually chant before eating and reflect upon the food that they are about to consume. I don't know the specific chants. Still, I do my best to bring mindfulness to my eating. In the moment of feeling hunger, I may be having a negative or positive experience of hunger. I want to attend to my hunger and when mackerel and cookies don't cut it, it's time for a walking meditation.

JOURNAL:

> As a practice, I pause to discern my impulse to eat. Is it motivated by loneliness, anxiety, a distraction from my pain? Am I attempting to comfort myself? What are the sensations that make up my feelings of hunger? What happens to those sensations as I am mindful of them? Do they become stronger or weaker, or do they stay the same?

Today, one of the Native inmates made tons of fried bread for all of us. It's rare, but wonderful, to have a guest cook (inmate) make food for us. While these occasional surprises were delightful in and of themselves, they did have a strange way of reminding us of the monotony of our menu.

JOURNAL:

> I want to empower myself to be myself, every moment. Otherwise, I'm trapped as a cog in a machine, ignoring who I am, ignoring the life I want to live. Freedom isn't a plethora of options; freedom is present even when there is only one option. Freedom is about being. Being is freedom.

Bringing mindfulness to my hunger and to my eating, I can breathe, take a step back, loosen the attachment to the hunger. I am not trying to escape the moment, but instead be here in the moment.

One day on my way to the track, I see women eating sushi-like rolls. "Hey, Bunkie! Who's the woman who makes sushi rolls?"

Once I find the woman who reportedly makes the best sushi rolls, cooked white rice with mackerel and imitation cream cheese, I ask if she will make me some sushi. She says she will make me a roll. We make a plan; she will make the roll and I will eat it out by the exercise equipment so that the guards don't see.

When the day arrives, I go over to pick up my sushi roll. She is leaving with her friends and tells me to pick out the one on top. I didn't want anyone to see me so I quickly grabbed one and left.

I'm hungry. I'm walking around, looking for a place to sit that is not crowded, and I take a bite. I stop suddenly, *What?! That's so creamy, almost buttery. Amazing! What is that taste? Oh, my God! It's avocado!*

Where did the avocados come from? We've never been served avocado, not once while I was down. We can't buy avocados from the commissary.

I see the sushi lady rushing over to me. "Have you eaten it yet?" she asks.

"I had a couple bites," I said. "It's amazing!"

"I think you got the wrong one."

"Because it had avocado?"

"Yes." She says nervously, "Please don't tell anyone that you ate avocado. My friend brought them from an officer training session that she was serving. She made guacamole for the officers and brought a couple avocado for us."

"Don't worry, I would never tell a soul! I said enthusiastically. "That is the best sushi ever!"

"Don't let anybody see that you have avocado," she said as she walked away.

As it happened, no one is around, I take my sushi roll to a concrete table and started eating it, slowly. *It is delicious!* I savor every single bite. I know I'm sitting in prison; however, I feel the sun, the breeze, and this amazing sushi is making me feel so good! *This can't be prison. I must be in a monastery!*

Fourteen:
WOMEN'S JOURNEY, DHARMA

M Y FIRST MONTH DOWN, I was walking around the track with Liz. She said that I don't look like I belong in prison. I started telling her my story. "I am here because my brother was a pot dealer."

She stopped suddenly and whispered, "Don't tell that to anyone else!" She cautioned me never to talk about what I did or didn't do. "Just leave behind everything that brought you to prison."

It reminded me of the rune Thurisaz, Gateway. There comes a time in every cycle when one reaches a gateway to the next chapter in life. "Visualize yourself standing before a gateway on a hilltop. Your entire life lies out behind you and below. Before you step through, pause, and review the past: the learning and the joys, the victories and the sorrows – everything it took to bring you here. Observe it all, bless it all, release it all. For in letting go of the past you reclaim your power." — Ralph Blum, *The Book of Runes*, St. Martin's, ©1993

To other inmates, I'm sure my case is of little consequence (except to the snitches). Snitches—inmates who pass information to staff in hopes to get time off their sentences—are always listening.

The Thurisaz rune also states that looking back, "you are being confronted with a true reflection of what is hidden in yourself…" So, it's best to leave your past behind when you step into prison and it's best to leave everyone you know outside. Of course, this intensifies the sense that you are here alone.

On the one hand, my past experiences seem to define who I am and how I respond to life. I react a specific way to each new experience because of whatever I've come to understand previously. Being a single mother, increased my level of resourcefulness. And resourcefulness is a useful tool to have in prison.

On the other hand, prison is a new experience. I feel it as if I've just been told that I have cancer. The outcome is unknown to me, and only by living moment to moment can I utilize the tools gained by my past experiences. What is right here in my present time makes me who I am.

What is the truth of my being? What is my Dharma? How does it become apparent? Dharma is much more than a teaching. Dharma is "what there is." It is what everything arises from–analogous to the atoms or quarks that make up all matter.

Physicists tell us that quarks have "flavor." And so does Dharma. In the present moment, my world has a prison flavor. My Dharma flavors my thoughts, my emotions, my life.

The distinction of Dharma allows me to separate the emotion, the memory of past events or experiences, from my authentic self. With observation and contemplation, I'm peeling back the layers until I uncover my beginner's mind—that attitude of openness, and lack of preconceptions, as if I am seeing myself for the first time. I want to choose my experience coming from a beginner's mind. It's tricky. Even how I react in this moment contributes to a new pattern. New experiences change my pattern so that in the next experience, I will react in a totally new way. *Is this growth?*

There is so little privacy of any kind in prison that inmates understandably protect every bit of privacy they can control. Our lifestyle is exposed. We're subject to constant intrusions, always vulnerable. We have no personal space to call our own and what little we may consider "property" remains always subject to search and seizure. Items must be carried in a mesh bag so guards can see what we have. Of course, this means other inmates can see it, too.

I'm living with three hundred women for two years. We have a lot in common: we are women, we're inmates, and most of us are mothers. The longer I'm here, the more people on the outside ask me, "Do you have a friend?" They ask me if I've come to know anyone on a deeper level. Or have I met anyone I can relate to? *Have I really gotten to know anyone?* The answer is no.

One day, I come back from work and Bunkie catches me up on the goings-on of the prison. "Did you know that Yoli's husband is filing for a divorce because when Yoli was outside, she had an affair with the next-door neighbor?" *How would I know that?! I'm never in the gossip loop.*

I asked Bunkie if she talked to Yoli. Bunkie tells me that Yoli told her bunkie, and her bunkie is friends with an inmate downstairs. The inmate downstairs wanted to use the microwave, but it was busy, so she came upstairs to use our microwave and then Bunkie talked to her.

Rumors and stories are always swirling around. Never is the water still. I can't keep up! The fierce gossip network represents another good reason to keep your past to yourself. And keep your opinions, observations, and thoughts to yourself as well. In here, people's reputations can be built by hearsay instead of intimate conversations.

An inmate across the hall occasionally says hi and we may talk for a couple of minutes. She asks if I have any children. "Yes, I have a son." She does too. Now we have something in common.

When I hung up a card from the aquarium visit my family went on, she came to talk to me. She tells me that she is terrified of water. She will not even wade at the edge of a lake or river. And now gets the heebie-jeebies walking by my room. I took down the card.

Sitting in my room with no doors, it's easy to hear my neighbors talking. We overhear everything in the unit, either directly or indirectly, other women talking about someone else.

No matter where I am, I can overhear inmates talking. Most of what I've learned directly are stories I've overheard while I was doing yoga, or while I was reading in my room. A woman next door talks to her bunkie about her education. She never finished high school. However, when she wanted to become a nurse's assistant, she found a place online to get a fake high school diploma and that allowed her to get the nurses' assistant training. *I'm glad she's working.*

Some conversations grab my attention. I overheard a nearby inmate say, "One day I beat up my cousin with a baseball bat, and she was pregnant."

Another inmate replied, "Did she lose the baby? How bad was it?"

"She went to the hospital but didn't lose the baby."

"What did she do to tick you off?"

"Oh nothing. I just didn't like her."

I make a mental note, *This is someone I don't want to piss off!* And I wonder, *Why didn't anyone pull her off? She only comes up to my chin.*

Another time I overheard the same inmate talking about being her daddy's favorite, how she would do mean things to her sister, but never get in trouble. Her parents were divorced, and her father had been a drug dealer. She was used to getting her way, so one time she tricked her sister to go into the backyard and locked her out of the house. The backyard was home to the very mean pit bull. Even though it was chained up, it was very scary to a small child. And when her father came home, she said she didn't do it.

JOURNAL:
> A female population without the rules and culture of the outside—who are we and what will we become? "To be or not to be?" Hamlet's question takes on a whole new significance here in prison. Inside here, it swims in a whole different cultural soup. We are peeling back the layers to discover ourselves.

Most inmates I see every day. If they don't live in my unit, I might see them at the mess hall, or out on the track, or waiting for the phone. There are a few inmates that stay in their room all the time. However, one inmate in my unit has a job within the unit and never went to the mess hall. She prepared all her meals in her room and didn't like to be in the sun. I never saw her outside. I would have had no reason to talk to her; however, one day she sees me reading and asks what kind of books I read. I end up giving her books occasionally.

Bunkie has been doing laundry for an inmate on our floor to make some extra money for food purchases. A new inmate, named Crystal, starts doing laundry for a few women. Bunkie decides to pay Crystal to do the laundry she is getting paid to do for the other inmate. (Bunkie sometimes has a bit of a lazy streak.)

One day, Bunkie comes to me in a panic. She is being accused of stealing a pair of ankle socks—the type of socks we pay for. She knows Crystal did it, but she can't tell anyone else because she is supposed to be doing the laundry herself.

Soon we start hearing stories about how Crystal is stealing everything: a cup, coffee, creamer, a dirty shirt out of someone's hamper. I am warned, "If you see Crystal in the halls, make sure your stuff is locked up," and "Don't let Crystal in your room."

One day in the food line, I am behind Crystal. She and her friend are talking. I overhear that she has *thirteen children*: six are hers while the other seven are her husband's. She looks so young, maybe late twenties or early thirties. She lives in a trailer, not a palace with maids! I imagine three or four bedrooms at the most. *Where does everyone sleep?*

Finally, Crystal is busted, and the officers search her room. They find things that are not her size, brand new things that she never opened, so many stolen items! I tell Bunkie that stealing is probably Crystal's habit. She comes from a place of incredible lack, and others' needs always must come before hers. She just couldn't help herself. Maybe for Crystal, prison feels like a palace with maids.

Mondays and Thursdays, we take our greens to the laundry to be washed. Our uniforms bleed green on everything. Tuesdays and Fridays, they do whites. Sheets get washed on Wednesdays. Inmates who do their own laundry or wash clothes for other inmates compete for the use of three normal washers and three dryers. Yes, that's three washers for three hundred inmates.

The first time the prison laundry broke down, we had to put our name on a list to use the next available washer. I went down on the second day, thinking there would be fewer people. I ran into a woman who tells me that she put her name on the list yesterday at 6:30 a.m. and didn't get to use a machine until 4 p.m. And we must be present when our name is called for the next available washer. I start looking for someone I can hire to do my laundry.

In addition to paying someone to do our laundry, we must buy our own detergent, but the benefit is that our clothes smell better than when they were washed by the laundry. And they will fold your clothes. After a while, I hire someone to do my whites. Eventually, I have someone picking up all my laundry every week.

Women also cook and clean for other women. Perhaps they have veiled themselves in "wifely" duties, but before I chalk this up to gender stereotypes, I remember that here it's only women doing everything for anyone. In a women's prison, gender expression easily gets confused and misinterpreted.

When I arrived in prison in January 2011, my concept of gender was flat, without dimension. Being in prison adds light, bringing out hundreds of colors in the picture that is gender. I quickly realized that my notion of gender needed to evolve, partly because prison culture demands it, and partly because of the new choices that inmates allow themselves.

Gender identity and gender expression, I learn, are not the same thing. Identity is the gender with which one identifies. It is central to one's sense of self. It's totally subjective and internal. Gender *expression* is what other people can see—the ways one expresses gender identity in the world. That's what people judge and evaluate based on the socially constructed roles and behaviors typically associated with males or females.

This gender issue reminds me of Buddhism's idea of duality: things are never only this or only that, nothing or everything. Rather, things are as they really are—Dharma. The Dharma is like the atoms at the core, beneath the many layers of creation. Who is the person underneath the layers?

I'm trying to understand my own gender bias. How much of my gender attachment comes from what I "have to be" or "want to be" for someone else? Prison strips us down. I journey down to my core: *who am I as a woman?* How much of my gender expression do I allow to be dictated by the "outside" presumptions?

JOURNAL:

> Gender is expressed in so many ways. Even though we all wear the same uniform, I am more aware here of gender expression. Some women convey maleness by expressing a quality of boldness, while some women totally "feel" like men. One inmate, Morgan, has been down for a long time. I hear inmates referring to Morgan as a "he." I hear about women trying to gain affections from Morgan. Women do his laundry, cook for him, or iron his t-shirts. Eventually, even without direct interactions with Morgan, I can't imagine referring to Morgan as "she."

This stereotypically masculine type seems to be in high demand in prison. I suspect women assume that *he* would give sexual favors. Also, they are known to get things for their gals, like taking a banana from breakfast or doing things like carrying the laundry. But more than anything else, I see women wanting to be treated like a woman—in the stereotypical way a man would treat a woman.

Another inmate, Mali, wore her very long hair in a braid rolled up on the back of her head. One day I saw her, and she had cut her hair into a very short, masculine style. The next week, I saw Mali upon release, completely dressed as a male: khaki pants and a buttoned-down shirt with a white t-shirt underneath. But unlike Morgan, I didn't know how she identified until I saw the street clothes, her—rather his—gender expression. Maybe it was me, but I never perceived his (male) gender expression before that day. Except that he constantly had women hanging all over him.

Before prison, I never considered myself a "domestic" woman. I don't consider cooking and cleaning to be my job; it falls under "household." Everyone under the roof must participate for the sake of the household. I also didn't think of myself as "feminine." No form-fitting feminine clothes, pink, or heaven forbid *dainty* items. Nor did I see myself as "masculine," and in prison, I didn't fit into the masculine category, even though I take on some "masculine roles" at times. In my house and my space, I go for comfort. This is where I put considerable effort.

Bunkie does all the cleaning in our room. For my part, I do the heavy lifting like taking our laundry down on laundry days. When it comes to cleaning, she wants things just right, her way. There are not a lot of things to clean in a small room, only the floor and the top of the locker. We were responsible for our own bunks as any guard could report a messy bunk and nobody is going down for anybody around here.

Outside, I didn't feel like my feminine qualities were visible: I did not consider myself emotional, creative (like my sisters who are both artists), or sensual in my manner of dress. Instead, I was analytical (twenty years as a research scientist), logical, and goal-oriented.

JOURNAL:
> I wonder who I am? Am I being true to My Dharma, the seed that Collin arises from?

I do a lot of inmate-watching. *What can I intuit about who these women are?* There are many large-breasted women here, more than I remembered outside in the general population. Many years ago, while living in Texas, I had a waitressing job where I was the only woman without breast augmentation. I wonder how many of these inmates are from Texas. Or is this just a peculiarity of this population?

One day, a young woman in her mid-twenties, Lily, moves in next door to me. She has *beautiful* tattoos on her chest, shoulder, and arm: lilies laid on her chest and draping over her shoulder. The tattoos are incredible, just gorgeous!

I hear her talking to her bunkie one day about men hiring her to go to parties. They want the most beautiful women at *their* parties and that's how she earns her living on the outside. Lily has every intention of going right back to that life when she gets out. She talks about a guy, the "nice" guy who helped her get the high-paying gigs. I am thinking, *Come on, really? This is the life you want?*

I hear Lily's voice and imagine her at a party. A "nice" guy offers her free drugs, a good time. Being arm candy, she becomes a regular, and the "nice" guy offers to pay for a tattoo, pay for breast enlargement, and always keeps her supplied with drugs.

I hear of women who have undergone one or more breast enlargement surgeries paid for by men. Not husbands, but really pimps (except that the women telling the stories never use the word 'pimp'). I feel like I am hearing about a domestic abuse issue where the woman keeps going back to an abusive husband.

JOURNAL:

The underbelly of a dark, obscure race of men. Women "of men, for men." There's a kind of power in it for both sexes, men creating women, and the women being revered. But this can't be true, it's not real? It's straight out of one of my Sheri Tepper science fiction books. Love her reflections! Outside prison is a novel of fiction. Here in prison, I see the truth. Wow! When one is being someone for someone else, where does the rest of you go?

These stories regularly involve drugs. Frequently, their own drug use or taking a drug rap for their man lands these women in prison. Lily went down for a man. I knew a woman that was in for her son's drug use. One gal was on a first date when the guy stopped at "a friend's" and the place was raided. Many women's stories begin with, "I didn't know."

Each time I hear one of these stories I wonder why she took the rap. Were you making this choice as a "better" person? Were you taking one for the team? Do you sacrifice for your kids and your man because it's the right thing to do? Or are you doing it because it's the woman's role—what's expected of a woman?

These choices get rationalized in many ways. Courts are easier on women, to some degree. And outside people entertain this fantasy that prison life is easier for women. There's also an expectation that women are more capable of adapting and therefore can handle the stress of prison better than men. The higher suicide rate for male inmates may support this view. Even if true, these justifications express a patently sexist bias.

Any way you slice this, it's gender abuse.

JOURNAL:

> Are we attached to an identity created before prison? Prison may actually offer an advantage—revealing who is underneath the conditioning, circumstance, and expectations. Does sacrifice make you a better person? Once in prison, a woman has been stripped of her role, who is she now? What if becoming her authentic soul is not sanctioned out there? The woman neglects her own soul. If I didn't want to feel anything, drugs would certainly distract me from feeling my soul's desires.

Lucia didn't like to be outside in the sun, she rarely walked the track. Many women of Hispanic descent didn't want to be in the sun. At first, I didn't see it. Then while hanging out with Lucia and Julia, I saw that "too brown" was a big issue. Anything to be lighter, fairer. Staying out of the sun, plucking all visible body hair.

I've read that one common unconscious stereotype among women is that fair skin equates to being attractive and lovable. Or is it unconscious?

I wonder, *how many of these dark-skinned women have been on the receiving end of a colorism slur?*

I don't share their concern; I love being outside. Every spare minute possible, I was outside.

JOURNAL:

Our authentic selves. I have always wanted to look like my mother, dark and beautiful, half Spanish from Spain and half Indian from Mexico.

I observe women here in different phases of discovering and recognizing themselves. It's as if there was a pattern everyone follows: birth, gradually creating an identity, wonder, question the adopted roles, awaken, and allow the authentic self to be truly conceived and birthed. Prison can be the do-over. Cultural and familial expectations are outside. In here, birth order is irrelevant. In here, one can experience a paradoxical freedom that isn't available outside. Freedom from the roles and expectations. Freedom to choose who we are going to be.

Not everyone makes that choice, of course. Even thinking about that kind of change can feel risky. It can seem dangerous to unfold into our authentic being. Holding on to our past and external circumstances that identify our core seems the safer path. It's easier to continue to blame circumstances for who we are. In the end, authenticity means accepting responsibility for who we are, for our choices and actions. Accepting responsibility is scary, but also powerful. You can't be responsible and still be a victim of circumstances. When I accept responsibility, I have freedom to choose, and I can truly reinvent myself and my life.

The women surrounding me have been forcefully removed from the environments that held their identities together and now there are no more drugs to distract. I expect that drugs can make the party, the household, one's life, feel okay. These women are not bound in the same way they were on the outside: inside they are free of the past conditions, and the environment that set up the conditions. Previous roles, responsibilities, and distractions are gone. *Now what?*

Many of these women have left abusive situations. Maybe their role has been wife, arm candy, or just a defenseless woman. How much acting has it taken to get through in life? In prison, there is the opportunity, a clear space without drugs, to contemplate the question, *am I an actor playing a role? Does my essence shine through?*

JOURNAL:

> Does the authentic self want to emerge? In prison, there are no drugs—not totally true; however, essentially true for most inmates. There's no one to be performing for. Women who have lived their lives in a second skin, now have the freedom to envision a new skin. What will she look like when she lives fully in her body? Be present. Live in the moment.

Bertilla bunks across the way from me. One day, it hits me how different she appears when she is sleeping. She sleeps on the top bunk, face to the wall, and her long hair loose. During the day, she is mostly "cholo-esque." Her pants are hanging down and baggy. Her hair is in a tight long braid down her back. Walking with her toes pointing out, that "cholo" swagger. A tough exterior to be sure. In contrast, when she is out of uniform with her hair down, there is such softness.

Bertilla becomes one of my workout gals. I always have two or three women who take me on as a personal trainer. I develop workouts and we all go work out together. When I meet Bertilla, she has been down a while, I think years, and she tells me that she has lost a lot of weight. In here, she is learning what her body wants in order to be healthy. I like her down-to-earth demeanor. I tease her about her cholo swagger, and tell her that a chiropractor, a rolfer, or anyone doing body work would say the walk was bad for her body. Maybe she should try walking with her feet pointing straight ahead. She laughs at me.

Bertilla has a wife on the outside. I find this to be surprisingly quite rare. For all the hype about most inmates being gay, I do not know many women that came to prison gay. Maybe it's our society, gay marriage is only legal in seven states at this time. Bertilla was someone I interviewed about my Gender in Society project, asking women if they had ever experienced violence toward themselves. Her answer surprised me. "No," she says, "my husband hit me all the time, but I'm gay."

I do a double take. *What? What is going on here?* I don't even know what to say. I clarify, "Have you experienced violence toward yourself, sexual or otherwise." There is another inmate present and Bertilla just laughs it off. I only know a little bit of Bertilla's background. From the local chatter, she married young and was only married for a short time.

Does Bertilla feel that her husband was justified to beat her? I thought that this data gathering was going to be straightforward. Another inmate says, "He only hit me once." I hear these (and other) women justifying violence. *What is justified violence?* A class reading asserts "there are more laws protecting animals than there are protecting women from violence."

I wonder if Bertilla having chosen the role of a man's wife, feels that her being gay somehow justifies this violence?

JOURNAL:

> We women have come from long-held, male-dominated cultural systems. And our brains are wired for survival! Our brain wants us to conserve energy, in times of stress, shut down all that is not essential for our survival. Are we not our thoughts, our feelings? Isn't my default perspective of who I am based on my past? If the culture and laws create roles for women, are our identities lost? We as women should define ourselves.

In prison, we can unravel our past identities and our self-concepts become malleable.

I read somewhere that when someone believes in you, you are more likely to succeed, to become that smart, generous, and admirable person the believer said you were. This idea has been with me for many years. Whenever my son would tell me that he didn't think he could do something or that he thought he was bad in some way, I always told him that I believed in him!

JOURNAL:

What is the opposite of the *believer*? (Abuser) Someone who always puts you down, tells you that you are nothing, valueless. I think that many of my fellow inmates come from a place where there was a prominent *non-believer*. Now in prison, that non-believer's influence is null and void. Ahh, now there is space to create. I am more than the sum of my past. I know that I am glimpsing my essence here!

My self-concept was static before I came to prison, but now I want to uncover my Dharma. I see I can move beyond my familiar past. I loosen the sticky connection to my past, and to my brain's "this is Collin" movie. My new practices and perspective make me feel like the blinds are up and light is everywhere.

Bertilla finds out unexpectedly that she has only one more week down. I ask her if I can do anything for her. She asks if I would make her a cake. The next day when I've made her cake, I let her know and she says that she only wants one piece. She has to go do something and when she comes back, I tell her that I will be sharing the rest of the cake with her friends.

I decide to give each woman a piece of cake and ask them to share something they value or appreciate about Bertilla, to Bertilla, when they say their goodbyes. Bertilla says "Ah, na don't do that." I do it anyway. I tell her that I value and appreciate her, she gets a little teary. I feel an impulse to give her a hug and hesitate. Always in the back of my head, *no touchy, touchy*! So what? Another rule broken. I give her a big hug.

One gal, Jessie, was on the outs with Bertilla. They had been friends, but Jessie wanted more. Bertilla didn't feel that way. "I'm in a committed relationship—I'm married," she said. When I gave Jessie a piece of cake, she thanked me profusely for the opportunity to share her feelings with Bertilla. She said she had been trying to find a way to talk to Bertilla for over a week now. After Bertilla left, Jessie told me it went really well. This had given her an opportunity to express her sorrow and gratitude.

JOURNAL:

How are these experiences shaping me? What of myself will be revealed here? Will I be different when I get out? How could I not be different?

After Marcia, my recycling work partner, and I have been working together for a while, she joins Sarah and me doing yoga. Sarah has helped me learn poses and we have been practicing together. For a few months, the three of us do yoga together.

One day while Sarah and I were working out, Sarah said to me, "I probably won't be able to do yoga with you anymore."

"What?" I ask, "why?"

"Well as long as Marcia isn't doing yoga with you, I would do yoga with you."

"What's going on between you and Marcia?"

"I found out that Marcia is a Jehovah's Witness. I'm an excommunicated Jehovah's Witness and when Marcia finds out she won't want to be around me."

I'm a little baffled. I've never seen any trouble between Sarah and Marcia. I said, "Let's go walking and talk about this, I don't understand why this is such a big deal. We're in prison together, maybe there are exceptions? Can we work something out?"

While walking around the track, Sarah told me stories of her religious upbringing, and it sounded harsh. After high school, when she became pregnant, she married the baby daddy and left the Jehovah's Witnesses. Her brother has not talked to her since. Her parents didn't talk to her for years, but then eventually decided to be in her life.

Once when I lost commissary privileges for a week, it was Sarah, not Marcia, that offered to buy food for me that week. Her compassion really made an impression on me. In here, it often seems everyone is out for themselves.

Once Sarah talked to Marcia, Marcia talked to the prison Jehovah's Witnesses leaders and that was the end of the three of us doing yoga together. Sarah would be leaving soon so she bowed out. Again, I wonder, *how does one decide what to leave on the outside when one is within a closed system? Do we choose to hold close an identity because letting go would force us to redefine ourselves?*

Now Marcia and I are doing yoga on my concrete mat when the new athletic director asks if we want to teach yoga, I say no, Marcia says yes. A week or so later, after Marcia's urging, I say yes we can team teach yoga. I ended up teaching yoga, while Marcia assists, for the last six months of my stay in prison. It is a wonderful experience!

I realize that I love teaching. I never would have thought that to be true of me. It's so fun to come up with new ways to explain something that is familiar to me. And that moment someone gets it, gets what I'm trying to say, gets what I'm asking of them, what a wonderful feeling!

When it gets close to my time to leave, I am told that I will have a month off before I leave. As the time approaches, we find someone to replace me at my recycling position. The first day she takes over for me, I sleep in. About 10 a.m., I go check on how they are doing. I go out there and the new gal is working by herself. She tells me that Marcia got hurt and is in the infirmary. *What the heck?!*

Someone accidentally ran into Marcia with one of the electric carts; the cart was in reverse when it should have been in forward gear. Marcia has hurt her shoulder pretty bad; they say it is not broken and send her to her bunk with plenty of painkillers. I have to start working again.

Marcia doesn't want to lose her job, so after the first week in bed and on serious pain killers, she wants to go back to work. After our boss talks to her, he wants to talk to me. She doesn't want me to talk to our boss. I tell him what I know: that her shoulder has been hurting for a long time and this just made it worse. My feeling is that she has suffered a major injury to her shoulder. He tells her to take another week off.

It has been almost two weeks since the accident when Marcia's husband comes to visit her. When I asked her about the visit and what he thought about her accident, she told me that she didn't tell him. I can't believe it; I ask her why? She doesn't give me a reason.

Because Marcia can't go back to work, we find someone new to take my place a week before I am leaving. Now that I'm off, I thought I would see Marcia more often; however, she is avoiding me. Even when I do see her in the dining hall, she ignores me. It's not permissible to go to her room because she lives in a different unit, and we are not allowed in a unit that we don't live in.

JOURNAL:

I can't stop thinking about Marcia. The whole thing blows me away! I wonder if somehow, she must feel that she deserves this pain. Doesn't she care for herself? Does Marcia's suffering play such an integral role in her identity that she can't let it go? I want her to rise above her suffering, the pain she is enduring, receive support and feel empowered. Bless you, Marcia, on your Dharma path.

What empowers one to reinvent the self? In a way, leaving the past behind is the opportunity to become authentic; suspend the past and have the freedom to be true to my essence. When I live in the present, I invent myself newly each moment according to my values. Will the truth I glimpse in here continue to live within me when I get out?

Phra Ajaan Lee Dhammadharo provided keen insight into the meaning of Dharma in a talk he once gave (translated by Thänissaro Bhikku). "The Dhamma (Dharma), in one sense, is a means of nourishing the heart to make it pure. In another sense, the Dhamma is our self. Every part of our body is a piece of the world, and the world is an affair of the Dhamma. But it's not the essence of the Dhamma. The essence of the Dhamma lies with the heart." *My heart is where I gain access to my essence.*

I never said goodbye to Marcia. When it is my time to walk out of prison, I walk out wearing the purple beaded necklace that she made for me. I wonder if she watches me leave.

Fifteen:
BIRDS AND FREEDOM

B UDDHISM TEACHES REVERENCE for all living things; we live inter-dependently with animals and all creatures in the web of life. A few creatures challenge my reverence. Scorpions, for example, just freak me out.

For the most part though, this aspect of Buddhism resonates with me. Even before I became a Buddhist, animals held a healing space for me.

In my late twenties, I began a daily practice of witnessing animals and the lessons they have to offer. I bought a set of David Carson and Jamie Sams' "Medicine Cards," which promised "The Discovery of Power through the Ways of Animals." Whenever I had questions or issues in my life, I would pick one of the animal cards to prompt a new mindset.

Now in prison, I follow the birds. Each species is a new meditation. I sit on my concrete mat, watching the birds, and my mind takes flight.

Birds have superpowers. Birds can fly to incredible heights and over incredible distances. They can create sounds and songs that are impossible for us humans. And they can survive dramatic seasonal shifts!

Contemplating the birds, I'm full of wonder at the birds themselves, the sky, and the air. As I watch them come and go beyond the limitations of prison walls and gravity, the birds evoke freedom. Through the miracle of flight, the air gives freedom to the birds. I want to feel the bird's freedom in my mind, body, and spirit.

Native American wisdom reveres animals as our teachers. Cultures have honored birds over the centuries, even worshiped them. Seeing this same connection between birds and humans, I view them as my access to higher states of mindfulness. Whether as messengers to the gods, or as instruments of knowledge, they are my teachers. *The birds make my world bigger.*

POCKET NOTE:

"Free your mind and the rest will follow."—En Vogue (from Free Your Mind, by Thomas McElroy, Denzil Foster @1992) What constraints of my mind keep me from flying?

From the time Kenge went on the run until I was indicted, I was in limbo. I felt his loss so intensely, and uncertainty was my constant companion. I started a practice of watching the sun rise every morning.

I remember a particularly cold winter month. I walked to a field near my house to watch the sun rise. I get there just before the sun rises so that I am not standing around in the zero-degree weather for very long waiting for the sun. I notice that there are a couple of red-tailed hawks up in the pines that line the field, waiting for the sun, just like me on this chilly morning. I wonder what kind of night they had and how much they must yearn for the warmth of the sun.

This inspired me to write a poem, "Birds & Death," about six months after Kenge left. My loss was so profound and somehow death, even an imagined death, always brings life into sharp focus. Little did I know how birds would become for me such a frequent subject of contemplation and reflection.

Watching the birds, I'm living the questions. Who am I? What is freedom? What's the difference between a crow and a raven?

When I got here, it seemed like there were lots of ravens. I'd see one by the track, then one by The Boneyard looking down at me, making a lot of noise. I wasn't adept back then at telling the difference between crows and ravens. I would look at a big black bird and think, *He's big. I bet he's a raven.*

I've heard that Ravens have a Roman beak. Not sure exactly what that looks like. Is it the curved-out nose like Barbra Streisand or Adrien Brody? Growing up, we had a horse that folks said had a Roman nose. It curved out a little bit.

Both ravens and crows have signature sounds, but I'm not sure I recognize the difference. According to the dictionary, ravens "croak." The American Heritage Dictionary describes the raven's sound as "commonly heard as the classic gurgling croak, rising in pitch and seeming to come from the back of the throat. It's much deeper and more musical than a crow's simple, scratchy caw."

JOURNAL:
Ahh! There are just two ravens here! The others are crows! Ravens have the big, curved beaks and they're definitely larger than the crows. They always hang out together. Hearing them talk to each other I get it. Now I hear the difference. That's a caw, and that's a croak!

I name the two ravens, Caesar and Beatrice. These two ravens have claimed this land with the two prisons as their territory. Caesar and Beatrice make this place their home.

There are a lot of crows, but they just show up in the morning to find food, hang out for a while, and in the evening they leave.

Crows contain the medicine of "Law," the laws of nature, laws of the universe. Ravens are the medicine of magic. I think it's their color, the iridescent black that imbues them with magic. I've heard women say, "Those birds are so ugly." I don't see that at all. Where's the ugly? The ravens are beautiful birds!

JOURNAL:

It's the first day over 100 degrees this year. I had oatmeal for breakfast and did yoga in the sun before it got hot. I see Caesar and Beatrice as individuals now. They were on watch this morning, trying their very best to scare off a hawk. They finally just leave the hawk alone and go about their business of getting some water from the track infield sprinklers. Caesar watches out for Beatrice when she is on the ground. He is up high, croaking.

One day as I am walking the track, Beatrice swoops down and catches a mouse. She flew over to the fence and started to eat it. Boom, a red-tailed hawk dives down toward her. Caesar, appears suddenly, and both ravens chase away the hawk. Without missing a beat, Beatrice goes back and picks up the mouse to finish her dinner.

Later when I talk to Greta about this, she tells me that the ravens are the smartest of the corvids and well-adapted to surviving. Clearly, these two birds have learned to survive and make this desert of dirt and cacti their home. Scavenging is still in their nature and checking out the dumpsters is still a must! And, they have become predators to survive.

JOURNAL:

How many ways am I adapting in response to my environment, my circumstance? I'm modifying myself and becoming someone different. What adaptations will I consciously and unconsciously change when I get out?

Some birds are easier to recognize than others. The noisy grackles, always yelling back and forth about something. The quiet flocks of small brown sparrows, always hang out in one particular type of tree. The doves coo while they scratch in the dirt. They all seem to have their own social circles.

> In this desert, my desert, lacking humaneness, lacking humans that I can seek comfort from, I seek out the animals. Why have the ravens chosen this place as their home? Aren't there better places to be? They could fly a hundred miles in any direction. Why here? I think it doesn't matter. I can look at this place as my home. The ravens are here. For now, I live in the present moment. I'm here.

I remember hearing a mom declare to her flock of children, "Get back here, you gaggle of geese." I found it hilarious that a flock of geese is called a gaggle. A flock of crows may be referred to as murder of crows and a flock of buzzards, a wake. Watching the buzzards circle high in the sky always makes me wonder if there is a dead animal for them to scavenge, so a wake makes sense. I especially like the "glittering" of hummingbirds and a "ballet" of swans.

Sometimes watching these birds, I think of the birds I see at home, but never here, like the kestrels. Kestrels are the smallest falcons, only about the size of a blue jay. Kestrels do not build nests; they look for cavities made by other birds or boxes built by humans to call home. At home, they fly swiftly to and fro, and I almost miss them because their small profile tricks my mind into thinking, *That's an insignificant bird.* No such thing.

I remember Jera showing me a video. "Mom, check this out, an epic fail!"

The video showed some birds flying low over the ocean. Suddenly a whale tail appears out of the ocean catching one of the birds, knocking it down out of the sky. "Isn't this an epic fail?"

"It is an epic fail for the bird," I replied, "but an epic win for the whale."

There are times when a single grackle hangs out in front of my unit. I find out that this grackle has formed a bond with one particular woman who feeds it all the time.

One day, I noticed the grackle was missing. I ask around and find out that someone killed it. Supposedly, she was throwing a rock at the pigeons and struck the grackle, killing it. This is not the end of the story. When she threw the rock at the pigeon, but killed the grackle, the same rock hit a wren. One rock, one throw, she also hit a tiny wren, killing it too! Literally, this woman killed two birds with one stone! I am appalled. *Epic fail!*

There are red-tailed hawks too. They do not live down here in the desert with me. They live in the air above. The red-tailed hawks break the upper limit of my prison, creating an added dimension to my boundaries. The sky is not just a glass ceiling—this is where the hawks live! When I see a red-tailed hawk, I can feel the energy of freedom. The wind under the wings, invisible, yet holding the capacity of freedom, freedom from gravity. To see a red-tailed hawk soaring above me, I long to have the sky as my home.

In falconry, a relationship is built between a bird and its human to the point that as long as the bird wears jesses, this bird will return to the human. A jess is a short leather strap attached to the leg of a hawk or falcon that allows a leash to be attached. When the jesses are removed, the bird is allowed to fly unrestricted. Now it's free, released into the wild.

JOURNAL:
> I am having a Buddhist moment. I know there are prison walls surrounding me and I am not trying to tear down the walls. I'm being released from my jesses. Liberated from my conditioned mindset.

Jeff, Jera's therapist, writes to me that one day while riding his bike in my neighborhood thinking and praying for me, he sees *three* eagles circling in the sky. As he watched in amazement, he realized that the eagles were circling directly over my house. Eagle medicine is the power of the Great Spirit, the connection to the Divine. It is the ability to live in the realm of Spirit, and yet remain connected and balanced within the realm of Earth. *This is a good omen!*

There are a lot of pigeons in our compound. They are always underfoot on our patio area. They are flying in, flying out, and if you are not used to them, there are times you might think that they will hit you, they are flying so close. I see a new inmate duck as the pigeons fly, and I realize I have become accustomed to them. We all experience the pigeons differently. Some women throw rocks at the pigeons all the time. Other women feed them.

Many pigeons have mangled feet, missing toes, etc. Of course, we hear stories that the male inmates set traps for them. *To eat them?* I know how to pluck and gut a chicken. Maybe somebody else here does too. Or is it a mishap with the razor wire? They must learn not to land on the razor wire.

One early spring morning, as I walk down to breakfast, I hear a sound that I don't recognize. The two tall eucalyptus trees are in bloom. It is cloudy and a bit cold. I look up and see hundreds of hummingbirds in the tops of the eucalyptus trees. I think the hummingbirds are hungry and in need of energy. Or maybe they are feeling spunky and have decided to play tag all morning so that I can see their amazing energy, their beauty, and hear their little chirps. I've never seen so many hummingbirds in one place at one time. *It's a glittering of hummingbirds!*

For this moment, I wish the trees were not so tall, or that I was taller, so I could take in this amazing sight. Hummingbird medicine brings joy, beauty, and love. The Mayan teachings tell us that the hummingbird medicine can solve the riddle of the contradiction of duality. This reminds me of Jera's story of the hummingbird and the forest fire. Oh, I wish I could share with him this incredible, spectacular display of hummingbird life.

The birds weave throughout my day. The noise from the shooting range pierces the tranquility of my concrete mat. My mind seeks out the sounds of the doves to ignore the sounds of shooting. *Listen to the doves. Come back to the doves.* Another mediation.

The doves hang out in the shorter eucalyptus trees near my concrete mat. This is a softer tree, without thorns. I spend anywhere from one to three hours per day right here at this spot. As the doves peck in the dirt under the tree, I find the sound the doves make soothing.

Doves are amazing birds. For a long time, I did not know that doves and pigeons belong to the same family. What we consider to be a "dove" versus "pigeon" is mostly our perception. Both dove and pigeon refer to the 308 species of birds from the Columbidae family. There's no difference between a pigeon and a dove in scientific nomenclature. However, they do exhibit different behaviors.

One of the most incredible things I know about doves is that when their chicks hatch, both males and females feed them "crop milk." Crop milk is like colostrum, the first milk that mammals produce for their young. Rich in protein and fat, it is secreted by the adults' crop lining and is regurgitated to the chicks. Feeding the chicks in this way boosts their chance at survival.

JOURNAL: Prison is isolation from life. However, the birds and their medicine reconnect me to Life beyond. The birds connect me to life, wholeness, and Spirit. That's freedom.

When I was nearing the age that my mother never lived, I decided to get a tattoo. To honor where I came from, I decided on a swallow tattoo. The swallow in Mexican folklore represents home, as swallows are said to always return to the same nest every year. They also represent happiness and love.

For a sailor, the swallow tattoo was historically used to show the sailor's experience. The first swallow tattoo on the arm or the chest demonstrates having been out on the water for at least five thousand nautical miles. The second swallow tattoo would be upon returning home after sailing at least ten thousand nautical miles. This tradition honors the incredible length of a swallow's migration of upward of eight thousand miles. And it is also said that if the sailor drowns, the swallows will carry their soul to heaven.

I had indeed put in many miles on my journey of life. Later, I learned from a Japanese chiropractor that the swallow represents the samurai's sword, for the way the swallow flies. He explained that the sword represents discernment. How wonderfully fitting for my Buddhist practice. Discernment itself is regarded as an intentional action.

JOURNAL:
How many times I've wondered what brought me here? Was there one thing that brought me here or many tiny deviations? What might have I done differently? Science, neurochemistry, and psychology stress the importance of not reliving our stories. Now I discover Buddhism corroborates this. It calls me to step outside of my suffering.

I imagine my mind like a bus passing from one place to another collecting thoughts along the way. At one stop, it gets filled up with worries of Jera. At another bus stop, my mind fills up with thoughts of how I will make it after I get out. I can choose to step off the bus, leave my thoughts on the bus, and now I'm not my thoughts. I'm full of emptiness, and a clean slate.

JOURNAL:
Emptiness is a freedom; in emptiness, all things are possible. Freedom can be seen from many different vantage points. A commitment provides freedom to have a path to run on. Freedom without commitment is being without direction. When birds mate for life it is a freedom! Isn't it interesting how perceived limits may not be the true limits?

Birds have always been important throughout my life. Maybe before prison, I just never saw them in all their wholeness. I'm always learning something about the birds, or from them.

In Samuel Taylor Coleridge's *The Rime of the Ancient Mariner*, a sailor kills an albatross, which brings bad luck to the crew, and subsequently, he is made to wear the albatross from a rope around his neck as penance. The albatross is a centuries-old metaphor for unbearable burdens. And it is considered extremely unlucky to kill an albatross.

The albatross comes to mind when I think of sentencing. A prison sentence is a sentence of disconnection. The prison society always finds a way to isolate. Nothing belongs to me. Touch is off-limits. There's no connection to living creatures. I've heard of prisons where the inmates raise and train guide dogs. That sounds incredibly wonderful. I even heard an inmate once say, "If I had my dog here, I'd be fine." *I miss my dog!*

When I'm confined to my room, it's hard not to feel claustrophobic. It has floor space of about five by eight feet with a small metal desk bolted to the wall and one plastic chair. Above the desk is a cork board, the left half for me and the right half for my bunkie. This is the only place we are allowed to put up pictures, drawings, and cards from home. When I sit here, I stare at my son, the beautiful cards from my sister, or turn to my right to look out of our window.

My window overlooks a triangle of dirt and the concrete path leading from our units to the outdoor fitness area and the track. I am looking down from the second floor at the top of a couple of acacia trees. Trees so thorny that no birds hang out there.

One day while looking out that window, I see something swaying from a branch, about half the size of my fist. A bird hanging by its feet in the tree outside my window! It is obviously dead. It looks like a small brown sparrow. I never see these sparrows in the acacia trees. *What is it doing there?*

It is well-camouflaged; I must look hard to find it. There are days I think that maybe it has disappeared. I look again and there it is. *How in the world did it get there?* What storm of perfect circumstances collided to leave this little bird dead, hanging upside down from this tree outside my window? It is the hanging bird.

There is no way to get it down from the tree. It's too high up. So, every day I look and there it is day after day, hanging by its feet, swaying in the breeze. Maybe this bird was working on building a nest, carrying a piece of string. When it stopped, for only a second, on this small branch and a gust of wind wrapped the string around the branch, entangling the bird's feet?

A koan is a riddle or puzzle that Zen Buddhists use during meditation to help them unravel greater truths about the world and about themselves.

My little, dead sparrow dangling by a string from a branch is like a koan. I can't come up with a scenario that makes sense.

I've got to learn to live the questions.

BIRDS & DEATH

Wake up!
Moving into the sun
The Red Tails share the first rays
Live the question, live everything
Even when it's too dark to see
Sorrow's light blinds me with the demise of another self

A murder of crows plays in the snow
Living the naive life on the battlefield
Surviving in the noise of a war
Not suspecting the mad outlaws around them
Until the whale wins and you are knocked out of the sky

The Kestrel feigns flying with a broken wing
Keeping my own safe through assault after assault
Hover and dive, holding the fear inside
Creating a gaping wound
Slowly bleeding to death looking for a nest to call my own

Golden eagles rise to meet Spirit and hunt
Talons effortlessly pierce the skull of a hare
Realization of potential to transmute damage
Allow yourself to be changed, commit yourself to change
Otherwise, you die with your eyes open, still searching

Ferruginous, "royal hawk"
Sky-dancers, grasping each other's beak and interlocking talons
Falling, spinning no control, screaming and calling

Buddha Behind Bars

Loosen ourselves, liberated from the jesses
Breaking open won't be such a shock

Merlins pluck prey out of the air, hunting on the wing
Magic in the existence of raw collisions
A lasting space to allow the Divine through
Missing you sneaks up on me, a hole in my universe
Even what sustains you can kill you, so let go

Albatross's flying heart rate near resting
Able to drink seawater, balance of life heartening
Live fully this precious short life
No need to bear a sentence around my neck
Pray as the albatross falls, opening up to see true beauty

Swallow's flight cutting like a samurai's sword
Nests of mud, holding me strong and warm, coming home
Make the journey, earn my mark
One breath separates us from the next life
Allow yourself to close your eyes content this life was lived

Doves echo the mourning sounds
Without delay the momentous process of death is revered
A bird with milk for their young
Prayer and the struggle for strength grants us hope
Keep my loved ones around me and let the harps play when I die

These birds mate for life!

—Collin Ruiz, ©2010

Sixteen:

BECOMING A CREATURE OF MY HEART:
HONORING SILENCE

A reconceived identity transforms perception and behavior.
A reconceived body transforms experiences and their meaning.

—Author Unknown

I FEEL THE FREEST WHEN I WALK around the track. It is (almost) alone time. I am in my own world unless someone is walking and talking to me. I am moving and moving has always helped ground me. One foot in front of the other, a simple walking meditation. For just a little bit more privacy and quiet I walk against the flow. Today, I'm using my newest mantra: *Going to open up to wonder today.*

At the center of the paved track is one of the very few grassy areas in our compound. And we are never allowed on the grass. They water the grass with the non-potable water from our water treatment ponds. They watered the grass this morning. I'm walking on the outer edge, far away from the grass because the stink is robust. When the sprinklers are on, they send the foul odor far and wide. This makes walking around the track almost unbearable.

I have three choices: walk on the paved track, walk on the dirt on the outer edge of the paved track, or cheat and walk on the grass just along the inner edge of the track. I like the feeling of connecting with the earth, so I try to stay off the pavement. Walking in the dirt isn't so bad, but I must watch out for the rattlesnakes. When I want to stare at the sky, I walk in the grass.

Move us, our mindfulness into a full embrace of life. Walking with mindfulness. Surfing the waves, a meditative attitude strengthens our capacity to handle life's difficulties, anger, and negativity. Be fearless meaning, dare to be, and be gentle.

In the Theravada Buddhism tradition of my teacher, mindfulness begins by paying attention to the breath. Then you notice everything that comes up in your consciousness: the body sensations, thoughts, and emotions. The various schools of Buddhism use different methods of meditation, incorporating mantras, walking meditations, breathing exercises all in the effort to clarify and illuminate the mind.

Walking around the track has become my daily ritual. I can't remember a day when I didn't walk, except during a lockdown. Or maybe it was one of the three rainstorms we experienced that put us in lockdown.

When I walk the track, I listen to my music, chant under my breath, think, or just listen. A couple times, I've walked and cried allowing my sadness to quietly flow onto the track. The track and the phones are the only places that I see other inmates crying.

Most people think of mindfulness as simply a relaxation technique. However, a calm, relaxed body and mind is just the first step. Attentive calmness in a meditative state enables the ability to notice everything without being hooked by whatever you experience. This "equanimity," as it's called, allows for the awareness of the big questions behind the thoughts or feelings. Questions such as *Why am I resisting change? What is my reality? And what does my reality offer me?*

Sam Harris, an author and teacher of mindfulness, captures the essence of mediation simply and clearly: "Meditation develops our capacity to prioritize what we pay attention to. We become what we pay attention to. Why not free your attention from all the trivial things that are clamoring for it? Why not pay attention to those things that make you a better person? The more you practice, the more degrees of freedom you will find in managing where you put attention."

At times, I walk around the track imagining myself lying on the grass in the middle of the track, arms-wide, staring up at the sky. The urge to lay in the grass can be strong at times, but I don't do it, not once, not one single time! Sometimes, I can see this as my quiet place; I imagine the silence at the center of the field.

I would love to roll up my short sleeves to feel the breeze on my arms. However, it stresses me out because the rules don't allow me to lie in the grass or to roll up my sleeves. And some guards are very strict and more than anything I don't want to stand out and be noticed.

Ugh! I don't want this to be my meditation for today! I take a deep breath to let go of the thoughts and I keep my sleeves unrolled. I really do want to "free my attention from all the trivial things that are clamoring for it," as Sam Harris said. *Spirit, what is here for me to learn? To unlearn?*

Today as I walk around the track, I work on a meditative visualization. I visualize light at my core, healing my pain. Then I imagine the light radiating outward from my core and I listen to whatever comes up. When a thought or feeling comes up, I mull it over for some time.

It's not that I mull my thoughts in a circular way or think about the one thought deeply. In a meditative space, when I notice thoughts as the arise, I don't go down the rabbit hole of thought as easily. I listen to what the newly arisen thought is trying to tell me. I listen as if listening to water in a brook: *what does the sound of water want to tell me about water?*

Whether meditating, chanting under my breath, or just being mindful, sometimes my observations can be quite amusing.

When I got to prison, I thought I would explore my habits and practices, like shaving my legs. *Why do I do it? What do I get out of it?*

My grandmother's generation was bombarded with ads persuading them to shave their legs and underarms. Marketers appealed to women's insecurities just as fashion exposed more of their bodies through shorter hemlines and sleeves. They even played on a stereotype that associated hairiness with "primitive" races. Sales of razors and blades boomed while new cultural norms shamed women to go to great lengths to remain "feminine, clean, and fair-skinned."

I see these norms persist even today as women pluck hairs from their faces, arms, and legs.

As I've begun to let my hair grow, I notice my prickly leg hairs poking through my socks. Well, this is something I've never experienced. It cracks me up, and I can't help smiling to myself.

As it starts to get warmer, the commissary offers some optional apparel (for purchase) such as silky men's basketball shorts to wear in our "free" time. Walking around the track I feel the wind in my hair. But it's my leg hair! Now that it's grown out, it's a totally different sensation. *That does it, I can't take it!* I decide to shave my legs for the remainder of my time. Wind in my hairy legs is such a distraction!

Today as I walk, I pass a woman I realize that she is crying. I don't say anything, I want to give her space to have her sadness. I've cried here before. I remember coming out to the track on Thanksgiving morning. It was my first major holiday spent in prison. A Thanksgiving not to be ignored. I didn't feel like saying, "Happy Thanksgiving." I was not happy.

JOURNAL:

Thanksgiving morning. The song in my head: "Whenever you call me, I'll be there. Whenever you want me, I'll be there. Whenever you need me, I'll be there, I'll be around." Of course, that's all I can remember of The Spinners' song and all I can think about is Jera so far away. I cry and go walking around the track before the sun rises. Yoga. Eating. Yoga. Writing. Reading. Listening to music. This is my Thanksgiving.

Prison is something I *do*. I follow the rules. In every culture, people feel a pressure to conform; however, prison *demands* that I conform. We wear the same clothes, and we have lost our names, all to standardize the women beneath the clothes. Prison tries to tell me I'm someone I don't know, someone as contrived as this environment. *What does "living authentically" look like in here?*

The guards and even the other inmates generally relate to me like an inmate, a criminal, as my essential identity. That alone is such a distortion.

Prison life often has a disorienting, hallucinatory quality. The limited connection to the outside world makes prison feel like a separate world, in and of itself, which of course it is. However, it's more than that. Something doesn't add up. I feel somewhat out of sync. Walking around the track I ask myself, *What am I? Who am I?* I feel that there is so much at the edge of my awareness that *this* experience and *this* perspective may allow me to discover.

Today, I woke up with a tear in my eye—it is my brother's birthday. The second of his birthdays since I've been here. It's hit me that celebrating with him might not ever happen again. We both have found ourselves in strange new worlds. If I ever do see him again, everything will be different. I long to have celebrations with him, if only in my dreams.

It occurs to me that identification comes (in part) from the observation of myself in relation to others. Observation of self in relation to others is just one layer of identity. My brother Kenge's absence becomes the first steppingstone in my re-conceiving of myself. As I wonder about Kenge's existence, questions arise about my own existence.

POCKET NOTE:

"Spiritual growth is a fine-tuning of our ear to the needs of our heart"—Rodney Smith

Kenge was the brother I cared for as he grew up. He slept in my bed when my mother was pregnant with our next sibling. From that point on, he was my kid. I was responsible for him. I'd carry him on my hip all day, making sure he was fed and cared for.

As an adult, he was my best friend and my brother. I could talk to him about the mundane. I would call him on my way to work at 8 a.m. and tell him about a funny license plate I just saw! Or I'd call crying when I was overwhelmed and had no idea how I was going to pay my mortgage. I wanted to be part of his life. He supported me and I wanted to do the same. He was there for me.

As our worlds fell apart, we both have had to deal with the unraveling of our identities. There is so much unlearning to do. I will never blame Kenge for my prison time. He's living his prison time, too.

JOURNAL: Events have ripped apart the fabric of my reality. Pieces of me come back together and a new shape takes form. Some pieces no longer have any use while new pieces add more dimension to my "self." Identity influences everything.

Stepping on the track, I can walk to the right or the left. Even such a simple choice creates a new meditation intention. I walk to the right when watching the sunsets. Walking around the track is the best way to watch the sunsets. We have *beautiful* sunsets! Walking right takes me farthest away from camp with a length of the track to look at the sky. It takes only a few clouds on the horizon to get amazing oranges and yellows. I keep walking and I watch the dark blues and purples come out.

Is Kenge watching a sunset, too? My walking meditation encourages me to go deeper than when I'm just thinking. The big questions want answers. When I contemplate the relationship between Kenge and me, I question myself. I question my Dharma.

Dharma, the seed from which my existence as Collin begins. My dharma includes the fact that I was born a first child, that I was born a female, born from my specific parents. How did my past shape me into the person that I am now? How mutable are my beginnings? Is my identity strictly based on the roles I've assumed, or adapted to, in life? How much of my identity is based on the expectations of my society, culture, and family?

Once, while I was talking with my lawyer, he said I was being a martyr. He added that he suspected I had always been a martyr within my family. I was not at all happy about this. Being here now, I think long and hard about what it might mean to be a martyr and about who I really was. *Did I go to prison for my brother?*

Pocket note:

"We're swimming upstream, against the current of habitual consciousness."

How many of my actions come from "habitual consciousness?" *All of them?* Perhaps only actions that come from my beginner's mind are new. However, I need to look deeper at this idea of my habitual martyrdom. Would I choose to suffer rather than contradict my beliefs? *Yes.* When does it come time to question my beliefs? Now, and always now.

Pocket note:

We exist as a thought believed.

Lifting one foot, setting the other foot down. Buddhism teaches to allow your feet to kiss the ground. As I walk, thoughts, feelings, and sensations arise and fall away. That's mindfulness. As Sam Harris says, "It's simply a state of clear, nonjudgmental, and undistracted attention to the contents of consciousness whether pleasant or unpleasant."

Let me put my "contents of consciousness" out into the light. What responsibilities, burdens are mine to carry? My responsibilities, my burdens are the ones that are mine alone. This prison sentence is my burden. I take ownership of this burden. I was born and subsequently became the oldest of five siblings; that is not a burden.

JOURNAL:

Labels can become burdens. "To practice nonattachment, we let go of the roles we've bought into and the labels we've stuck to ourselves. When we shed all our stories, with their limiting roles and confining identities, and become a mystery unto ourselves, we're practicing non-attachment. In many spiritual traditions, to become a monk or a nun you have to shed your nice clothes, shave your head, and don a simple and cheap robe so that you won't be perceived by anyone as a person of any importance. You're forced to find your reference point internally instead of externally. You detach from the labels you've created for yourself or that you allowed to be created for you."—Alberto Villoldo

I've often wondered, *is going to prison my karma? Am I paying dues for something I've done?* And if so, when did my karma in all this begin? Was it six months ago when I got indicted? A year prior when my brother Kenge ran? Or when I killed the spider that ran across my kitchen floor?

Or am I thinking about this all wrong? What if karma is circular instead of our past-present-future rut of linear thinking? Maybe karma lives outside of time and space so that cause and effect happen simultaneously in every moment.

What I have accepted as my karma certainly plays a role in my identity. Was I meant to suffer? I create a new mantra: *I choose to embrace happiness, be peaceful, be serene, learn to let go, accept whatever comes, have the courage to face my fears, be forgiving.*

The roles I fell into or held onto have shaped my perspective. There was a time that being responsible for my younger siblings was required, *but is it anymore?* Can holding my family sacred look different than it has in the past?

Becoming mindful of our perspectives and past thoughts creates an opening for something new.

As I look over at the men's prison, I think about my brother and feel a void inside. Which is the crueler prison? I am most certain that he thinks that prison is worse for me than whatever life he is living. I believe that wherever he is, it must be a worse prison than the one I am in. I have a light at the end of my tunnel—Jera is waiting for me.

My mindset is shifting. The level of dread has begun to release. I can do very little to change the reality of being imprisoned. Perhaps prison is just the container I sit in. Who and what I am within this container, determines my experience.

POCKET NOTE:

"We are not here to change the world; the world is here to change us" —Shantideva

Kenge was fiercely loyal to those he considered friends. They were like family to him. He felt that friends should look out for each other. But when he ran, that didn't happen. The court proceedings revealed that almost all the people indicted rolled on everyone else. I read a statement from one of them. He claimed he saw me at my brother's birthday party. *How ridiculous is that?* What does that prove? Why wouldn't I be at my brother's party?

Kenge must have felt very alone and betrayed by his friends, those he considered his "family." If his people didn't step up, what did that say about him? After all this went down, what was left of his identity, family, and home? He has been stripped of being a father and a sibling. The path he took looks so bleak from here.

I remember a great passage on "emptiness" from *Clouds in Each Paper* by Thich Nhat Hanh. "Emptiness is not nothingness, emptiness is not, the not, it's everything. A flower, a bird, the sky is full. Full of the sun and the moon, full of water and earth, full of our own consciousness and the universe." There are so many ways to describe emptiness. I think I get it, then my understanding evaporates, and I'm not so sure.

Thich Nhat Hanh continues, "There is a cloud hovering within this sheet of paper. Without a cloud, there cannot be any rain; without rain, the trees cannot grow; and without trees, we cannot make paper. The cloud is essential for the paper to exist. If the cloud is not here, the sheet of paper cannot be here either." *Okay, so the paper is full. And empty. It's empty of anything that is only "paper."*

What a beautiful day for a walking meditation! The sky is empty. The sky is full. I do think that it would be so cool if I could bottle up some sky. Just grab even a handful of that blue sky. If I had a handful of blue sky, would anyone believe that is what I had in my hands? Emptiness *is* the sky. Prison is emptiness. Prison cannot be one thing; therefore, it is empty. I am here and I can be the sky, much more expansive than prison. The track never fails to offer up insights.

My music playing through my earbuds can be the best feeling. The earbuds can block out the noise of prison, which creates a silence within the music. When I hear Flo Ride sing, "Sometimes I get a good feeling," I'm singing along. I'm reimagining who I am, someone with this new good feeling. I have that good feeling now! (Good Feeling, © 2011 Flo Rida, et al.)

Dreaming that I'm still a sister to my brother Kenge, he is present in the way my feet kiss the earth, this walking meditation. It's time for me to reimagine the individual relationships between me and my siblings, peel back the expectations and assumptions, to look at the heart of our relationships, my heart. Kenge's absence is of major consequence in my life. He has had a hand in shaping my heart. With so much love in my heart, I imagine it bursting with happiness and joy if I saw him again. In my imagination, we sit and talk for hours, share wonderous meals, and celebrate. Could we be more real with each other? Can we work more happiness into our new identities?

Kenge's children all tell me that they are the best humans ever because of what their dad taught them. "He taught me how to work hard, play hard and how rewarding snowboarding, fishing, hunting, even bowling could be." They all say, "Of course, we had to earn it, but with hard work, we learned that we could stand on our own two feet." "Our dad, Kenge, showed us that we are capable of making a life for ourselves."

"He taught us not to be afraid." My nephew tells a story of when he was eight years old and walking home by himself in the dark. He's walking from one house on our family's three-hundred-acre land to another house across a stream and by a stand of oak trees.

"I was scared, wondering what could jump out of the dark. Then I tightened my hands into fists and thought, *Whatever comes out of the dark is going to get a fight.* After that, I wasn't afraid. My dad taught me, 'Don't waste time being afraid.'"

Most of all Kenge taught us how important family is. "Family before anything else."

For Jera, Kenge was the "big, strong uncle with lots of cool things like his tanks of big fish." Jera called him, "The man with the plan." He rescued us when we wrecked our car. He initiated and organized great trips, to the Renaissance Festival, skiing, birthday parties. Even going out to eat dinner was fun.

One time, he took the kids to get a car wash at the local car wash fundraiser. Jera had eaten something that disagreed with him, so while the young women were washing the outside of the car, Jera was puking inside. Kenge just laughed it off. He paid extra for the young women to clean out the inside of the car once Jera was done puking. Jera was so relieved and appreciative that Kenge didn't get mad at him.

He always made Jera feel he was part of the group. I remember how he had Jera chalk his cue stick between each shot. Jera loved Kenge so dearly.

POCKET NOTE:

Transformation—shedding from the ordinary womb and transforming into the immortal bones. Zen of the Wild Foxes

JOURNAL:
Who am I? Who am I? I ask my heart, Who am I? I ask the being at my core as she sits on a lotus flower. Who am I? I ask the Universe. I am no one thing.

As I go deeper into silence, first I imagine a happy place, a clearing in the woods with the soft sounds of the wind in the trees. This is the still place inside me. I imagine that one day I can sit with my brother, my head on his shoulder, in silence. The first word I would offer is, grace.

I don't know where I read the words "creature of my heart." I wrote down, "becoming a creature of my heart." My heart feels bigger than my head, and closer to my skin than ever before. It feels raw. I used to experience life mostly through my thoughts and mind. Now I can't help but feel everything through my heart.

Oh, I miss you, brother!

Seventeen:
ALMOST HOME

JOURNAL:

I wonder what it looks like out there. The world has no doubt changed, because I have changed.

TOMORROW, I LEAVE THIS PLACE! Finally!

I'm leaving prison, but I won't be going home just yet. They are sending me to a halfway house to reacclimatize me to society. Fortunately, they count time in the halfway house toward my sentence. I'm sent there three months prior to my release date. My probation sentence of three and a half years of supervision begins *after* my release date. The halfway house and probation offer only a taste of freedom.

Many dreadful stories circulate in prison about halfway houses and probation officers. I have seen inmates return after breaking probation. One gal went to see her ailing mother in another state. She stayed a day later than expected and ended up back in prison. However, I haven't met any inmates who have been to the halfway house where I am headed to in Colorado. So, I'm not sure what to expect.

Even though there is an option to have a friend or family member transport you from prison to the halfway house, I'll be taking a bus. I talked to my siblings about picking me up, but it is not going to work out for anybody to do that. The bus ride from prison to the halfway house will take over twenty-four hours.

I will live in a halfway house for an undetermined amount of time. Jera will continue to stay with my siblings over seven hours away. In all likelihood, I won't see him until I'm allowed back into my own house, weeks or months from now. Even though my house now sits empty, I'm not sure when I will be allowed to go home.

Between Phoenix and Fort Collins, I'll have a four-hour layover in Albuquerque. Mesa has offered to bring Jera to Albuquerque to be with me for a few hours. It's been over a year and a half since I've been with Jera without guards, without the prison surroundings. I'm looking forward to the layover with every fiber of my being!

I can't imagine myself—who I would be—without my son. I've learned so much about love by loving him. I've been moved to tears watching him, filled with pride, gratitude, and awe. I am looking forward to being his mom again!

When I talked with Jera about getting out, he seemed a little worried and a little concerned. He said, "Maybe you could move up here?" When we left Fort Collins, he was in junior high school, and now he'll be in high school. A new school again. I know even small changes have always been very challenging for him. One thing will be familiar—we will be back to the same house, our home.

Jera has had to go on living more and more of his life without me in it, without my direction and daily presence. I feel that I've missed so much of my son's life. My heart aches.

JOURNAL:

What's *being home* going to be like? I feel a tightening throughout my whole body. Breathe, practice being present. Being present means I must be here, until I'm not. How can I bring my mind back here when there is so much to anticipate and even dread?

Word of someone's release date spreads very quickly. I had someone asking for my Wolverine boots the day after I found out my release date. I think my bunkie told her friends so that they have first crack at my best stuff. Now inmates are coming by all the time. "Can I have your footlocker when you leave? Your boots?"

My bunkie tells me what I need to be released. I should get a duffle from the commissary and that's all I will walk out with. What will I wear at the halfway house? I have packed a few things. My gray clothes, they are the clothes I bought in prison. I also have some papers including several pages of rules stating how I am still a ward of the state and all the things I can't do. I was able to send my notes, letters, and pictures that I had in prison to Vida so they would be safe. Everything else I give away.

Tonight, I'm going to bed for the last time in prison. It's routine and different at the same time, I'm very tense. I can't stop thinking, *Are they going to call my name? Will I really be able to walk out of here?* Just like I couldn't imagine what walking in would be like, I can't picture myself walking out of here.

How am I going to handle all the stresses outside? I've heard inmates express real distress as their release date nears, questioning if they are going to make it *out there*. Inmates don't always *want* to leave when the time comes. I've even seen inmates break rules to get additional time. *What kind of job will I get as an ex-con? Will I be able to pay my bills? What will my probation officer be like?*

JOURNAL:

Prison has been an experience of living out loud from my core, even though mostly in silence. I'm not the same person who walked in here. A lot of women leave as Christians. I leave as a Buddhist. Did this time turn me into a Buddhist? Has my time in this "monastery" made any difference in who I am? Or was Buddhism just a crutch? I wonder who I will be when I'm out there?

And what am I going to wear? I've had lots of dreams in the last couple months about jewelry. I've read many different opinions about adornment. Buddhism considers adornment, jewelry, as material attachment. Someone said jewelry represents the desire to make things appear different than they really are. *Is that always the case?* I want to be true to myself. I see Buddhism as the practice of *awakening to who we really are.* I like the idea of adornment for the purpose of defining myself, expressing who I truly am. I'm eager to discover my sacred adornment.

As soon as I get my release date, I am allowed to have someone on the outside send me clothes. I have heard inmates talk on and on about what they want to wear out. One friend sent her husband a very detailed list, clothes to walk out in and clothes for the halfway house. She also had a list of makeup, even the specific shade of lip liner to go with the color lipstick she wanted. I saw inmates with clothing catalogs their significant others had sent in so that they could pick clothes they wanted to wear out.

My sister sent some of my old clothes that I had left at her house right before I went to prison. The clothes that I didn't care that much for. However, I won't see them until I dress out. After every part of my life was packed away, I had just a few clothes that were comfortable and I wasn't worried if they weren't there when I got out. *Will they fit me?*

Another thing that hasn't crossed my mind in a long time: *what do I look like?* There are no scales to weigh oneself. The only mirror is the reflective metal in the bathroom. Our uniforms are baggy, so gaining or losing a little bit of weight is not noticeable.

JOURNAL:

Now I'm upset. What am I upset about? Is it that I want new clothes? Is it that I feel totally dependent on my family? Of course, I'll do whatever my family needs of me. That's what family is all about, right? Is it that I don't have a significant other? I've been alone and I feel alright with that. Yet, I still imagine a person asking me what I want. Not what is *sufficient,* but *what do I want.* I just want someone to care about what *I* want.

I'm awake, I'm leaving today! My bunkie asked to do my makeup. Sure! Why not? I leave my hair down, wear the necklace that Marcia made me. I have the small cheap duffle packed. I can't wait in my room; it feels so claustrophobic. I go to the art classroom.

Sitting alone in the art room, watching through the windows the other inmates going about their daily routines. Knots in my stomach. As I sit here, I'm already an outsider—not part of this group. As inmates, we always want the best for someone leaving. It's just hard that you are staying and it's not you leaving.

Finally, I hear my name on the intercom. I leap up and walk to the office. The guard gives me my clothes and I change. Jeans, t-shirt, underwear, bra, and a gray Colorado State hoodie. The gray hoodie just makes me laugh. I've been wearing nothing but shades of green and gray since I've been here. Of course, the guard says, "I hope I never see you again," he chuckles, and hands me fifty dollars in cash.

Then I am finally walking the walk. There are more people out than I expected, maybe a dozen. They yell at me and I hold back tears, I wasn't expecting this. I don't know what to say. I yell out, "Finally, underwear that fits!" They laugh. I see a friend waving with tears falling down her face. *Wow, they are here for me?* I know tears of sorrow are usually shed when no one is looking. I wish I could bring them with me. However, we each walk out into a different world, carrying different burdens. Being an ex-con on the outside looks different for each person.

I cried the most watching a woman leave who had been down over fifteen years. Even though I never got to know her, it felt like such a momentous occasion, like watching a birth. A new being going out into the great big world. This place has to change you. Because I felt a subtle shift in the prison environment when someone left, I wonder what the outside does with this new person in it. *How will the world change with me in it?*

Inmates, ex-cons, a group that nobody wants to be a part of. However, I've been doing my time, this world became mine, now I'm leaving. It's over, so quickly, I'm outside. I take a deep breath. And then I step into the van.

An inmate is driving the van taking me to the bus stop. I just stare out the window, not saying anything. I don't know what to say. I am watching normal people driving by in their normal lives and I feel very removed from normal. I can't imagine driving a car, being normal. Everything is going by so fast. Then we are there, and the driver must hurry back to prison.

There I am, standing in a parking lot, in the hot sun, in front of a very small office that says, "Greyhound Bus." I walk in, ask about my ticket, which the prison has purchased for me, then I have almost an hour to wait. There are only three chairs in the bus station. One is occupied and I feel like everyone is staring at me.

Across the street is a drugstore. I go in and I'm overwhelmed by the smell of beauty products, shelves with not one, not five, but seemingly hundreds of every type of beauty and household product. The notion of what I *need* versus what I *want* runs through my mind. Too much stuff, too many products that seem to leap out at me saying, *You need me*! I bought blueberry yogurt and a pair of earrings.

The bus is already quite full of people as I board and I look for someone not too scary, preferably a woman. I see a young woman playing a video game and sit next to her. Jeanie introduces herself to me. Then we are moving and I'm on my way to Colorado.

Jeanie is wearing a tube top. It is over a hundred degrees today, but the bus is freezing from the air conditioning. Jeanie talks a lot and I have nothing to say. I don't tell her I'm "fresh out." I tell her I'm going to see my son. I borrow her phone to call Mesa to find out if they are still going to be there when I get to Albuquerque. He says yes and is glad I'm on the road.

When we get to Albuquerque, Jeanie will continue overnight to the east while I'm going north. It was beastly hot in Phoenix, but now we're in Albuquerque in an ice-cold bus and Jeanie is chilly in her tube top. I give her my hoodie.

"Really? Are you sure you don't need it?" I assure her I will be fine and it's all hers. I think I made a friend for life.

I stand in front of the station under a streetlight, in a dreamlike state. Then out of the dark night, I see Jera and Mesa running toward me. Hugs as we rush away. I'm thinking, *Let's go be by ourselves for a little while.*

"I know a restaurant here," Mesa says, and he drives us there. Eating a late dinner, I marvel at the food. I'm eating salmon over salad and drinking earl gray tea! Choices and food made to be palatable and enjoyable, for the first time since going to prison. So many choices, I can hardly wait until I'm buying and cooking my own food and eating whatever I want.

Despite almost being overwhelmed by the good food, I can't get enough of my son. I watch Jera as if he is a newborn. I picked a bench to sit on so that I can be right next to him, with Mesa across from us. I can't get enough of Jera's voice. I hang onto his every word. I am looking with new eyes, seeing how much he has grown. He's not the boy I left. *This is my son!*

We are back at the station. Our time has gone by so quickly. "Oh, did you bring my clothes?" I ask Mesa. He opens his trunk and hands me the small suitcase I had packed with my clothes before I left for prison. He hands me some money, too. I still have an overnight bus ride to Colorado.

I feel a lump in my throat and tears welling up. I want so badly to go home with them. I want this prison experience to be over now! I don't want to let go of Jera. I want to keep touching him.

We don't know how long it will be until we are together again. Once again, it's so hard to say goodbye.

263

The overnight bus ride is blissfully uneventful. I arrive at the halfway house at midmorning.

Escorted to my room, I am assigned a top bunk. The windows are frosted so I can't see anything outside. There are five bunks, ten women in this one room. The bunk beds are so close together, if I reach out, I could touch the other bunk. There is a locker in between the bunks. We share one tiny bathroom. We share one sink, one toilet, and one shower stall. There is a whiteboard next to the bedroom door with names and chores listed. Country music is blasting out of a small radio sitting beneath the whiteboard.

When I arrive, there are only a few women in the room. Three women sleeping and one young gal sitting on a bunk, greets me abruptly. "Who the fuck are you?"

"Collin, and your name?"

"Sherry. See this list?" Pointing to a paper on the wall, she continued, "These are all the daily chores. Your job is to sweep the room every day and then check it off the list."

"Okay, got it," I said.

"We have to do a fucking piss test, nearly every goddamn day. So, check at the front desk to see if your name is on the list."

I go to walk the halls and check out whatever is available. The TV room is past the front desk, and I learn it is not always open. It is also used as the visiting room. There is a small closet-sized room with two washers and dryers. I'm guessing these are always busy. And last but not least is a room on a corner with windows on the two sides. It's the cafeteria. There's no kitchen here and they bring the food in on trays from the outside for every meal.

I'm starving. The minute I hear over the intercom "food is here," I go pick up a tray. A big glob of mush, a roll—I don't even bother tasting it. I drink the small carton of milk and wonder if it's going to get any better. Oh, now that's a laugh! The cafeteria room has a vending machine and a microwave. Not very many options in the vending machine, besides microwavable popcorn.

It's nothing new to me to have a lot of rules; it's just hard to figure out what they are. We have to check one list for our daily duties. Another list announces if we must take a piss test or if we have lost privileges. We hear other rules like "no dating ex-cons" from other inmates.

The front desk is the only place to get any information. However, when I ask how long I will be staying at the halfway house, I don't get a definitive answer. "You have to have a job before you can leave the halfway house." Or "You can stay here until your release date." My official release date isn't for three more months!

Unfortunately, I can't go back to working for myself as a nutritionist. Self-employment is not an option, so I set about applying for anything and everything. The computer room is open only a few hours per day. I find out I must sign up for a thirty-minute block and only four people are allowed in there at a time. It's the only place to use computers or check emails.

Sitting on my bunk, I notice that a gal has an energy drink that is not sold in the one vending machine. I go to the front desk and ask about bringing food in. She tells me that I'm allowed to walk to the nearby grocery store once a week. However, we are permitted only five canned food items and whatever dry items we can fit in our very small mailbox.

I get to go to the store! Walking outside into the grocery store is my first normal thing I've done in so long. I feel like everybody is staring at me. *What will I say if I will bump into someone I know?* I'm amazed as I walk up and down the aisles. All I've been eating is popcorn from the vending machine. Canned apricots and peaches are as close as I'm going to get to fresh fruit. Instant oatmeal will have to do. At least there are a variety of new flavors, blueberry cinnamon flax, chia oatmeal with brown sugar—well it's different than what I've been eating for years.

As women come in after work, I meet Mama J. She is about my age, whereas most of the other women are younger. Most seem to be in their twenties. Mama J tells me about her job. She works at a company that makes cell phone covers and she is so happy to be working. She wears the color purple. Her t-shirts have butterflies on them.

My first week feels dreadfully long. When I'm lying on my bunk that night, I can't imagine this place more insane. I'm used to the lights on, snoring, and someone coming in to count us. Now I am starving, I can't go outside except for an hour per day, and I get my first write-up for missing a piss test. I had looked at the sheet at the front desk first thing in the morning, but it had not been updated for that day. I failed to notice it later when they added my name.

I'm always cold because of the air conditioning. One gal tells me there is a closet of donated clothes I can go through. I rummage around in there, finding some jeans and a couple sweaters, indoors in July.

One day I walk into the bathroom while Mama J is getting out of the shower. Her whole body, front and back, is covered in one to two-inch scars. Later, I learned that her husband would duct tape her to a chair and stab her. She thought her husband would abuse their child, so she killed him. She hadn't told the authorities about the torture because her husband said he would kill her mother, and she believed him. She went to prison for twenty years.

I was only written up once in prison. Here, it seems like I'm always being written up. One time, I'm written up because when I was out applying for jobs. I stopped at a gas station to get gas in the car I borrowed from a friend, and I didn't bring back the receipt. I bought a yogurt, which is against the rules, and I was so stressed out, I forgot I had to turn in the gas receipt. I'm on the printed sheet the next day. There is no one to talk to, I've lost privileges, and I must be reviewed. I *really* dislike the halfway house. The halfway house seems like purgatory; the "purging" place halfway between heaven and hell. I prefer prison!

One day in the TV room, a gal is talking to her friends and it's impossible not to overhear the conversation. She is upset because she just found out that she could be sentenced to six months to a year in the halfway house. Her friends are telling her that she should consider doing her time in prison instead of here. I butt in, "Yes, prison is much better than here!"

My second month, I'm in the employment office. A man comes in to talk to the director. He asks her about guys needing jobs. He wants to hire a couple guys to dig ditches for Comcast cables. I overhear this and immediately jump in to say, "I'll do it! And I know another gal, Jessie very tough, she will work with me."

Once I go fetch Jessie, we introduce ourselves and he says "Okay, you're hired!"

Now I'm working! I can go home!

Not so fast. I learn that I can't go home right away. With good behavior, I can earn time to spend at my house. Certain requirements must be met before I even go visit my house, like have a landline installed. Once there is a landline, they can call me randomly to make sure I'm there.

Within two weeks, I've earned three hours per week at my house. I don't have a car so a gal lends me a bike to get over to my house. It's about a thirty-minute bike ride to get to my house. I must include the bike time in the three hours.

Finally, I visit my empty house. It's so quiet! I take off my shoes and go sit in the backyard. The sun, the grass, the privacy, it's a morsel of heaven. And then the phone rings. I jump up, race inside to answer it, again a weird phenomenon, I haven't had a phone for almost two years. The officer from the halfway house says, "Where have you been?"

"Here, at my house, by myself." *Where else would I be?*

"Why didn't you call in when you got there?

"What?" *You are calling me on a landline, at my house, where I'm supposed to be.*

"You were supposed to call in when you *arrived* at your house. I'm going to have to write you up." *Crap! Seriously?! We're playing a game of "Mother, may I?"*

One visit and I've already lost the privilege of coming home. I must earn back those privileges, and in the meantime, I'm only allowed one hour per day outside. *Oh my gosh, I'm at the end of my rope!*

Eighteen:
GO YOUR OM WAY

"This was the beginning of my understanding of lay Buddhism. A lay Buddhist is one who fully embodies his or her entire life of work, family, and relationships without spiritually prioritizing any activity. From this perspective all moments are equally precious, and whether we are practicing formal meditation on retreat or showing up for ordinary moments of our lay life, freedom is never diminished. The unequivocal resolve not to move away from where we are is essential. Once we abandon the belief that there is a more spiritually useful moment than the one we are in, we have embraced our life and infused it with the energy for awakening."

—Rodney Smith, *Undivided Mind,*
Becoming Whole

I'M ALMOST HOME, yet here I am in this frustrating halfway house. *Okay, breathe. Focus on my new job.* Digging ditches is hard, but I'm not complaining! I'm outside, we stop at the grocery store every morning on the way to work, and I'm getting paid!

And best of all, it means I get to go home! I ask around and I can't find anyone who will tell me definitively when I can go home.

The second week of work, Mike, who runs this crew, runs into some personal hardships. He has a young son who has many health issues and is in the hospital. That leaves just his partner, Tony, Jessie, and me.

Monday morning, Mike doesn't pick us up for work, and when I try calling, the phone just goes to voicemail. The next day, Tony comes to pick us up and we work with him for the next few days.

Friday, no one comes to pick us up and we don't get paid. Hmm. I leave messages, but never hear back. Days go by and I assume I don't have a job anymore.

Without a job, I ask what I can do to earn more home time. They tell me to ask the janitor if I can help clean. A week of mopping floors and washing windows and I have earned time to be at my house again.

Ahh. Back to my quiet, empty house. Everything I own is in my shed, so I start unpacking. Table, chairs, kitchen things, and clothes. Slowly it starts to feel right, like my home. While unpacking, I find some purple hair clips with butterflies on them. I don't remember them as mine. I give them to Mama J and her eyes well up with tears as she warmly thanks me.

When I meet my probation officer, he tells me that he is a former police officer and that he doesn't believe in going easy on criminals. *Oh boy.* I'm used to being treated *less than*; but this process is supposed to support me and integrate back into my new and improved life. *Doesn't feel like it.*

I keep wondering, *What monkey wrench will they'll throw in next?* As the stress increases, I think, *No wonder the recidivism rate is so high.* I can't help thinking about the women who have dealt with drug addiction. If I ever had a drug habit, I would definitely want to use now. Anything to relieve this overwhelming stress.

I seem to be waiting for something. I guess I'm waiting to get settled and I'm not sure how long I'll be here. This place is so static, and not in a good way. Everybody's squeezed into a tiny space. Everybody's tense and on edge. I'm tense. What's going on?

> Waiting—and reacting to waiting, I want to be done with all this! My one goal is to be home with my son, living a normal life. What am I supposed to be doing? Am I doing it right? I feel myself resisting structure, and yet my mind is more focused. That's good. Waiting is just another meditation, whether I'm leaning against a wall, sitting outside, or lying on my bunk.

I need my rituals, but my attempts to practice are thwarted. Even when I'm allowed outside, there is nowhere to walk; it's a small grassy area, a picnic table, and a rocky water area. I found out I could check out a yoga mat, however doing yoga between bunks or in front of our door doesn't work well with women always coming and going.

Here at the halfway house, I feel like I've been in a constant state of *what's next?* I've dropped out of the present moment. I left my monastery back in prison. Time to start back at the beginning: breathe.

Luckily, after only one week without a job, I got a new job in the deli department at Safeway.

And I have a counselor now. A couple days ago, the staff gave me a workbook and scheduled my first appointment with the counselor. At our first meeting, Claire asked if I wanted to go for a walk for my one-hour session. *Yes!* I jump at the chance to get outside and move!

In the two days I've had the workbook, I've almost finished it. She tells me that normally it would be a six-week project and we would be talking about each section. Claire tells me she's happy to talk about the workbook if I have any questions, but she just wants to get to know me and talk about getting out. I'm fine with that!

Calling Jera is more difficult these days. Jera is spending time between Greta and Mesa in New Mexico on his summer break. Even though I have my cell phone now, I can't keep it with me. I must check it out from the front desk. When Jera and I talk, I tell him I've been to our house, and that I'm working at Safeway, and that soon we will be home together.

I've been here two months and things are settling in a bit. I look forward to my Thursday walks with Claire. This week she greets me and says, "Let's go for our last walk." *What?!*

Claire sees my concern and chuckles. "You get to go home next Monday! I sigh. "Finally! That makes my day! Wow, I can't wait to tell my son."

To check out, I meet with another counselor who fits me with an ankle monitor. He tells me that I will have to call in daily to find out if I have a piss test. I had no idea that I would be going home with an ankle monitor. I will be on home arrest for a couple months.

My first night alone in my house is this clash of feelings. I'm very happy, comfortable, and at the same time feeling apprehensive. *Is this for real?!* I haven't been alone in so long, I feel awkward. I will feel better when Jera is here with me.

Finally, Jera can come home! We have so much to do because school starts in a week. I'm juggling family logistics so that Jera can pick up our dog and the rest of his things and come home.

A friend is driving my car from New Mexico. These small freedoms like having a car and being in my house feel strangely unsettling. Eventually I realize I'm entertaining a subtle fear that my freedoms could be taken away again.

Time for a new mantra: I am safe in my own home.

It's a beautiful day when they finally pull up. They arrive in a car and a pickup truck with sideboards full to the top with Jera's things.

Jera and our dog, Daphne, jump out. Daphne acts like she never left. I give Jera a big hug! I shout, "You're finally here!"

We are all milling about, unpacking the vehicle, and talking excitedly. "Look, Jera," I say, "We both have a mattress on the floor in our *own* rooms. We have a table and chairs. We even have a television. Can you believe it? We made it! We are home!"

It's time to find our new normal. I go to work. Jera rides the bus to and from school. We start living again.

I got a new probation officer, and she thinks it's cool that I'm a nutritionist. Every time she stops by she has a nutrition question for me. "What should I put in my smoothies?"

I don't socialize much yet, even at work. I don't feel comfortable hanging out with the other employees and I haven't met anyone I want to be friends with. I am appreciating the fact that I get to choose my population now. I'm still thinking in prison terms like *population*. What's the right word outside for my people? My community? Peeps?

I walk up and down the Safeway aisles appreciating the variety of products available. It's almost overwhelming. *Oooo, ravioli! I haven't had ravioli in forever.* At least a dozen varieties to choose from. *What type of spaghetti sauce will I get?* I grab the mushroom ravioli, a jar of mushroom spaghetti sauce and... *Wait! Chocolate chips! Jera and I can make chocolate chip cookies!*

We also have a coffee shop in the store. On every break, I get tea and a snack to take to my car and enjoy in my own private bliss. I have a book in my car. And I always park my car under a beautiful tree on the edge of the parking lot. Reading, sipping my tea, and eating a slice of pumpkin bread feels so peaceful.

Jera's best friend still lives across the street. He is making new friends at school. Jera even seems to have outgrown many of his old behavioral patterns. He's less reactive, more easygoing. I notice little things like improved control of his emotional reactions.

He's smiling, laughing, and optimistic. When I ask him how he's liking school, he tells me, "It's great!" Jera will surprise me by saying mature things like, "Mom how can I help?" Or "Mom, what do *you* want to do today?" Each day with Jera my heart fills with joy.

We experienced fewer challenges between us. It's so easy to be with him. We both say "thank you" and "I love you" all the time. I got Jera a special Halloween plastic cup that he found delightful. It came with a lid and straw, and had a skull shaped into its inner wall. He uses it as his water cup for the next couple years. He said, "Mom it's so nice!" (Nice is one of Jera's favorite adjectives.) "You are *always* thinking of me," he said, "I've missed you!"

As I watch Jera, everything seems easier, he's stepping into life with confidence. He acts refreshed, ready, and able to conquer any challenge. Jera grew in bone and Spirit just as I did while I was away.

I still feel a little anxious at times. The ankle monitor reminds me I'm still somewhat caged. Whenever I must go in for a piss test, I get really stressed out. I drink lots of water and try to get there right before I think I'm going to burst.

Whenever I'm out on an errand, I still feel a sense of dread. *Will something bad happen?* I sense a subtle level of anxiety and panic every time I leave the house. It feels like a lingering conditioning of prison life, I worry about stepping outside the lines. My home is my *safe zone.* I read an article and realized I had a subtle form of agoraphobia. (Definition: a panic response in a variety of situations, including traveling, being in a crowd, or a confined area. A fear of leaving one's house altogether.) *I refuse to let my house become my new prison!*

Going through the motions of daily life, everything begins to feel brand new. I'm no longer listening for my name over the intercom. As I wash dishes by hand, I look out my window at the birds eating at the bird feeder. I'm eating real food with real utensils. No more cooking in plastic containers and eating with plastic utensils. I drink out of glasses, eat on ceramic plates, and cook on a stove with heavy pans. When I sit down with a salad on my plate, it's the heft of the silverware, the beautiful pottery, and the taste of my food that make it a mindful experience, like never before.

No prison noise to block out. Noise is completely different for me now. The noises around my home are not a threat to me and even less annoying than prison noise. If I have my window open, I can hear a little traffic, and the train somewhere around 11 p.m. It sounds so far away, just the echo of noise.

No prison light either. I have curtains and I get to decide when to turn on the lights. I don't have to sleep with a light on as I did in prison. I can relax.

Sleeping in my bed is the most delicious experience ever! I can't get enough. It's not that I want to sleep all day; it's just that I want to go to bed and get up on my terms. I can shut my door and it is just me in my bed. Just me in my room.

I revel in waking up in my bed at various times in the morning with no alarm clock. Safeway has me on afternoon and evening shifts. There is no breakfast call at 5:30. I sleep in comfortable shorts and a tank top. I get Jera breakfast and send him off to school, then I walk around, slowly. *What will I do next?*

While I was putting away my box of papers from prison, I noticed my final pocket note. It said, "All moments are equally precious…The unequivocal resolve not to move away from where we are is essential. Once we abandon the belief that there is a more spiritually useful moment than the one we are in, we have embraced our life and infused it with the energy for awakening."

A lay Buddhist is one who fully embodies her entire life of work, family, & relationships & also spiritually prioritizing any activity. All moments are equally precious. The unequivocal resolve not to move away from where we are is essential. Once we abandon the belief that there is a more spiritually useful moment than the one we are in, we have embraced our life + infused it with energy for awakening. (are doing. The sacred

I discovered the article this pocket note was quoting: Rodney Smith's *Undivided Mind*. Like most of my pocket notes, I modified the quote a bit. (See the full quotation at the start of this chapter.) When I reread the article, I recognized my new perspective was about more than leaving prison. My time and practice in prison began to awaken me to the preciousness of each moment. That's what the monastery taught me.

As I practiced Buddhism in prison, it felt like my struggle was all about the hard things: not wanting, being okay with what is. Here at home, it feels like Buddhism has become easier; it's all about appreciation, gratitude, and kindness. My practice has given me new eyes and a deeper appreciation of living.

In prison, I counted the weeks with a view to my release. Routines in prison seemed like tedious things to be endured. Now I see that we all have our prisons. My practice teaches me that I have a choice of how I experience each moment. Every moment can be a moment of awakening.

JOURNAL:

I'm home! My home is my sanctuary. How do I make my home into my new monastery? Living fully. Awakening amid the mundane. Being present in my routine means living my dream.

Life is full of routines, but now they represent life being fulfilled. I choose to enjoy these moments. I look forward to everyday moments. Prison gave me this awareness—this is what I discovered in my monastery.

Let life wake you up.

Let's Connect!

Collin Ruiz, Author

Before my imprisonment, I applied my education in nutrition, anatomy, and physiology both in research laboratories and in clinical work.

Since my time in prison, I have included more mindfulness practices and life coaching skills in my health and wellness work. I'm still very passionate about food as medicine and the capacity food has to take us out of pain, anxiety, and depression.

All of my work with groups and individual clients is grounded in bio-individuality—uncovering each person's unique profile and requirements and discovering the right foods, supplements, and practices to support their goals.

You can reach me at CollinRuiz.com and download my free ebook, *Breaking Free of Life's Prisons.*

Max J. Miller, Developmental Editor

People frequently ask me, how did you go from producing Disney theme park attractions to writing and coaching other writers? Like so many of my clients, I found myself yearning to make a greater impact. I wanted to find a way to create a more meaningful legacy.

Since then, helping others create their own "wisdom legacy" is by far the most rewarding work I've ever done. I help people fashion their life lessons and stories into books, talks, and other media so they feel a sense of fulfillment, meaning, and contribution.

People work with me one-on-one and in group programs. For more information, reach me at maxjmiller.com and download my free *Guide to Creating Your Wisdom Legacy.*

www.ingramcontent.com/pod-product-compliance
Lightning Source LLC
Chambersburg PA
CBHW071144130626
46553CB00004B/1515